R.J. Delahunt

Is NAFTA Constitutional?

▼

Is NAFTA Constitutional?

▼

Bruce Ackerman
David Golove

HARVARD UNIVERSITY PRESS
Cambridge, Massachusetts
London, England
1995

Library of Congress Cataloging-in-Publication Data

Ackerman, Bruce A.
Is NAFTA constitutional? / Bruce Ackerman and David Golove.
p.   cm.
Reprinted from: 108 Harv. L. Rev. 799 (1995).
Includes bibliographical references.
ISBN 0-674-46712-4 (alk. paper)
1. Free trade—North America.   2. Canada. Treaties, etc. 1992 Oct. 7.
3. United States—Foreign relations—Executive agreements.
4. Treaty-making power—United States.   I. Golove, David.
KDZ944.A41992A74   1995
382'.71'097—dc20   95-41094
                                                                          CIP

Contents

I · *The World We Have Lost*   *4*

II · *The Twenties*   *37*

III · *The New Deal Abroad*   *45*

IV · *The Great Transformation*   *61*

V · *The Era of Codification*   *97*

VI · *The Bigger Picture*   *107*

VII · *The Future Debate*   *116*

Is NAFTA Constitutional?

IS NAFTA CONSTITUTIONAL?

Article 2, section 2 of the Constitution requires treaties to be approved by two thirds of the Senate. But many international accords, including the North American Free Trade Agreement (NAFTA) and the World Trade Organization, are approved as congressional-executive agreements by simple majorities of both Houses.

This is a modern development, departing radically from the constitutional practice of the first 150 years of the Republic. The congressional-executive agreement arose as part of the constitutional revolution of the Roosevelt years. Using the transformative techniques developed during the conflict between the New Deal and the Old Court in the 1930s, the President and House of Representatives gained the consent of the Senate to a revision of the foreign affairs power in the aftermath of the Second World War. The end of Roosevelt's fourth term saw the dawn of the modern Constitution — in which President and Congress have the authority to commit the nation on any important matter of domestic or foreign policy.

Ackerman and Golove's story challenges originalist accounts that suppose the Treaty Clause to have a plain meaning that cannot be altered without formal amendment. It also challenges theories that suppose that the last war to generate a major constitutional change ended in 1865. And yet, the processes of twentieth-century transformation can be ignored only by mystifying the ways in which modern Americans exercise their popular sovereignty.

B y a vote of sixty-one to thirty-eight,[1] the Senate resolved that "Congress approves . . . the North American Free Trade Agreement."[2] The vote was virtually unnoticed, because the real battle over NAFTA was in the House.[3] But there is a puzzle here, obvious to any reader of the constitutional text. The President, the Framers assure us, "shall have Power, by and with the Advice and Consent of the Senate, to make Treaties, provided two thirds of the Senators present concur."[4] Whatever happened to the Treaty Clause?

This is an expanded and revised version of the Inaugural Lecture presented by Professor Ackerman in a new series sponsored by the Order of the Coif and organized as part of the Centennial Lecture program at the University of California at Berkeley Law School (Boalt Hall) in November 1994.

[1] *See* 139 CONG. REC. S16,712–13 (daily ed. Nov. 20, 1993).

[2] North American Free Trade Agreement Implementation Act § 101(a), 19 U.S.C. § 3311(a) (Supp. V 1993).

[3] The House voted first, on November 17, 1993. Although the vote was not as close as had been expected, the bill passed only by a margin of 234 to 200. *See* 139 CONG. REC. H10,048 (daily ed. Nov. 17, 1993).

[4] U.S. CONST. art. II, § 2, cl. 2.

No less puzzling is why this obvious question was never raised during the long hard battle over NAFTA.[5] The opponents were grimly determined to gain victory at all costs. They could well have mustered the thirty-four Senators needed to defeat NAFTA if it had been treated as a treaty rather than a congressional-executive agreement.[6] And yet the obvious questions were left unasked. How did Americans come to the point where they undertake the most solemn international obligations through a procedure in which the House of Representatives joins the Senate, and simple majorities in both Houses serve to commit the nation? Is this alternative to treaty-making constitutionally legitimate? The real mystery, then, is not merely whether NAFTA is constitutional, but how and why we have gotten to the point where the foundational questions have become unaskable.

It was not always so. During the first 150 years in the life of the Republic, NAFTA would never have slipped by without fierce controversy. We begin with an exploration of this earlier constitutional world, now entirely obscured from view. We then turn to the transformation accomplished during the Roosevelt years. The climax came with the Second World War. As Allied armies swept through Europe, Americans recalled the disastrous denouement of the First World War. The Senate's rejection of the Treaty of Versailles had become a symbol of failure in the original constitutional design. The Senate's prerogative was now linked with an isolationism that was out of step with American public opinion.

The question was how this mobilized consensus would express itself in constitutional law. The movement went down two tracks. In May of 1945, two thirds of the House of Representatives approved a constitutional amendment requiring all treaties to be approved by majorities in both Houses rather than by two thirds of the Senate. But this movement was short-circuited by an informal process, which yielded the modern congressional-executive agreement. During and af-

---

[5] The fact that 38 Senators voted against NAFTA does not imply that 34 naysayers could have been found if the agreement had been processed as a treaty. The Administration might have induced five of the opponents to change their votes if they were crucial. But the auguries are not especially auspicious. If one looks at the House vote, where the Administration used every bit of its political influence, there were no fewer than 21 state delegations which cast a majority vote against the agreement. Five other delegations were equally divided. *See* 139 CONG. REC. H10,048 (daily ed. Nov. 17, 1993). Against this background, persuading two thirds of the Senate to approve a treaty would have been a formidable task.

[6] We use the term "congressional-executive agreement" more narrowly than is usual in the literature; for us it includes only those agreements negotiated by the President and then submitted to the Congress for its ex post review and approval. It does not include presidential agreements authorized by statute but not subject to ex post review by the Congress. The *Restatement*, in contrast, uses the term to include all agreements other than treaties that are generated by either form of congressional-executive collaboration. *See* RESTATEMENT (THIRD) OF FOREIGN RELATIONS LAW § 303 cmt. e (1987) [hereinafter RESTATEMENT]. As we shall see, this broader usage obscures distinctions of overriding historical and theoretical significance.

ter the War, the President won the constitutional authority to substitute the agreement of both Houses for the traditional advice and consent of the Senate. It is this historical triumph that laid the foundation for NAFTA.

But not without a further step, taken a generation later. The Trade Act of 1974[7] made a comprehensive effort to restructure the modern two-House procedure to suit the needs of economic diplomacy. This framework has proved remarkably successful — to the point where it is now taken for granted by all foreign-trade professionals. This professional consensus accounts for the constitutional silence surrounding NAFTA. After two decades, it was only natural to negotiate NAFTA through the two-House procedure that had been perfected in a series of sweeping trade agreements.

The construction of a new framework for trade in 1974, however, could not have occurred without the constitutional breakthrough won by the internationalist generation who fought the Second World War. Without this earlier transformation, NAFTA would have been processed as a treaty — and condemned to defeat by thirty-four isolationist Senators.

The intentions of the Framers have been redeemed — so long as we recognize that the relevant Framers were the Americans who fought the Second World War and not those who fought the Revolution. These Americans were determined to avoid the tragic mistake of the Versailles Treaty — in which the United States turned its back on the world just as its ideals seemed to have triumphed. In the aftermath of the Cold War, the Versailles dilemma is once again upon us. The victory of American ideals in 1989 has provoked a renewed debate between isolationists and internationalists on the need for further engagement in the new world order. Like Versailles, NAFTA became a symbol of new-fangled internationalist entanglements that threaten to compromise our "sovereignty." Only this time, the contest was not conducted on a playing field that gives isolationists a decisive advantage. The Founders' "antidemocratic" and "outmoded" decision to privilege "one third plus one" of the Senate no longer monopolizes our constitutional vision. It remains available as an option but is no longer a requirement.

This does not mean that internationalists are destined to sustain the political momentum they gained during the Cold War era. But as NAFTA suggests, rules of the game do make a difference, and sometimes a large one, in the evolution of politics. If the Senate had rejected the North American Free Trade *Treaty*, this defeat would have jeopardized prospects for American involvement in the World Trade Organization. It also would have changed the face of American politics: rather than retreating from public view, Ross Perot might have

---

[7] Pub. L. No. 93-618, 88 Stat. 1982 (1975) (codified at 19 U.S.C. §§ 2111–2242 (1988)).

been catapulted by his triumphant leadership in the NAFTA struggle to the center of the stage of presidential politics. These sorts of things can add up.

This essay is part of a larger project sketched in *We the People*.[8] Like the earlier work, it protests against a view that emphasizes the constitutional creativity of the American people during the eighteenth and nineteenth centuries, but looks upon twentieth-century Americans as more passive political creatures, who rely upon lawyers and judges for their heavy constitutional lifting. *We the People* focused on the domestic side of the twentieth-century story, urging a revision of the conventional understanding of the struggle between the New Deal and the Old Court in the 1930s. This essay considers the international side. It also focuses on the Roosevelt years, though the 1940s bulk larger than the 1930s.

Before moving into the details, reflect on the way the two stories — domestic and international — are related to one another. Before 1933, Presidents were hemmed in on two sides. Domestically, they were constrained by the Supreme Court's insistence that the federal government was one of carefully limited powers. Internationally, they were constrained by the Senate's insistence on the Treaty Clause, which the Senate had systematically used to frustrate presidential leadership.

By the end of Roosevelt's fourth term, all this had changed beyond recall. Acting with the assent of simple majorities in Congress, Presidents could lead the nation to embrace large new commitments on any matter of domestic or foreign policy. Americans were now living under a Constitution that authorized state activism at home and abroad.

We conclude by locating the rise of the congressional-executive agreement within this larger story, as well as looking ahead to future controversies. Though NAFTA glided through both Houses without constitutional debate, opponents of the next great initiative — the World Trade Organization — challenged the constitutionality of the Clinton Administration's decision to commit the nation through the two-House procedure. It may only be a matter of time before the Supreme Court gets into the act: what should it say?

I. The World We Have Lost

The President initiates a congressional-executive agreement by negotiating terms with one or more foreign governments. He then invites Congress to approve the terms through one of several procedures:

---

[8] Bruce Ackerman, We the People: Foundations (1991).

it may pass an ordinary statute or a joint resolution,[9] or enact implementing legislation necessary for the agreement's legal effectiveness.[10] Congress is also free to impose conditions or "reservations," just as the Senate does for treaties.[11] The President then signs the legislation and ratifies the international agreement in accordance with its provisions.

According to the *Restatement of Foreign Relations Law*, the result binds the United States under international law on any subject "that falls within the powers of Congress and of the President under the Constitution."[12] It also functions as the supreme law of the land, trumping inconsistent state laws and prior federal laws and treaties.[13] In other words, there is no significant difference between the legal effect of a congressional-executive agreement and the classical treaty approved by two thirds of the Senate.[14]

A. The Mythic Pedigree of the Modern Doctrine

We do not dispute this modern constitutional consensus. Our aim is to understand its historical origins and its contemporary claim to constitutional legitimacy. The rise of the congressional-executive agreement challenges originalist accounts that suppose the Treaty Clause to have a plain meaning that cannot be altered without formal amendment. It also challenges theories that presume that the last

---

[9] *Compare* 19 U.S.C. § 3311 (Supp. V 1993) (regular legislation "approving" NAFTA and authorizing the President to bring it into effect) *with* S.J. Res. 144, 80th Cong., 1st Sess. (1947) (joint resolution authorizing the President to bring into effect the United Nations Headquarters Agreement).

[10] *See, e.g.*, H.R.J. Res. 192, 78th Cong., 2d Sess. (1944) (implementing the United Nations Relief and Rehabilitation Agreement).

[11] *See, e.g.*, S.J. Res. 144, 80th Cong., 1st Sess. (1947) (adding reservations to the United Nations Headquarters Agreement); S.J. Res. 77, 80th Cong., 1st Sess. (1947) (adding reservations to the International Refugee Organization Agreement).

[12] RESTATEMENT, *supra* note 6, § 303(2); *see also id.* § 303 cmt. e (elaborating on the interchangeability of treaties and congressional-executive agreements). The *Restatement* expresses the widely prevailing view. *See, e.g.*, LOUIS HENKIN, FOREIGN AFFAIRS AND THE CONSTITUTION 173–76 (1972); Phillip R. Trimble & Jack S. Weiss, *The Role of the President, the Senate and Congress with Respect to Arms Control Treaties Concluded by the United States*, 67 CHI.-KENT L. REV. 645, 650–53 (1991). The executive branch has repeatedly affirmed this view, *see, e.g.*, Memorandum from Monroe Leigh, Legal Adviser to the State Department (Sept. 24, 1975), *reprinted in* 121 CONG. REC. 36,718, 36,721 (1975), and it was recently reaffirmed by the Congressional Research Service in an authoritative study for the Senate Foreign Relations Committee. *See* CONGRESSIONAL RESEARCH SERV., LIBRARY OF CONGRESS, TREATIES AND OTHER INTERNATIONAL AGREEMENTS: THE ROLE OF THE UNITED STATES SENATE 58–59 (Comm. Print 1993). For dissenting opinions, see, for example, THOMAS M. FRANCK & EDWARD WEISBAND, FOREIGN POLICY BY CONGRESS 141–45 (1979); MICHAEL J. GLENNON, CONSTITUTIONAL DIPLOMACY 183 (1990); Memorandum from Michael J. Glennon, Assistant Counsel, Office of the Legislative Counsel, to Sen. Dick Clark (Sept. 24, 1975), *reprinted in* 121 CONG. REC. 36,724, 36,726 (1975); and the views of Professor Laurence H. Tribe discussed below at pp. 917–23.

[13] *See* RESTATEMENT, *supra* note 6, § 111(1) cmt. d & rptr. note 2; *id.* § 115 cmt. c.

[14] *See id.* § 303 cmt. e.

armed conflict to generate a major constitutional change was the Civil War.

At the same time, we hope to contribute to the study of foreign relations law. Recent work has tended to accept the conclusions of an earlier generation for whom the status of congressional-executive agreements was a matter of desperate urgency.[15] For scholars like Edward Corwin, Wallace McClure, Myres McDougal, and Quincy Wright,[16] the fate of the entire world hinged upon establishing the interchangeability of congressional-executive agreements with treaties. They were met on the field of academic battle by defenders of an older tradition, led by Professor Edwin Borchard of the Yale Law School.[17] The modernists' triumph has been so complete that we have

---

[15] Modern scholars have generally accepted the myth of continuity without serious inquiry. *See, e.g.*, HENKIN, *supra* note 12, at 173–76 (recognizing the deep constitutional questions but affirming the prevailing consensus without returning to the foundations); John F. Murphy, *Treaties and International Agreements Other Than Treaties: Constitutional Allocation of Power and Responsibility Among the President, the House of Representatives, and the Senate*, 23 KAN. L. REV. 221, 233 & n.73 (1975); Solomon Slonim, *Congressional-Executive Agreements*, 14 COLUM. J. TRANSNAT'L L. 434, 436–37 (1975); Trimble & Weiss, *supra* note 12, at 650–51; Armen R. Vartian, *Approval of SALT Agreements by Joint Resolution of Congress*, 21 HARV. INT'L L.J. 421, 425 n.9, 429 n.27 (1980). But there are exceptions. *See, e.g.*, *Congressional Review of International Agreements: Hearings Before the Subcomm. on International Security and Scientific Affairs of the House Comm. on International Relations*, 94th Cong., 2d Sess. 74–75 (1976) (testimony of Professor Raoul Berger).

[16] We call this group — together with associated lesser lights — the "revisionists" or "modernists" or "New Dealers." It should be understood, however, that these writers held different political convictions. The striking similarity in their views extended only to a common embrace of the need to justify an alternative to treaty-making. While their thinking was shaped by the New Deal revolution in constitutional law, moreover, we shall see that this domestic transformation did not, by itself, necessitate a similar transformation in foreign affairs. *See infra* Parts III and IV. The leading New Deal works include: EDWARD S. CORWIN, THE CONSTITUTION AND WORLD ORGANIZATION 31–54 (1944) [hereinafter CORWIN, WORLD ORGANIZATION]; Edward S. Corwin, THE PRESIDENT: OFFICE AND POWERS: HISTORY AND ANALYSIS OF PRACTICE AND OPINION 232–40 (1940) [hereinafter CORWIN, THE PRESIDENT]; WALLACE MCCLURE, INTERNATIONAL EXECUTIVE AGREEMENTS: DEMOCRATIC PROCEDURE UNDER THE CONSTITUTION OF THE UNITED STATES (1941); Myres S. McDougal & Asher Lans, *Treaties and Congressional-Executive or Presidential Agreements: Interchangeable Instruments of National Policy* (pts. 1 & 2), 54 YALE L.J. 181, 534 (1945); Quincy Wright, *The United States and International Agreements*, 38 AM. J. INT'L L. 341 (1944).

[17] Borchard was tireless in his defense of the Senate. *See* Edwin M. Borchard, *Against the Proposed Amendment as to the Ratification of Treaties*, 30 A.B.A. J. 608 (1944); Edwin Borchard, *The St. Lawrence Waterway and Power Project*, 43 AM. J. INT'L L. 411 (1949) [hereinafter Borchard, *The St. Lawrence Waterway and Power Project*]; Edwin Borchard, *Shall the Executive Agreement Replace the Treaty?*, 38 AM. J. INT'L L. 637 (1944); Edwin Borchard, *Shall the Executive Agreement Replace the Treaty?*, 53 YALE L.J. 664 (1944) [hereinafter Borchard, *Shall the Executive Agreement*]; Edwin Borchard, *Treaties and Executive Agreements — a Reply*, 54 YALE L.J. 616 (1945) [hereinafter Borchard, *A Reply*]; Edwin Borchard, Book Review, LAW. GUILD REV., Sept.–Oct. 1944, at 59 (reviewing CORWIN, WORLD ORGANIZATION, *supra* note 16). Other notable defenders of the Senate included Charles Cheney Hyde and Herbert Briggs. *See* 2 CHARLES C. HYDE, INTERNATIONAL LAW CHIEFLY AS INTERPRETED AND APPLIED BY THE UNITED STATES § 509A, at 1416–18 (2d ed. 1945); Herbert W. Briggs, *Treaties, Executive Agreements, and the Panama Joint Resolution of 1943*, 37 AM. POL. SCI. REV. 686 (1943) [hereinafter

lost sight of the polemical character of their path-breaking work. In their struggle to vindicate interchangeability, these scholars engaged in a characteristic form of common law argument. They attempted to create a long and illustrious pedigree for their assault on the senatorial monopoly over treaty-making. They searched history for "look-alikes" that might serve as plausible precedents for the modern congressional-executive agreement. By piling one "look-alike" upon another, they sought to convince the world that their great transformation was not such a radical change after all.

We will show that these "look-alikes" looked very different to the Americans who actually created them. Rather than developing an all-purpose alternative to the treaty, earlier Americans thought they were acting on principles different from, and more modest than, the interchangeability doctrine, which serves as the foundation of modern practice. Indeed, the very word "interchangeability" is a creation of the New Deal scholars who constructed its long and august historical pedigree.[18]

We do not suggest that the scholars who created this myth of continuity rested their case solely upon its historical accuracy. They took a lawyerly approach to their precedents. Rather than placing them in historical context, they used them as suggestive analogies in an effort to justify their innovation. This meant, of course, that the disanalogous features of previous practice were suppressed from view.

Nor were these New Dealers particularly embarrassed by this common law approach. Their jurisprudence placed a high value on learning the lessons of experience and deploying them in the service of a President who had gained a sweeping popular mandate for constitutional transformation. They thought it ridiculous to suppose that two thirds of the Senate would voluntarily surrender its treaty-making prerogatives by supporting a formal constitutional amendment. Rather than accepting defeat at the hands of an arid formalism, they believed that the American Constitution provided far more supple instruments to test and legitimize constitutional change.

And so do we. The problem comes only if one takes the scholarly myth of continuity as serious history. Since the cutting edge of scholarship has moved beyond these historical questions, it has lost sight of the extent to which the New Dealers were playing with the precedents. Leading critics like Edwin Borchard were on solid ground in emphasizing the gap between older practices and the emerging doctrine of interchangeability.[19]

Briggs, *Panama Joint Resolution*]; Herbert W. Briggs, *The UNRRA Agreement and Congress*, 38 AM. J. INT'L L. 650 (1944) [hereinafter Briggs, *The UNRRA Agreement*].

[18] To our knowledge, the term first appears in McClure's ground-breaking 1941 book. *See* MCCLURE, *supra* note 16, at 32.

[19] *See, e.g.*, Borchard, *A Reply, supra* note 17, *passim*.

They were wrong, however, in asserting that this delegitimized the enterprise. The work of the New Deal scholars fed into a larger enterprise in constitutional reconstruction — one in which the American people reexamined their traditional isolationism amidst the sacrifices of the Second World War and resoundingly repudiated the Versailles precedent and the constitutional order that made it possible. It was only this decisive shift in public opinion that permitted the President and Congress to give constitutional substance to New Deal jurisprudence and introduce the congressional-executive agreement as a legitimate alternative to treaty-making.

To appreciate this larger process of transformation, we must return to a world we have lost — a world in which Woodrow Wilson never imagined he could come home from Versailles and make an end-run around the Senate by asking Congress to endorse the League of Nations through a joint resolution of both Houses.

B. *Original Understandings*

One of the glories of the 1787 text is its brevity. But all virtues are vicious when carried to extremes. The Founders established a very complex law-making machine: one system for constitutional amendment, another for treaty-making, a third for statute-making. But they failed to answer some obvious questions raised by the coexistence of three distinct systems.

For us, the most pressing question is interchangeability. To what degree could statute-making substitute for treaty-writing, and vice versa? The Supremacy Clause provides part of an answer by stipulating that a treaty could serve as the "law of the land" and take immediate effect as a federal law. But the text is not equally clear about the opposite relationship. Could a majority of both Houses, in the exercise of its statute-making powers, approve international agreements? The Treaty Clause does not say Yes or No, and so constitutionalists are left to construe the sounds of silence. For a long time, this silence did not seem very problematic. Until Versailles, American constitutional practice was remarkably consistent. The Constitution's special treatment of treaty-making was understood to imply that *only* the Senate, and not the Congress, had the power to commit the country to binding international agreements.

This practical construction of the text had deep roots in the original understanding. The Continental Congress had managed foreign relations with considerable skill. It had not only concluded treaties with the French but had won English recognition of American independence in the Treaty of Paris of 1783. Under the Articles of Confederation, all such treaties required the approval of nine out of thirteen states — with each state casting one vote.[20]

This practice served as a baseline for the Constitutional Convention.[21] During its first phase, everybody assumed that the Senate would continue to direct negotiations without presidential assistance.[22] Rethinking was required once the Convention reached its Great Compromise, which split Congress into two Houses and retained voting equality for the small states in the Senate. Nationalists like James Wilson believed that treaty-making, no less than statute-writing, was a fit subject for the House. But this proposal was rejected overwhelmingly,[23] as was a proposal by Gouverneur Morris that would have avoided binding the United States by any treaty "not ratified by law."[24] The stakes were made plain by Dickinson, who supported the latter motion "tho' he was sensible it was unfavorable to the little States; w[hi]ch would otherwise have an *equal* share in making Treaties."[25]

By confiding treaty-making power exclusively in the Senate, the Convention seems, then, to have been motivated by a commitment to federalism. This was why Madison wanted to get the President involved. He "observed that the Senate represented the States alone, and that . . . it was proper that the President should be an agent in Treaties."[26] Only later did the delegates approve a last-minute proposal for presidential participation presented by the Committee of Postponed Parts.[27] At this point, the exhausted delegates were no longer in an arguing mood. They approved the proposal "[w]ith surprising unanimity and surprisingly little debate."[28]

In contrast, the prior selection of the Senate seemed quite deliberate. While a commitment to states' rights played a role,[29] functional

---

[20] *See* ARTICLES OF CONFEDERATION AND PERPETUAL UNION arts. IX, X.

[21] The best modern accounts of the Founders' deliberations on treaty-making are provided by Bestor and Rakove, but they do not focus extensively on the role of the House. *See* Arthur Bestor, *Respective Roles of Senate and President in the Making and Abrogation of Treaties — The Original Intent of the Framers of the Constitution Historically Examined*, 55 WASH. L. REV. 1, 73–132 (1979); Jack N. Rakove, *Solving a Constitutional Puzzle: The Treatymaking Clause as a Case Study*, 1 PERSP. IN AM. HIST. (n.s.) 233, 236–50 (1984). The best study that emphasizes this narrower issue is Slonim, cited above in note 15. Our analysis is broadly consistent with all three accounts.

[22] *See* 1 THE RECORDS OF THE FEDERAL CONVENTION OF 1787, at 20–22 (Max Farrand ed., 1966) [hereinafter RECORDS] (the Virginia plan); *id.* at 242–45 (the New Jersey plan); Slonim, *supra* note 15, at 437.

[23] *See* 2 RECORDS, *supra* note 22, at 538.

[24] *Id.* at 392, 394.

[25] *Id.* at 393.

[26] *Id.* at 392.

[27] *See id.* at 498–99.

[28] MAX FARRAND, THE FRAMING OF THE CONSTITUTION OF THE UNITED STATES 171 (1913).

[29] *See* Slonim, *supra* note 15, at 437.

arguments were no less important.[30] Unlike House members, Senators would have six-year terms and could confront foreign policy problems from a long-range perspective. The Senate's small size would also permit the secrecy and speed necessary in foreign negotiations.

The grant of a senatorial monopoly proved one of the Convention's most controversial decisions.[31] The prospect of a few distant Senators disposing of the fate of the nation struck terror in many hearts. It is here that the two-thirds rule was repeatedly invoked to assuage anxiety. The rule's importance had been recently brought home by the Continental Congress's negotiations with Spain over a commercial treaty. A bare majority of northern states had supported instructions to John Jay, Secretary of Foreign Affairs, authorizing him to bargain away American rights of free navigation on the Mississippi in exchange for trading privileges of interest to the north. In southern eyes, this was an enormous betrayal of the national interest.[32] Because the Articles of Confederation required the approval of nine states for ratification, however, southerners could block any such treaty; the Treaty Clause of the new Constitution offered them a similar assurance. For friends and foes alike, the two-thirds rule served as a fundamental protection for minority interests.

Indeed, the serious question raised in the debates was whether the rule went far enough. When Virginia ratified the Constitution by a very close vote,[33] it appended a series of proposed amendments, including a revealing modification of the Treaty Clause.[34] In the Virginia Convention's view, the Constitution was too weak in allowing commercial treaties to be approved by two-thirds of the Senators who happened to be present at the vote; it proposed an amendment requiring the assent of "two thirds of the whole number of the Senate."[35] As for the House, the Virginians wanted it to enter the process only as a special obstacle to the enactment of certain treaties in specially sensitive areas — including restrictions upon navigation on the Mississippi. Within suspect categories, their amendment required the approval of three quarters of both Houses before a treaty could be validated. Given this proposal, we have no doubt that the Virginia Convention

---

[30] *See* THE FEDERALIST No. 64, at 391–93 (John Jay) (Clinton Rossiter ed., 1961); Rakove, *supra* note 21, at 246, 248, 249.

[31] Debate on this subject consumed 10% of the journal pages left by Virginia's ratifying convention. *See* Charles Warren, *The Mississippi River and the Treaty Clause of the Constitution*, 2 GEO. WASH. L. REV. 271, 297 (1934).

[32] *See* Bestor, *supra* note 21, at 60–68; Slonim, *supra* note 15, at 443.

[33] The key role of Virginia in the overall ratification process is discussed further in Bruce Ackerman & Neal K. Katyal, *Our Unconventional Founding*, 62 U. CHI. L. REV. (forthcoming Apr. 1995) (manuscript at 73–78, on file at the Harvard Law School Library).

[34] *See* 3 DEBATES ON THE ADOPTION OF THE FEDERAL CONSTITUTION 660 (Jonathan Elliot ed., 2d ed. 1888).

[35] *Id.*

would have been alarmed to learn that commercial agreements like NAFTA would one day pass on the basis of a bare majority in both Houses.

Nonetheless, it is important to emphasize that the text does permit an interpretation that supports modernist practice. This alternative reading begins by emphasizing that the Constitution does not explicitly say that international agreements can *only* be ratified by the Senate. This silence seems more meaningful once the Treaty Clause is situated among other constitutional texts. Most fundamentally, Article I gives Congress the power to "regulate Commerce with foreign Nations," to "declare War," and to "raise and support Armies."[36] If both Houses find that statutory approval of an international agreement is a "necessary and proper"[37] way of exercising such powers, why should they be barred from approving the agreement merely because two thirds of the Senate could achieve the same end under the Treaty Clause?[38]

It is too bad that such a textualist line was not vigorously articulated at the Founding, for it would have provoked a furious counterattack. We have seen that friends of the Constitution did not merely oppose House participation on functional grounds — that is, the need for speed, secrecy, and the sober consideration of long-run interests. The Treaty Clause also expressed principles that then seemed paramount to many Americans: the equality of states and the protection of regional interests against easy sacrifice by the dominant majority.[39]

Indeed, the Senate's monopoly was seriously challenged only once in the early years, with results that emphasize the distance between the eighteenth and twentieth centuries. The Jay Treaty with England provoked bitter political resistance from the rising Jeffersonians. As their struggle with President Washington reached new partisan heights, they led the House to demand access to all official papers connected with its negotiation.

But Washington refused to establish such a "dangerous precedent." Citing his experience at Philadelphia, he emphasized that "the power of making treaties is exclusively vested in the President, by and with the advice and consent of the Senate."[40] To support this view, he relied on "the opinions entertained by the State conventions."[41] He also elaborated the principles at stake:

---

[36] U.S. CONST. art. I, § 8, cls. 3, 11, 12.

[37] U.S. CONST. art. I, § 8, cl. 18.

[38] For further discussion, see below pp. 913–14, 919–22.

[39] *See supra* pp. 809–10.

[40] Message from George Washington to the House of Representatives of the United States (Mar. 30, 1796), *in* 1 A COMPILATION OF THE MESSAGES AND PAPERS OF THE PRESIDENTS 1789–1897, at 195 (James D. Richardson ed., Washington, D.C., Government Printing Office 1899) [hereinafter PRESIDENTIAL COMPILATION].

[41] *Id.*

[I]t is well known that . . . the smaller States were admitted to an equal representation in the Senate with the larger States, and that this branch of the Government was invested with great powers, for on the equal participation of those powers the sovereignty and political safety of the smaller States were deemed essentially to depend.[42]

Washington's defense of the senatorial monopoly expressed the overwhelming constitutional consensus for the next century and a half.[43] This is not to suggest that the role of the House in treaty-making was settled, but the nature of the early controversies reveals how far eighteenth- and nineteenth-century understandings fell short of modern practice. Even as early as the Jay Treaty debate, Jeffersonians in the House, most notably Madison, disputed Washington's suggestion that the House was morally bound to adopt legislation implementing Senate-approved treaties. Nothing in the treaty power, they countered, reduced Congress to such a ministerial position.[44] Yet, their claim was not that Congress could substitute for two thirds of the Senate, as modern doctrine accepts. Theirs was a much more modest goal: to establish that the House could exercise legislative discretion in deciding whether to adopt laws necessary to put treaties into effect.[45]

---

[42] *Id.* at 196.

[43] Story made an elaborate defense of the Senate's treaty role, which he thought superior both to unilateral executive, and joint congressional, decision-making. *See* 3 JOSEPH STORY, COMMENTARIES ON THE CONSTITUTION OF THE UNITED STATES § 1503, at 356 (Ronald D. Rotunda & John E. Nowak eds., Carolina Academic Press 1987) (1833).

[44] *See, e.g.,* 4 ANNALS OF CONG. 427–28 (1796) (summary of remarks of Rep. Livingston); *id.* at 465–74 (summary of remarks of Rep. Gallatin); *id.* at 487–94, 772–82 (summary of remarks of Rep. Madison); LOUIS FISHER, CONSTITUTIONAL CONFLICTS BETWEEN CONGRESS AND THE PRESIDENT 261–62 (1985); 2 ASHER C. HINDS, PRECEDENTS OF THE HOUSE OF REPRESENTATIVES OF THE UNITED STATES § 1509, at 982–84 (1907); Chalfant Robinson, *The Treaty-Making Power of the House of Representatives*, 12 YALE REV. 191, 195–96 (1903). Madison observed "that the Constitution had as expressly and exclusively vested in Congress the power of making laws, as it had vested in the President the power of making treaties." 4 ANNALS OF CONG. 774 (1796).

[45] *See, e.g.,* 4 ANNALS OF CONG. 427–28 (1796) (summary of remarks of Rep. Livingston); *id.* at 465–74 (summary of remarks of Rep. Gallatin); *id.* at 487–94, 772–82 (summary of remarks of Rep. Madison). Gallatin expressly disclaimed any power in the House to make international agreements. *See id.* at 467 (claiming "for the House [not] a power of making Treaties, but a check upon the Treaty-making power — a mere negative power").

The Jay Treaty dispute marked the beginning of a century of constitutional controversy over these issues. *See, e.g.,* FISHER, *supra* note 44, at 261–64; 2 HINDS, *supra* note 44, §§ 1506, 1509, 1523, 1524, 1526–1530, at 975–79, 982–84, 988–94; Robinson, *supra* note 44, at 192–200. The debate's high-water mark came in the 1870s and 1880s when the House finally prevailed on the Senate to condition the international effectiveness of reciprocity conventions with Hawaii and Mexico on Congress's prior adoption of implementing legislation. *See* FISHER, *supra* note 44, at 264; Robinson, *supra* note 44, at 201–02. Even at its most assertive, however, the House claimed only the right to exercise its own judgment in deciding whether to implement treaties to which the Senate had already given its advice and consent. *See, e.g.,* H.R. REP. NO. 2680, 48th Cong., 2d Sess. 7 (1884) (enunciating, in an elaborate report of the House Foreign Affairs Committee, the

At the same time, it is important to note that Washington's broader point did not go entirely unchallenged. Jefferson himself denied that treaties could ever be used for subjects falling within Congress's legislative powers.[46] Although this extreme claim has been consistently rejected, it suggests that the modernist reading of the text was within eighteenth-century interpretive horizons. Still, if that reading is legitimate, it is not because it represented the prevailing view of the Founding generation, but because it expresses the considered judgment of Americans of our own century.

C. *Modernity's Tangled Pedigree*

As twentieth-century reformers took aim at the traditional consensus, they sought to lift the weight of the past from their shoulders by developing a scholarly counter-narrative. Their aim was to deny that history was as monolithic as conservative opponents claimed. By elaborating this revisionist account, the reformers could portray the congressional-executive agreement as continuous with the best of preexisting practice.

In criticizing this myth of continuity, we do not suggest that the reformers' account was utterly without factual foundation. Nonetheless, they greatly exaggerated the extent to which the congressional-executive agreement evolved organically from the main lines of previous development. To make this point, we shall emphasize four features of the modern congressional-executive agreement and show how the precedents used by the myth-makers fell short of fulfilling these key characteristics.

Once we have rediscovered the contours of an older constitutional world, we can proceed to our main inquiry: given the large gap between yesterday and today, how did the twentieth-century reformers win the constitutional authority for their fundamental innovation? Does their achievement deserve continued acceptance by the new generation of Americans coming to power today?

1. Four Distinctions. — First, the congressional-executive agreement involves interbranch collaboration. This simple point does great damage to the myth. Many of the standard cases the New Dealers used to build their pedigree did not involve any form of institutional interaction. Instead, the New Dealers cited countless cases of unilateralism, executive or legislative, as if they served as precedents

---

House's perspective but conceding that Congress "cannot make compacts or agreements" and that "the *nexus* of international faith must be bound by the treaty-making power").

[46] *See, e.g.,* THOMAS JEFFERSON, A MANUAL OF PARLIAMENTARY PRACTICE § 52, at 110 (New York, Clark & Maynard 1873) ("[T]he Constitution must have intended . . . to except those subjects of legislation in which it gave a participation to the House of Representatives.").

for a novel form of congressional-executive interaction that could substitute for the traditional treaty.

Second, the two-House procedure yields agreements that generate
binding international obligations identical to those of a classical treaty.
This was not true in an earlier era. Though we may find it surprising
today, even Presidents and their Secretaries of State were remarkably
candid in conceding their lack of constitutional authority to bind the
nation without the Senate.[47]

The third point involves a matter of timing. For most of American
history, only the Senate reviewed the President's agreements after he
negotiated them. While Congress was always passing forward-looking
statutes, it invaded the Senate's treaty-making power if it reviewed
presidential agreements ex post. This simple point also undercuts the
myth of continuity. The precedents the myth-makers invoked often
involved cases in which Congress authorized the President to take certain steps in foreign affairs, but not cases in which Congress displaced
senatorial advice and consent regarding agreements that the President
had already negotiated.

Finally, modern doctrine asserts that the two-House procedure is
appropriate for any subject within the powers of Congress. But at no
time before the New Deal did diplomats imagine that any non-treaty
form could serve as an all-purpose alternative to the treaty.

In constructing their myth of continuity, New Deal scholars ignored two or more of these four points in their treatment of individual
precedents. By piling dissimilar cases on top of one another, they
could construct a pedigree for a previously unknown practice — one
in which the President could gain constitutional legitimacy for any international agreement he negotiated by appealing for the support of
Congress rather than the Senate.[48]

There is nothing unusual or illegitimate about this process of ana-
logical reasoning. When married to considerations of principle, and a

---

[47] To avoid confusion, it is critical to distinguish between two questions. The first, central to
our inquiry, is whether the President, acting under congressional authorization, has the *domestic*
constitutional authority to take acts that generate binding commitments under international law.
The second is whether *international law* will nevertheless impose binding obligations even when
the President and Congress are acting beyond the scope of their domestic constitutional authority.
This latter question has been the subject of tremendous historical controversy among international
scholars. *See infra* pp. 844–45; *infra* note 464.

It is also important to distinguish our problem from one raised when Congress passes a statute
that violates the country's preexisting international obligations. Although courts enforce the statute in such cases, *see, e.g.*, Whitney v. Robertson, 124 U.S. 190 (1888), this has never been taken
to imply that Congress may also create international obligations. It means simply that American
courts will not protect aggrieved parties when Congress places the country in violation of its
international commitments, leaving them to pursue their remedies in other fora.

[48] Characteristically, the creators of the myth overwhelmed the reader with an impressive
mass of historical detail but failed to provide the reader with any basis for distinguishing one
kind of agreement from another. *See, e.g.*, McClure, *supra* note 16, at 35–190; *infra* p. 868.

fundamental shift in public opinion, it can make for a persuasive case for constitutional change — as it did in the 1940s. If, however, we are to understand how much creativity was involved in this process of constitutional construction, we must scrutinize each line of precedent with greater care.

We begin with precedents that would, in time, provide a supportive context for the twentieth-century breakthrough. These involved presidential decisions to conclude international agreements without seeking the advice and consent of the Senate. When we measure these early executive accords along our four key dimensions, they fall short of the modern congressional-executive agreement. Nevertheless, conventional wisdom is not altogether wrong in emphasizing their importance. Though these precedents are discontinuous with modern practice, they provided important resources for the legal imagination as it struggled with twentieth-century demands for a more democratic alternative to the classical treaty. We turn afterwards to other lines of precedent that have little organic connection to modern developments. Nonetheless, conventional wisdom often gives them great importance, and so we must take them seriously — if only to suggest how much must be forgotten before they can be treated as serious legal analogies for the congressional-executive agreement.

   2. *Executive Unilateralism.* — From the very beginning, Presidents confronted countless foreign problems that required solution without the aid of either the Senate or Congress. These sometimes required them to enter into unilateral executive agreements. By the early twentieth century, a typology had grown up to define and confine this on-going practice.[49]

---

[49] It was uniformly agreed that the President could enter into some kinds of agreements under his independent constitutional powers. *See* 2 CHARLES BUTLER, THE TREATY-MAKING POWER OF THE UNITED STATES § 463, at 367 n.2 (1902); EDWARD S. CORWIN, THE PRESIDENT'S CONTROL OF FOREIGN RELATIONS 116–25 (1917); SAMUEL B. CRANDALL, TREATIES: THEIR MAKING AND ENFORCEMENT 85–87 (1904); SAMUEL B. CRANDALL, TREATIES: THEIR MAKING AND ENFORCEMENT §§ 56–61, at 102–20 (2d ed. 1916) [hereinafter CRANDALL, TREATIES 2D]; 2 CHARLES C. HYDE, INTERNATIONAL LAW CHIEFLY AS INTERPRETED AND APPLIED BY THE UNITED STATES §§ 505–509, at 27–34 (1922); QUINCY WRIGHT, THE CONTROL OF AMERICAN FOREIGN RELATIONS §§ 161–172, at 234–46 (1922); Simeon E. Baldwin, *The Entry of the United States into World Politics as One of the Great Powers*, 9 YALE REV. 399, 406–07 (1901) [hereinafter Baldwin, *Entry*]; Simeon E. Baldwin, *The Exchange of Notes in 1908 between Japan and the United States*, 3 ZEITSCHRIFT FÜR VÖLKERRECHT UND BUNDESSTAATSRECHT 456, 456–58 (1909) [hereinafter Baldwin, *Exchange*]; James F. Barnett, *International Agreements Without the Advice and Consent of the Senate II*, 15 YALE L.J. 63, 63 (1905); John W. Foster, *The Treaty-Making Power Under the Constitution*, 11 YALE L.J. 69, 77–79 (1901); Charles C. Hyde, *Agreements of the United States Other Than Treaties*, 17 GREEN BAG 229, 233–37 (1905); Francois S. Jones, *Treaties and Treaty-Making*, 12 POL. SCI. Q. 420, 430–33 (1897); John B. Moore, *Treaties and Executive Agreements*, 20 POL. SCI. Q. 385, 389–92 (1905). The President's independent powers derived from his authority as Chief Executive, as Commander-in-Chief, and as sole organ of the nation in the conduct of its foreign affairs. Some controversy arose, of course, over the scope of these powers and over the classification of particular agreements.

One capacious category was the modus vivendi. This involved executive agreements of a temporary nature, effective pending the completion of some other process, like the resolution of an international arbitration or the conclusion of a formal treaty. Modi vivendi were sometimes very important, and lasted for considerable periods, but their stop-gap character was their raison d'être.[50] After all, somebody had to handle problems quickly when they arose, and who else could do it but the President?[51]

A second category involved the President's delegated powers, most importantly those of Commander-in-Chief. These permitted him to make military agreements of all kinds, including those terminating hostilities.[52] But even these powers were not unlimited, especially during peacetime. For example, President Monroe unilaterally agreed with the British to demilitarize the Great Lakes in the aftermath of the War of 1812.[53] Initially, Monroe believed he could conclude the agreement as Commander-in-Chief.[54] A year later, he had second thoughts, and submitted it to the Senate, inquiring whether it was "such an agreement as the Executive is competent to enter into by the powers vested in it by the Constitution, or is such a one as requires the advice and consent of the Senate."[55] The Senate gave its consent,

---

[50] Oft-cited examples include an 1885 agreement between the United States and Great Britain for a temporary extension of a fisheries treaty that was to terminate in the middle of the season and an 1899 agreement provisionally settling a boundary dispute with Canada pending the results of an arbitration. *See, e.g.*, 2 BUTLER, *supra* note 49, § 463, at 369–70 n.2; CRANDALL, TREATIES 2D, *supra* note 49, § 59, at 112–14; Moore, *supra* note 49, at 397–98. The Supreme Court for the Washington Territory was willing to give provisional effect to a modus vivendi in Watts v. United States, 1 Wash. Terr. 288, 294 (1870).

[51] A closely related category, incident to the President's power to negotiate international agreements, permitted him to enter into provisional arrangements. These were agreements to negotiate a treaty or to set preliminary terms for a future, definitive treaty. *See, e.g.*, 2 BUTLER, *supra* note 49, § 463, at 370–72 n.2; CRANDALL, TREATIES 2D, *supra* note 49, § 58, at 111–12; 1 WESTEL W. WILLOUGHBY, THE CONSTITUTIONAL LAW OF THE UNITED STATES § 200, at 469–70 (1910).

[52] Important early examples included: President Madison's Cartel for the Exchange of Prisoners of War with Great Britain during the War of 1812, described in MCCLURE, cited above in note 16, at 48–49; a series of agreements with Mexico, made between 1882 and 1896, permitting each country's military forces to cross the border in pursuit of Indians, described in WRIGHT, cited above in note 49, § 169, at 242; and President McKinley's August 12, 1898 armistice agreement with Spain, described in CRANDALL, TREATIES 2D, cited above in note 49, § 56, at 103–04. In Tucker v. Alexandroff, 183 U.S. 424, 434–35 (1902), the Supreme Court assumed that the President's agreements with Mexico were based upon his powers as Commander-in-Chief.

[53] *See* 2 HUNTER MILLER, TREATIES AND OTHER INTERNATIONAL ACTS OF THE UNITED STATES OF AMERICA 645 (1931) (Rush-Bagot Agreement of 1817); *see also* MESSAGE FROM THE PRESIDENT OF THE UNITED STATES, S. EXEC. DOC. NO. 9, 52d Cong., 2d Sess. (1892).

[54] *See* CRANDALL, TREATIES 2D, *supra* note 49, § 56, at 102–03; 5 JOHN B. MOORE, A DIGEST OF INTERNATIONAL LAW § 752, at 214–15 (1906).

[55] S. EXEC. DOC. NO. 9, *supra* note 53, at 12 (quoting a communication of President Monroe to the Senate); *see* Barnett, *supra* note 49, at 71.

and the President then proclaimed its validity.[56] Later on, this episode would be cited as a precedent for the congressional-executive agreement. To us, it suggests how narrowly early Presidents construed their leeway under the Treaty Clause. Even when acting as Commander-in-Chief, Monroe felt obliged to gain the consent of the Senate to his peacetime agreement with the British.[57]

A final category involved the settlement of American claims against foreign governments. These were sometimes rather ambitious agreements, with Presidents entering into conventions for the arbitration of large groups of claims.[58]

As America emerged as a world power at the turn of the century, this neat system came under predictable stress.[59] President McKinley

[56] *See* CRANDALL, TREATIES 2D, *supra* note 49, § 56, at 102; 5 MOORE, *supra* note 54, § 752, at 214–15. Although the President proclaimed the agreement, he never exchanged ratifications with Great Britain. *See* CRANDALL, TREATIES 2D, *supra* note 49, § 56, at 102.

[57] Whether the agreement was properly a treaty or an executive agreement has been the subject of countless debates. *Compare, e.g.,* CRANDALL, TREATIES 2D, *supra* note 49, § 56, at 103 (characterizing Rush-Bagot as an executive agreement) *and* Barnett, *supra* note 49, at 72 (same) *with* WRIGHT, *supra* note 49, § 169, at 243 (characterizing it as a treaty, as agreements of its character "doubtless" ought to be).

[58] For particularly noted early agreements, see CRANDALL, TREATIES 2D, cited above in note 49, § 57, at 108–11; Hyde, cited above in note 49, at 233; and Moore, cited above in note 49, at 403–17. The executive also had recognized authority over a more general administrative category of minor agreements incident to the conduct of American foreign affairs.

One of the most troublesome precedents for the early scholars was President Fillmore's executive agreement obtaining the cession from Canada of Horseshoe Reef, a small spit of land in Lake Erie. Thinking that Horseshoe Reef was American territory, Congress made an appropriation for the erection of a lighthouse. *See* Act of Mar. 3, 1849, ch. 105, 9 Stat. 380. When it became evident that the useable portion of the Reef belonged to Canada, President Fillmore reached a cession agreement with Britain on condition that the United States erect a lighthouse. *See* 1 WILLIAM M. MALLOY, TREATIES, CONVENTIONS, INTERNATIONAL ACTS, PROTOCOLS AND AGREEMENTS BETWEEN THE UNITED STATES OF AMERICA AND OTHER POWERS, S. DOC. NO. 357, 61st Cong., 2d Sess. 663–64 (1910). Congress then appropriated the necessary funds. *See* 5 MOORE, *supra* note 54, § 752, at 215; WRIGHT, *supra* note 49, § 164, at 237. Early writers had difficulty classifying the agreement, with some suggesting that the President had acted without constitutional authority. *Compare* WRIGHT, *supra* note 49, § 164, at 237 (noting that "[i]t would seem properly a subject for treaty, rather than executive agreement") *with* CRANDALL, TREATIES 2D, *supra* note 49, § 60, at 114–15 (classifying it as "[m]iscellaneous") *and* 1 WILLOUGHBY, *supra* note 51, § 204, at 478–79 n.19 (attempting no classification) *and* Hyde, *supra* note 49, at 235 (same). Simeon Baldwin accepted the agreement as a minor "once for all" transaction. Baldwin, *Exchange, supra* note 49, at 457–60. The extended commentary generated by this trivial matter suggests how closely the borderlands of senatorial prerogative were scrutinized.

[59] As the new precedents accumulated, scholars began to rework the old categories. By 1922, Quincy Wright suggested that the President, as head of the administration, could make international agreements on any subject without statutory or treaty-based authority, "though it would seem that such agreements should not go beyond his own powers of execution." WRIGHT, *supra* note 49, § 164, at 237. Wright also argued that the President's power to receive ambassadors and to negotiate treaties gave him the authority to make agreements "defining executive policy." *Id.* § 170, at 243. Corwin took a similar view, presciently predicting that the President's prerogative to make unilateral agreements "is likely to become larger before it begins to shrink." CORWIN, *supra* note 49, at 125; *see also* CRANDALL, TREATIES 2D, *supra* note 49, § 58, at 111–12 (adding a new category for "agreements as to a foreign policy"); *id.* § 60, at 114–17 (adding a "miscellane-

unilaterally reached an armistice agreement with Spain that did more than end hostilities. It arranged for the Spanish withdrawal from Puerto Rico, Cuba, and other former possessions.[60] From McKinley through Wilson, Presidents used unilateral agreements to define America's burgeoning interests in the Far East. The Open Door Policy,[61] the Boxer Rebellion,[62] and our relationship with Japan[63] were all subjects of unilateral presidential action that strained existing categories. This did not pass unnoticed at the time. These actions regularly provoked constitutional debate in the Senate and among scholars.[64]

---

ous" category, which dealt with some of the more troublesome of the new and old precedents); 1 WILLOUGHBY, *supra* note 51, § 200, at 469–71 (including many new precedents within the President's power to conclude "protocols"). In 1909, Simeon Baldwin, generally friendly to expanding executive power, sought to limit the President's unilateral authority by invoking a distinction originally suggested by Vattel. *See* EMMERICH DE VATTEL, LE DROIT DES GENS OU PRINCIPES DE LA LOI NATURELLE, §§ 152, 153, 192 (Leyden, 1758). According to Baldwin, many Framers were familiar with Vattel, who distinguished sharply between agreements lasting considerable periods or in perpetuity and agreements of a temporary nature, "executed once for all." Baldwin, *Exchange*, *supra* note 49, at 458 (citation omitted). Only the latter, which Baldwin limited to agreements of "comparatively slight importance," *id.* at 457, could be concluded on the President's sole authority. Vattel's distinction became a theme in future discussions, *see infra* notes 70, 246, 250, and a subject of intense controversy, even as to the proper translation of the original. *Compare* Borchard, *Shall the Executive Agreement*, *supra* note 17, at 667–71 (relying on Professor Weinfeld's corrected version of an earlier translation) *with* McDougal & Lans (pt. 1), *supra* note 16, at 226–34 (quibbling over the accuracy of Weinfeld's revision and disputing Borchard's interpretation of the Framers' intentions).

[60] *See* Protocol — Spain, Aug. 12, 1898, 30 Stat. 1742; 2 MALLOY, *supra* note 58, at 1688; Moore, *supra* note 49, at 391–92.

[61] *See* 1 MALLOY, *supra* note 58, at 244–47, 249, 253–56.

[62] The Boxer Protocol of 1901 ended the military intervention suppressing the Boxers. Like the armistice with Spain, it went far beyond ending hostilities. *See* 2 MALLOY, *supra* note 58, at 2006–12. In contrast to the Spanish agreement, however, the President never intended to embody its terms in a subsequent peace treaty. *See* Moore, *supra* note 49, at 392.

[63] There were a number of important agreements with Japan during the first two decades of this century. The first was the Taft-Katsura Agreement of July 29, 1905, defining American and Japanese interests in the Far East. *See* McCLURE, *supra* note 16, at 96. The second was the so-called "Gentlemen's Agreement" of 1907 in which Japan checked emigration in return for President Roosevelt's agreement to refrain from urging exclusionary legislation upon Congress. *See* 65 CONG. REC. 6073–74 (1924); 1 WESTEL W. WILLOUGHBY, THE CONSTITUTIONAL LAW OF THE UNITED STATES § 287, at 528 (2d ed. 1929). The third was the Root-Takahira Agreement of November 30, 1908, which further defined the policies of the two governments in the Far East. *See* 1 MALLOY, *supra* note 58, at 1045–47. The final agreement was the notorious Lansing-Ishii Agreement of November 2, 1917, recognizing Japan's special interests in China. *See* 3 MALLOY, *supra* note 58, at 2720–22; 1 WILLOUGHBY, *supra*, § 302, at 546–47.

[64] Even those scholars with close ties to the State Department, like John Bassett Moore (the author of that department's official treatise on international law), considered the 1898 armistice with Spain and the 1901 Boxer Protocol "remarkable exercise[s] by the president alone of the power to make agreements." Moore, *supra* note 49, at 392; *see also* WRIGHT, *supra* note 49, § 168, at 241 (taking the view that an armistice should not affect the "political terms of peace"); Hyde, *supra* note 49, at 234–35 (remaining neutral about whether the 1898 armistice fit within the President's wide discretion as Commander-in-Chief, but arguing that "agreements in the form of capitulations, of a political character, and of such far-reaching consequence," require approval by

What is more, even activist Presidents were remarkably modest about their innovations. Consider the controversy surrounding President Theodore Roosevelt's intervention in Santo Domingo. With European powers threatening to intervene militarily on behalf of their creditors, Roosevelt negotiated a treaty that placed Santo Domingo under American receivership.[65] When the Senate refused to approve, he put a similar executive agreement into effect anyway[66] — declaring it a necessary modus vivendi pending Senate reconsideration. This decision was widely criticized, though the Senate consented to the treaty two years later.[67] The most striking point was Roosevelt's understanding of his authority:

> The Constitution did not explicitly give me power to bring about the necessary agreement with Santo Domingo. But the Constitution did not forbid my doing what I did. I put the agreement into effect, and I continued its execution for two years before the Senate acted; and I would have continued it until the end of my term, if necessary, without any action by Congress. But it was far preferable that there should be action by Congress, so that we might be proceeding under a treaty which was the law of the land and not merely by a direction of the Chief Executive *which would lapse when that particular executive left office*.[68]

This is a remarkable act of self-limitation coming from an activist President.[69] Roosevelt could give his own word to Santo Domingo,

---

the Senate). Willoughby, and others, thought the Boxer Protocol justified because the urgent circumstances left the President no other choice. *See* 1 WILLOUGHBY, *supra* note 51, § 200, at 470. Simeon Baldwin launched a scathing attack on the constitutionality of the Root-Takahira Agreement of 1908. *See* Baldwin, *Exchange, supra* note 49, at 456–65.

[65] *See* 1 HYDE, *supra* note 49, § 21, at 31–32. Under the proposed treaty, the United States was to guarantee the territorial integrity of the Dominican Republic, adjust the claims of its foreign creditors, and administer its finances. *See* PAPERS RELATING TO THE FOREIGN RELATIONS OF THE UNITED STATES 1905, at 342–43 [hereinafter FOREIGN RELATIONS xxxx, where "xxxx" stands for the year in which the reprinted diplomatic correspondence was exchanged]; Moore, *supra* note 49, at 386–87.

[66] The executive agreement was to be effective pending Senate action on the treaty. *See* FOREIGN RELATIONS 1905, *supra* note 65, at 360.

[67] After a "famous constitutional debate," HENKIN, *supra* note 12, at 177 n.16, the Senate agreed to the treaty with some minor face-saving amendments. *See* 40 CONG. REC. 1173–80, 1417–31, 2125–48 (1906); 40 CONG. REC. 433–36 (1905); W. STULL HOLT, TREATIES DEFEATED BY THE SENATE: A STUDY OF THE STRUGGLE BETWEEN PRESIDENT AND SENATE OVER THE CONDUCT OF FOREIGN RELATIONS 212–30 (1933).

[68] THEODORE ROOSEVELT, AN AUTOBIOGRAPHY 510 (1920) (emphasis added).

[69] Presidents Taft, Wilson, and Harding all apparently subscribed to this view. *See, e.g.,* WARREN G. HARDING, MESSAGE FROM THE PRESIDENT OF THE UNITED STATES TO THE SENATE, S. DOC. NO. 150, 67th Cong., 2d Sess. 3 (1922) (affirming the non-binding character of the Lansing-Ishii agreement); *The Treaty of Peace With Germany: Hearings Before the Senate Comm. on Foreign Relations*, 66th Cong., 1st Sess. 222 (1919) (testimony of Robert H. Lansing, Wilson's Secretary of State) (affirming the non-binding character of the Lansing-Ishii and Root-Takahira agreements); WILLIAM H. TAFT, OUR CHIEF MAGISTRATE AND HIS POWERS 111–12 (1916) (affirming the limited power of the executive in the context of a modus vivendi with Panama); *see also* 5 GREEN H. HACKWORTH, DIGEST OF INTERNATIONAL LAW 431–32 (1943) (reprinting Presi-

but he did not think he could bind the next President, let alone the United States.

Indeed, even when the President acted within his traditional rubrics of authority, he could constitutionally bind the country only under a narrow set of circumstances. Broadly speaking, it was only when he was acting as Commander-in-Chief and when he was settling American claims against foreign nations that most writers conceded the President's power to obligate the country.[70]

In short, while there were hundreds of unilateral executive agreements between the American Revolution and the First World War, they do not provide strong precedents for the congressional-executive agreement. They did not involve the collaboration of the executive with the other branches; they were not conceived as all-purpose substitutes for treaties; and they did not typically bind the country in the manner of treaties.

3. Interbranch Collaboration. — We turn next to cases in which the executive and the Congress did collaborate, but did not use the treaty form.[71] Once again, despite superficial similarities, it is

dent Harding's message regarding the Lansing-Ishii agreement and a State Department statement characterizing the Panama agreement as non-binding).

[70] In the aftermath of the Spanish-American War, Charles Henry Butler, the greatest authority on treaties of his time, went so far as to deny that *any* executive agreement could impose binding legal obligations upon the United States. *See* 2 BUTLER, *supra* note 49, § 463, at 370–71 n.2. Butler's discussion established the baseline for the next two decades, but leading writers often nibbled around the edges of his absolutist doctrine. *See, e.g.,* 1 WILLOUGHBY, *supra* note 51, §§ 199–202, at 468–72 (arguing that the President has authority to make binding claims settlements and binding agreements under the Commander-in-Chief power); GEORGE SUTHERLAND, CONSTITUTIONAL POWER AND WORLD AFFAIRS 120–21 (1919) (expressing a similar view). In 1905, Hyde appeared to suggest that executive agreements did impose binding obligations, *see* Hyde, *supra* note 49, at 236, but in 1922 he retreated, seeming to accept the possibility that "important protocols," like the 1898 armistice and the 1901 Boxer Protocol, were binding only on the administration that concluded them. *See* 2 HYDE, *supra* note 49, § 508, at 33. Even Corwin, a strong supporter of presidential power, recognized in 1917 that agreements like the Santo Domingo receivership were "of a temporary nature" and required Senate confirmation in order to achieve a "durable basis." CORWIN, *supra* note 49, at 125, 122; *see also* EDWARD S. CORWIN, THE CONSTITUTION AND WHAT IT MEANS TODAY 55–56 (1924).

Other writers were somewhat more open to the possibility that the President could impose binding obligations on the nation. Moore, Crandall, and Barnett did not explicitly address the issue, but the tenor of their discussions suggests that such a presidential power existed in an ill-defined class of cases. *See* CRANDALL, TREATIES 2D, *supra* note 49, §§ 56–61, at 102–20; Barnett, *supra* note 49, at 70–82; Moore, *supra* note 49, at 389–420. But these ambiguous suggestions did not gain general acceptance. Quincy Wright's great treatise, *The Control of American Foreign Relations*, published in 1922, revealed the continuing influence of Butler's doctrine. *See* WRIGHT, *supra* note 49, § 161, at 235. Wright recognized the President's power to bind the country only in claims settlements and agreements reached under the Commander-in-Chief power. Even as to military agreements, Wright felt that those "of permanent character, and limiting Congress as well as the President ought, doubtless, to be by treaty." *Id.* § 169, at 243. Overall, then, there was no broad-ranging reconsideration of the traditional view.

[71] Another recognized collaborative category was executive agreements made ancillary to treaties. *See, e.g.,* WRIGHT, *supra* note 49, § 163, at 236–37; Moore, *supra* note 49, at 417–20. An

much too quick to view such cases as strong precedents for the modern practice.

(a) Proclamation Statutes. — Begin with a standard situation with roots in our earliest history. Congress passes a statute that has an impact upon foreign relations. But the law's precise operation is contingent upon one or another set of facts. Congress therefore delegates the fact-finding job to the President.

A typical case involves the problem of discriminatory tariffs. From early on, Congress followed a policy of commercial reciprocity: if country X did not discriminate against American products, the United States would not discriminate against X's exports. To implement this policy, Congress required a fact-finder capable of determining whether X was discriminating. Early statutes imposed this duty on the President, typically requiring him to issue a proclamation giving each complying country a clean bill of health. We call these "proclamation statutes,"[72] and they have been very common.[73]

These statutes did not expressly authorize the President to engage in negotiations with foreign powers. He was simply to find the facts and issue the appropriate proclamation. Nevertheless, the statutes engendered negotiating activity. Foreign countries were eager to fall on the right side of the legal line. If their conduct was problematic, the President often explained how they might comply with the statutory requirements. When an executive officer exchanged notes with a foreign government, and the foreign government complied with its terms, things began to look contractual.[74] What, then, was the status of these arrangements?

This question was raised clearly under the McKinley Tariff of 1890.[75] While previous proclamation statutes had generated ad hoc negotiations,[76] this was the first to provoke a programmatic effort to

---

enormous controversy about the scope of this power erupted over the Hague Arbitration Treaties of 1904 and 1905. *See, e.g.*, CORWIN, *supra* note 49, at 122–25; 1 WILLOUGHBY, *supra* note 51, § 203, at 473–76. The Senate effectively killed a series of mandatory arbitration treaties designed to promote the peaceful settlement of international disputes. *See* TAFT, *supra* note 69, at 106–08; HOLT, *supra* note 67, at 204–12. While the Senate's action serves as a prelude to the story of Versailles, the subject is otherwise tangential here.

[72] Butler called them examples of "Reciprocal Legislation and Executive Proclamation." 2 BUTLER, *supra* note 49, § 463, at 372 n.2.

[73] *See, e.g.*, Field v. Clark, 143 U.S. 649, 682–92 (1892) (cataloguing a number of these provisions); *Reciprocal Trade Agreements: Hearings on H.R. 8687 Before the Senate Comm. on Finance*, 73d Cong., 2d Sess. 82–98 (1934) [hereinafter *1934 Senate Hearings*] (same); CRANDALL, TREATIES 2D, *supra* note 49, § 62, at 121–27 (same).

[74] For an early example, see Proclamation of Oct. 5, 1830, 4 Stat. 817, 817, discussed in MC-CLURE, cited above in note 16, at 58–59, and Second Annual Message (Dec. 6, 1830), *in* 2 PRESIDENTIAL COMPILATION, cited above in note 40, at 501, 502–03.

[75] Act of Oct. 1, 1890, ch. 1244, § 3, 26 Stat. 567, 612.

[76] After the Civil War, presidential negotiations under proclamation statutes increased, especially under the Trademark Act of 1881, ch. 138, 21 Stat. 502, and the Copyright Act of 1891, ch.

induce many countries to act in a non-discriminatory way.[77] Within a short time, the Secretary of State negotiated twelve reciprocal trade agreements with foreign powers.[78]

Their fate reveals the very different world in which they were made. Consider the Secretary's negotiations with Brazil.[79] After passage of the Act, Secretary Blaine sent the Brazilian Minister a diplomatic note advising that the new law allowed the free entry of certain products so long as Brazil granted reciprocal concessions.[80] If an agreement could be reached, it would remain in force "so long as

---

565, 26 Stat. 1106, 1110, which was succeeded by the Copyright Act of 1909, ch. 320, 35 Stat. 1075, 1077. *See, e.g.,* CRANDALL, TREATIES 2D, *supra* note 49, § 64, at 129–31; 1 MALLOY, *supra* note 58, at 557–58 (copyright agreement with Germany); 2 *id.* at 1265–66 (trademark agreement with the Netherlands); *id.* at 1687–88, 1710–12 (copyright agreement with Spain); *id.* at 1769–70 (trademark agreement with Switzerland). The President also entered into agreements under other miscellaneous proclamation statutes, including (1) a discriminatory tonnage duty statute, *see, e.g.,* Proclamation of May 11, 1829, 4 Stat. 816; 2 MALLOY, *supra* note 57, at 1680–87 (agreements with Spain to establish national treatment of trade between the United States and Spain's Caribbean colonies); 3 MILLER, *supra* note 52, at 521 (agreement with Austria), (2) a provision permitting the President to waive the requirement of readmeasurement of foreign vessels, *see, e.g.,* Act of Aug. 5, 1882, ch. 398, 22 Stat. 300; FOREIGN RELATIONS 1894, *supra* note 64, at 636–45; 1 MALLOY, *supra* note 57, at 386–87, and (3) a provision, amended by Congress to meet Canadian demands, authorizing the President to extend on a reciprocal basis to Canadian vessels the right to come to the aid of vessels wrecked or disabled in contiguous waters, *see, e.g.,* Act of Mar. 3, 1893, ch. 211, 27 Stat. 120; FOREIGN RELATIONS 1893, *supra* note 64, at 276–308, 327–40.

[77] The McKinley Act followed a decade of intense controversy over whether the House was obligated to implement reciprocity treaties that had received the Senate's advice and consent. *See, e.g.,* 2 HINDS, *supra* note 44, §§ 1524–1530, at 989–94; *see also supra* p. 812. The debate culminated in 1886 with the House's refusal to implement a Senate-approved reciprocity convention with Mexico. *See* 1 MALLOY, *supra* note 58, at 1146, 1151, 1156; Robinson, *supra* note 44, at 202. This demonstrated how difficult it was to obtain not only senatorial but congressional approval of agreements lowering protectionist trade barriers. *See* McCLURE, *supra* note 16, at 83–84. Section 3 of the McKinley Act was a modest attempt to address this problem. To encourage mutual reductions in customs duties, it gave the President power, without further legislative approval, to retaliate against countries imposing reciprocally unequal and unreasonable duties on products of the United States. Congress limited the President's power, however, by allowing him to remove an unimpressive set of commodities from the free list. *See* Act of Oct. 1, 1890, ch. 1244, 26 Stat. 567, 612. In the event that the President issued a proclamation finding that a country discriminated against American commerce, the free list items would be subject to specified tariff rates.

[78] *See Extension of Reciprocal Trade Agreements Act: Hearings on H.R. 1211 Before the Senate Comm. on Finance,* 81st Cong., 1st Sess., pt. 2, at 1095–1121 (1949) [hereinafter *Hearings on H.R. 1211*] (reprinting the exchanges of diplomatic notes); McCLURE, *supra* note 16, at 85; U.S. TARIFF COMM'N, RECIPROCITY AND COMMERCIAL TREATIES 27, 150–57 (1919). In only three cases did the President issue proclamations imposing penalty duties. *See id.* at 27.

[79] *See Hearings on H.R. 1211, supra* note 78, at 1095–98; FOREIGN RELATIONS 1891, *supra* note 65, at 43–48.

[80] *See Hearings on H.R. 1211, supra* note 78, at 1095–96; FOREIGN RELATIONS 1891, *supra* note 65, at 43–44 (note from Secretary of State James G. Blaine to Salvador de Mendonca, Nov. 3, 1890). For Brazil, the free introduction of coffee, one of the items included in section 3 of the Tariff Act, was a matter of importance.

neither Government shall definitely inform the other of its intention and decision to consider it at an end."[81]

The Brazilian Minister responded affirmatively,[82] but proposed a termination clause requiring three months notice.[83] The Secretary assented,[84] only to create embarrassment when Congress repealed the McKinley Tariff in 1894 without providing comparable authority in its successor.[85]

The new Secretary of State, Walter Gresham, informed the Brazilian Minister that Congress had terminated the previous arrangement, effective immediately.[86] Brazil protested that termination could occur only after three months' notice, as provided in the executive agreement.[87] The Secretary responded with a lesson in constitutional law:

> The Constitution of the United States, like the constitution of Brazil, points out the way in which treaties may be made and the faith of the nation duly pledged. In the United States treaties are made by the President, by and with the advice and consent of the Senate; in Brazil they are made by the President, subject to the approval of the Congress. Of such provisions in each other's constitutions governments are assumed to take notice. . . .
>
> In view of these well-known principles of law and matters of fact, it can not be supposed that it was intended, by the simple exchange of notes on January 31, 1891, to bind our Governments as by a treaty . . . .[88]

The Brazilians were out of luck.[89] Though they had bargained with Blaine on the termination clause, they should have known that the

---

[81] 1 FOREIGN RELATIONS 1890, *supra* note 65, at 44. Similar provisions, which we call "lapse clauses," appeared in a number of Secretary Blaine's agreements. *See, e.g.*, Letter from James G. Blaine, Secretary of State of the United States, to Miguel Suarez Guanes, Envoy and Minister Plenipotentiary of Spain (June 10, 1891), *reprinted in Hearings on H.R. 1211, supra* note 78, at 1100 ("always reserving the respective right of the Congress of the United States and of the Cortes of Spain to modify or repeal said arrangement whenever they may think proper"); Letter from James G. Blaine, Secretary of State of the United States, to Sir Julian Pauncefote (Dec. 29, 1891), *reprinted in Hearings on H.R. 1211, supra* note 78, at 1108.

[82] *See* FOREIGN RELATIONS 1891, *supra* note 65, at 44–46.

[83] *See id.* at 46.

[84] *See id.* at 46–47.

[85] *See* Act of Aug. 27, 1894, ch. 349, § 71, 28 Stat. 509, 569.

[86] *See* FOREIGN RELATIONS 1894, *supra* note 65, at 77. Gresham asserted that the arrangement was not a binding treaty and that, as a result of Congress's repeal of the authorizing statute, "the arrangement actually exists no longer." *Id.*; *see also id.* at 332 (proclaiming the similar expiration of the reciprocity agreement with Guatemala).

[87] *See id.* at 77–78, 79, 82.

[88] *Id.* at 79–82. President Cleveland explicitly referred Congress to the Secretary's correspondence with the Brazilian Minister. *See* Second Annual Message (Dec. 3, 1894), *in* 9 PRESIDENTIAL COMPILATION, *supra* note 40, at 524.

[89] So were the 10 other countries that had negotiated agreements with Blaine. *See* CRANDALL, TREATIES 2D, *supra* note 49, § 62, at 122. In 1895, however, he did enter into another agreement with Spain, *see* FOREIGN RELATIONS 1894, *supra* note 65, at 621–35; 2 FOREIGN RELATIONS 1895, *supra* note 65, at 1185–86, under another proclamation statute. *See* Act of Aug. 30, 1890, ch. 839, § 5, 26 Stat. 414, 415–16.

executive agreement could not bind the United States without the Senate's consent. At most, Gresham explained, it merely guaranteed that the executive would not change its mind without giving the requisite notice.[90] But once Congress had repealed the underlying statute, Brazil could not claim that the United States had breached its international obligation. Only treaties could have this consequence.[91]

These kinds of cases, then, do not provide much precedential support for NAFTA — which is very much intended as a solemn international obligation of the first importance.

(b)   Ex Ante Authorizations. — Proclamation statutes provided the most common form of interbranch collaboration, but Congress occasionally used a more self-conscious technique. These ex ante authorizations explicitly empowered the executive to make agreements under specified circumstances.

A good example was the Dingley Tariff of 1897.[92] Congress authorized the President to reach reciprocal trade agreements on a very

---

[90] Gresham explained that the termination clause was merely "a declaration of the manner in which [the executive] would, in the particular case, exercise the special power conferred upon him [by statute]." FOREIGN RELATIONS 1894, *supra* note 65, at 81.

[91] The State Department's 1906 *Digest of International Law* reprinted Gresham's note in full. *See* 5 MOORE, *supra* note 54, § 774, at 359–63. New Deal scholars labored mightily to explain away the note. McDougal and Lans, for example, claimed that it furnished "no authority whatever" for the proposition that the President and Congress could not collaborate to generate international obligations. *See* McDougal & Lans (pt. 1), *supra* note 16, at 349. To do so, however, they had to ignore the main point of Gresham's disquisition.

In any case, Gresham later made precisely the same point in an official letter to Congress concerning United States membership in the International Union of American States (later the Pan American Union). Congress had authorized the President to adhere to the Union, but subsequently inquired whether the United States was bound under international law to continue its participation. In response, Gresham wrote that despite the agreement's express 10-year termination provision, "it has not the binding force of a treaty made by the President, by and with the advice and consent of the Senate." H.R. EXEC. DOC. NO. 116, 53d Cong., 3d Sess. 5 (1894).

[92] Act of July 24, 1897, ch. 11, 30 Stat. 151. Another precedent sometimes cited as an ex ante authorization is the infamous Platt Amendment establishing the terms of United States-Cuban relations in the aftermath of the Spanish-American War. *See* Act of Mar. 2, 1901, ch. 803, 31 Stat. 895, 897–98. The amendment authorized the President to withdraw the American military from the island but only on condition, inter alia, that the new Cuban state agree to lease lands for naval or coaling stations, "to be agreed upon with the President of the United States." *Id.* at 898. This commitment was to be embodied "in a permanent treaty with the United States." *Id.* In 1903, President Roosevelt entered into executive agreements with Cuba to lease two sites as naval and coaling stations. *See* 1 MALLOY, *supra* note 58, at 358, 360. Virtually contemporaneously, on May 22, 1903, the President signed a treaty with Cuba that included the stipulation that Cuba would lease lands necessary for naval and coaling stations, "to be agreed upon with the President of the United States." *Id.* at 362, 364. The Senate did not approve the treaty until March 22, 1904, and it became effective on July 2 of that year. *See id.* at 362.

Some contemporary writers viewed the executive agreements as ancillary to the treaty. *See, e.g.,* WRIGHT, *supra* note 49, § 62, at 107. In strictness, however, the treaty did not become effective until the agreements had already been concluded. As a result, other writers viewed the agreements as made pursuant to statutory authorization. *See, e.g.,* CRANDALL, TREATIES 2D, *supra* note 49, § 67, at 139; Barnett, *supra* note 49, at 69. Even if the latter view were correct,

limited number of commodities.[93] Dingley's repeal in 1909[94] revealed once again the limited character of these ex ante agreements.[95] This time it was France that was left holding the bag: "I have the honor to remind you," wrote acting Secretary of State Huntington Wilson, "that these commercial agreements, not being treaties in the constitutional sense, . . . in the absence of enabling legislation by Congress, have been terminated ipso facto."[96] So far as the United States was con-

---

Congress itself had contemplated the necessity of a treaty in order to make the requirements set forth in the Platt Amendment "permanent." Although the agreements undoubtedly stretched existing categories, they are best viewed as applications of the principle underlying the modus vivendi doctrine. The President no doubt anticipated that the Senate's imminent approval of the treaty would cure any defect in his authority.

[93] *See* Act of July 24, 1897, ch. 11, § 3, 30 Stat. 151, 203–04. Section 3 of the Act included two different authorizations. One was a proclamation provision similar to § 3 of the 1890 Act, *see* Act of Oct. 1, 1890, ch. 1244, § 3, 26 Stat. 567, 612, though the list of commodities was even less impressive. More significant was the second authorization, which empowered the President to negotiate commercial agreements with a view to obtaining "reciprocal and equivalent concessions" on specified commodities. Act of July 24, 1897, ch. 11, § 3, 30 Stat. 151, 203. Congress established two tariffs for each commodity, limiting the President's discretion to making agreements that would place a country's imports on the more advantageous schedule. *See id.* at 204.

[94] *See* Payne-Aldrich Tariff Act of 1909, ch. 6, § 4, 36 Stat. 11, 83.

[95] Under this provision, the President entered into a number of commercial agreements. *See, e.g.,* 1 MALLOY, *supra* note 58, at 542–44, 547–48 (France); *id.* at 558–59, 562–65 (Germany); 2 *id.* at 1463–66 (Portugal).

[96] FOREIGN RELATIONS 1909, *supra* note 65, at 251. For the entire correspondence between Secretary of State Knox and the French Ambassador, see the same source at 248–54. In the 1909 Act, Congress directed the President to abrogate all of the agreements reached under the Dingley Act, but provided that they should be terminated in accordance with their termination clauses. *See* Payne-Aldrich Tariff Act of 1909, ch. 6, § 4, 36 Stat. 11, 83. For those agreements that had no termination clause, such as the French agreement, termination was to be made effective after six-months notice. *See id.*

Significantly, France accepted the Secretary's basic premise that these agreements were not binding under international law. Its complaint was not so much that Congress had unilaterally terminated the agreement but that it had discriminated against France by granting one-year extensions to other countries while extending the French agreements by only six months. On this point, the French could effectively turn Secretary Knox's own doctrine against him. After all, if the termination clauses only applied during the time when the Dingley Act was still in effect, as the Secretary claimed, then Congress had extended the agreements on an ad hoc basis. What justification was there, then, for discriminating between different countries? *See* FOREIGN RELATIONS 1909, *supra* note 65, at 250.

This diplomatic exchange, as in the earlier case of Brazil, presented McDougal and Lans with a difficult problem. In this case, they simply ignored the substance of the diplomatic notes. Adopting a legal realist mode, they emphasized that rather than simply voiding the agreements, Congress had expressly provided that they be terminated in accordance with their terms. *See* McDougal & Lans (pt. 1), *supra* note 16, at 350–51. Because Congress had used its discretion to extend the agreements, they argued, it had clearly treated them as the functional equivalents of treaties. *See id.*

But there is a fundamental difference between extending the terms as a matter of legislative grace and extending them because they were constitutionally incurred international obligations. It is this critical point that McDougal and Lans, by ignoring the Secretary's efforts to justify American conduct, refused to confront. From our perspective, the incident's most revealing feature is that the French Minister agreed with the Secretary of State on the point of constitutional law, even though this concession was against French interests.

cerned, foreigners would have to insist on a treaty if they wished to bind America under international law.[97]

With one exception. In 1792, Congress authorized the Postmaster General to "make arrangements with the postmasters in any foreign country for the reciprocal receipt and delivery of letters and packets."[98] While many postal agreements were reached since the late eighteenth century,[99] they were almost never ratified by the Senate.[100] In 1890, William Howard Taft, then Solicitor General, was asked to comment upon this procedure. The most important point about his opinion[101] is its candid recognition that postal agreements were constitutional anomalies. The "ordinary rule of construction," Taft announced, "would make the grant of power [in the Treaty Clause] exclusive" and condemn the postal practice.[102] But Taft persuaded himself that the "long usage, dating back to a period contemporary with the adoption of the Constitution, sanctions" this special case.[103]

---

[97] Nevertheless, so long as the Dingley Act was in force, the courts had no trouble giving domestic effect to the President's reciprocal tariff agreements. *See, e.g.*, La Manna, Azema & Farnan v. United States, 144 F. 683, 683 (2d Cir. 1906); Mihalovitch, Fletcher & Co. v. United States, 160 F. 988, 989 (C.C.S.D. Ohio 1908); Migliavacca Wine Co. v. United States, 148 F. 142, 142–43 (C.C.W.D. Wash. 1905).

Section 4 of the Dingley Act also authorized the President to negotiate tariff reciprocity treaties within certain specified parameters. *See* Act of July 24, 1897, ch. 11, §4, 30 Stat. 151, 204–05. Pursuant to this provision, Presidents McKinley and Roosevelt negotiated the "Kasson Treaties," but the Senate failed to approve a single one of the series. *See* U.S. TARIFF COMM'N, *supra* note 78, at 28–30. By the time of the New Deal, the Kasson Treaties had become an important symbol justifying Roosevelt's innovative claim that the President should be given the power to make legally binding reciprocity agreements. *See infra* note 210.

[98] Act of Feb. 20, 1792, ch. 7, § 26, 1 Stat. 232, 239. This provision was reenacted by the Third Congress, *see* Act of May 8, 1794, ch. 23, 1 Stat. 354, 366, and many times thereafter in identical or similar language. *See* CRANDALL, TREATIES 2D, *supra* note 49, § 65, at 131–33; MC-CLURE, *supra* note 16, at 38–40, 75–77.

[99] *See* CRANDALL, TREATIES 2D, *supra* note 49, § 65, at 132–33; McCLURE, *supra* note 16, at 75–77; 1 MILLER, *supra* note 53, at 7–8. Prominent among these were the 1874 treaty forming the General Postal Union (later the Universal Postal Union), *see* 19 Stat. 577 (1874), and the 1897 and 1906 Universal Postal Union Conventions, *see* 35 Stat. 1639 (1906); 30 Stat. 1629 (1897).

[100] Only five postal agreements were processed as treaties before 1931. *See* 1 MILLER, *supra* note 53, at 7. The Supreme Court found a postal convention concluded under statutory not senatorial authority effective as domestic law in Cotzhausen v. Nazro, 107 U.S. 215, 217 (1882).

[101] *See* 19 Op. Att'y Gen. 513 (1890). New Deal scholars used this opinion as another precedent. *See, e.g.*, James W. Garner, *Acts and Joint Resolutions of Congress as Substitutes for Treaties*, 29 AM. J. INT'L L. 482, 486–87 (1935).

[102] 19 Op. Att'y Gen. at 513–14.

[103] *Id.* at 515, 520. Writers at the time widely perceived postal conventions as *sui generis*. Butler, for instance, did not include postal agreements in his list of agreements of the United States. *See* 2 BUTLER, *supra* note 49, 405 app. at 405–531. As late as 1931, the State Department's treaty adviser likewise declined to include postal conventions in his compilation, on the ground that they are largely "business arrangements between offices of transport rather than agreements between governments in the ordinary sense." 1 MILLER, *supra* note 53, at 7. Other legislators and writers took a similar view. *See, e.g.*, 48 CONG. REC. 2600–01 (1912) (remarks of Sen. Lodge); Baldwin, *Entry, supra* note 49, at 414; Barnett, *supra* note 49, at 68–69; Hyde, *supra* note 49, at 230.

It is especially revealing that Taft treated these agreements as authorized *by the Treaty Clause* as interpreted with the aid of historical practice.[104] He did not suggest that Congress's enumerated powers might provide a majority of the House and Senate with an all-purpose source of power to authorize binding international agreements.[105]

This narrow exception, then, proves the rule: the fact that Congress explicitly gave its advance authorization for an executive agreement by no means transformed the agreement into the constitutional equivalent of a treaty.

(c)   Ex Post Approvals. — We come next to the cases most similar to NAFTA. Here Congress does not merely authorize the President to reach a future agreement. Instead, it approves a deal he has already worked out. Were there any precedents of this type before Versailles?

The only significant episode came in 1911. Taft, now President, hoped to win congressional approval for a sweeping tariff reduction with Canada.[106] Although not on the same scale as NAFTA, this was a very ambitious program by the standards of the day. Moreover, Taft negotiated with Canada first, seeking congressional — not senatorial — support afterwards.[107]

But Taft was a first-class lawyer, and the way he structured his deal speaks eloquently about the limits of his constitutional universe. The notes exchanged with Canada contained only one promise: that the President and Prime Minister would make their best efforts to convince their legislatures to enact the statutes necessary to realize their dreams of a sweeping and reciprocal reduction in tariffs.[108] Indeed, the notes stated that

> it is distinctly understood that we do not attempt to bind for the future the action of the United States Congress or the Parliament of Canada, but that each of these authorities shall be absolutely free to make any change of tariff policy or of any other matter covered by the present arrangement that may be deemed expedient.[109]

---

[104] *See* 19 Op. Att'y Gen. at 520.

[105] Indeed, in subsequent years, as Roosevelt's Secretary of War, as President, and thereafter, Taft repeatedly confirmed the view that Congress has no power to approve binding international agreements.

[106] A wealth of relevant materials, including the fierce congressional debates, is compiled in S. DOC. No. 80, 62d Cong., 1st Sess., pts. 1–3 (1911).

[107] This led some New Deal scholars to emphasize the episode. *See, e.g.,* McCLURE, *supra* note 16, at 91–92; Garner, *supra* note 101, at 486.

[108] The notes are printed in S. DOC. No. 80, cited above in note 106, pt. 3C, at 4679–89.

[109] Letter from W.S. Fielding and William Paterson, Canadian Ministers, to P.C. Knox, Secretary of State of the United States (Jan. 21, 1911) [hereinafter Fielding Letter], *reprinted in* S. DOC. No. 80, *supra* note 106, pt. 3C, at 4679. Taft repeated this understanding some years later. *See* TAFT, *supra* note 69, at 111.

In short, Taft hoped to achieve a condition of *conscious parallelism*. The exchange of notes would mark the beginning of a coordinated campaign to win domestic legislation, with the hope that both legislatures would like the result.[110] Given this limited ambition, Taft did not believe it was necessary to ask for the Senate's consent. Instead, he called upon both Houses to enact legislation by the vote of a simple majority.[111]

Taft's elegant innovation proved attractive. Not only did Congress enact the President's proposal,[112] but it invited him to repeat his performance.[113] But the Canadian Parliament did not act out its parallel role, and the initiative died.[114]

Apart from this special case, the only other ex post approval cases involved American participation in a number of early international organizations.[115] Characteristically, these were merely organs for consultation. The participating states were under no obligations except,

---

[110] *See* TAFT, *supra* note 69, at 111; Fielding Letter, *supra* note 109, *reprinted in* S. DOC. NO. 80, *supra* note 106, pt. 3C, at 4679.

When he was Secretary of War in the Roosevelt Administration, Taft devised a similarly creative legal solution to handling relations with Panama during the construction of the Canal. For a detailed recounting of the incident, see TAFT, cited above in note 69, at 111–12. Ultimately, Panama followed in the footsteps of Brazil and France. In 1923, Congress authorized the President to abrogate the so-called "Taft Agreement." *See* Act of Feb. 12, 1923, ch. 69, 42 Stat. 1225, 1225–26. In response to Panama's vigorous protest, Secretary of State Hughes reminded the Panamanians that the agreement was nothing more than "a *modus vivendi* to serve as a temporary basis for the settlement of difficulties" and thus did not in any way limit the United States's freedom of action. 5 HACKWORTH, *supra* note 69, at 432–33; *see* 2 FOREIGN RELATIONS 1923, *supra* note 65, at 638–87; 2 FOREIGN RELATIONS 1922, *supra* note 65, at 751–62; *supra* note 69.

[111] Although the reciprocity agreement itself was controversial, Taft's clever procedural move generated little debate. Only the dissenting minority in the House Committee on Ways and Means challenged the procedure. *See* H.R. REP. NO. 3, 62d Cong., 1st Sess., pt. 2, at 1–2 (1911). The Senate was silent. *See* S. REP. NO. 63, 62d Cong., 1st Sess. 12 (1911).

[112] *See* Act of July 26, 1911, ch. 3, 37 Stat. 4.

[113] As ultimately enacted, the bill authorized the President to negotiate further trade agreements with Canada, which were to be submitted to Congress "for ratification or rejection." *Id.* at 12. Two years later, Congress generalized the procedure, authorizing the President to negotiate reciprocity agreements with other foreign countries. *See* Act of Oct. 3, 1913, ch. 16, § 4, 38 Stat. 114, 192. Again, before becoming operative, these agreements were to be submitted to the Congress for ratification or rejection. *See id.*

Nothing came of these initiatives. Congress repealed the 1911 Act some years later. *See* Act of Sept. 21, 1922, ch. 356, 42 Stat. 858, 947–48. The 1913 provision was also a failure, never giving rise to any actual agreements. We are thus left to speculate about the character of the agreements Congress was contemplating. Nevertheless, in light of traditional understandings and coming on the heels of Taft's Canadian agreement, there is every reason to suppose it had his non-binding agreement model in mind.

[114] *See* MCCLURE, *supra* note 16, at 91–92.

[115] Before World War I, Presidents most often sought congressional approval of American participation in international organizations through submission of the organizations' constituent charters to the Senate for approval as treaties. *See* LAURENCE F. SCHMECKEBIER, INTERNATIONAL ORGANIZATIONS IN WHICH THE UNITED STATES PARTICIPATES 5–7 (1935) (providing detailed descriptions). But in a number of cases, Congress authorized American participation through passage of statutes or joint resolutions appropriating, or authorizing appropriations for, the expenses

perhaps, to pay their share of the administrative costs.[116] Nonetheless, some mechanism was needed to regulate these engagements, and an ex post approval procedure evolved as one means of doing so. Typically, the executive decided to participate and then asked Congress to approve by appropriating the necessary expenses. Prior to Versailles, this was a trivial matter, but in 1913 Congress passed a statute to regularize the practice.[117] This statute reappears later in our story, but in 1913 it was seen as an uncontroversial measure regulating appropriations for participation in any "international congress, conference, or like event."[118]

(d) *The Role of the Courts.* — Courts generally play a secondary role in the transformation we are describing. The twentieth-century story has been dominated by the President and the State Department, the Senate and the House, the mass media and the citizenry. Nevertheless, judicial opinions — especially as they were interpreted by the main players — were also important in the process of legitimation.

Unsurprisingly, the judicial pickings from this early period are slim. But it is important to place them in historical context because in the 1930s and 1940s, the inventors of the modern congressional-execu-

---

of the American delegation and the country's share of the organization's (always quite limited) budget. *See id.*

[116] *See id.* at 13–25, 75–112, 144–57, 283–303, 321–30. These modest organizations were designed to facilitate international cooperation in areas of mutual interest and were limited to gathering and disseminating information, making recommendations, proposing treaties and conventions, and coordinating activities. The United States could typically withdraw at will.

The most important of the organizations was the Pan American Union, about which the New Deal scholars sought to make much. *See, e.g.,* McDougal & Lans (pt. 1), *supra* note 16, at 271–72. A resolution of the First International Conference of American States of 1889–1890 called for the creation of an International Union of American Republics charged with responsibility for collecting information about the customs laws and regulations of each of the American republics and disseminating the results through a trilingual publication called the *Bulletin of the Commercial Bureau of the American Republics.* Congress approved United States participation in an appropriations statute. *See* H.R. Exec. Doc. No. 116, 53d Cong., 3d Sess. 2–4 (1894); SCHMECKEBIER, *supra* note 115, at 77–79. Even though the participating states had agreed that no state could withdraw until 10 years had passed, the Secretary of State later informed Congress that the United States's only obligation to continue its participation was one of good faith. Because the Senate had never given its advice and consent to United States adherence, the country was not bound under international law. *See* H.R. Exec. Doc. No. 116, *supra,* at 4–5. In the following years, the Union's duties were expanded to include keeping the official records and planning the agendas of the International Conferences of the American Republics, making arrangements for special conferences, assisting in the ratification of conventions adopted by the Conferences, and performing other similar functions. *See* SCHMECKEBIER, *supra* note 115, at 81–83.

[117] *See* Act of Mar. 4, 1913, ch. 149, 37 Stat. 912, 913 ("Hereafter, the Executive shall not extend or accept any invitation to participate in any international congress, conference, or like event, without first having specific authority of law to do so."). This effort to control the President's conduct of foreign affairs is still on the books. *See* 22 U.S.C. § 262 (1988).

[118] Act of Mar. 4, 1913, ch. 149, 37 Stat. 912, 913; *see also* Act of Mar. 3, 1897, ch. 376, § 1, 29 Stat. 624 (recording a similar provision dealing with appropriations for monetary conferences).

tive agreement used them to create the legalistic illusion of a pedigree.[119]

There are only two Supreme Court decisions that have the remotest relation to our problem. *Field v. Clark*[120] considered a challenge to the proclamation provisions of the McKinley Tariff of 1890.[121] The statute authorized the President to determine whether foreign tariffs were "reciprocally unequal and unreasonable" and to impose by proclamation punitive duties on recalcitrants "for such time as he shall deem just."[122] Such vague standards, according to appellants, were unconstitutional delegations of both the power of Congress to make statutes and the power of the Senate to consent to treaties.[123]

Appellants' reference to treaties was rather mysterious, because the statute made no mention of international agreements of any kind, and none of the reciprocal trade agreements generated by the Act were before the Court. Appellants' primary challenge was to the vague standards Congress had used in delegating the power to impose penalty tariffs to the President.[124] It is perfectly understandable, then, that the Court treated the treaty issue as parasitic on the claim that Congress had unconstitutionally delegated its legislative authority.[125] This claim was roundly rejected by a vote of seven to two. After upholding the legislative delegation in a lengthy opinion,[126] Justice Harlan added: "What has been said is equally applicable to the objection that the [proclamation provision] invests the President with treaty making power."[127]

This single sentence was later read as an authoritative Supreme Court vindication of the modern congressional-executive agreement.[128] But it merely upheld the proclamation power of the President, and did not address the question whether he could make agreements, rather than treaties, with foreign nations. It is true that Secretary Blaine used the provision challenged by *Field* to launch the first program of reciprocal trade agreements in the history of the United States. But

---

[119] *See infra* notes 220, 224, 241, 266–67, 302, and accompanying text.

[120] 143 U.S. 649 (1892).

[121] *See id.* at 650 (stating the case); *see also supra* notes 75–77 and accompanying text.

[122] Act of Oct. 1, 1890, ch. 1244, 26 Stat. 567, 612.

[123] *See Field,* 143 U.S. at 656–59 (summarizing argument for appellants).

[124] The appellants were importers seeking a refund of duties exacted under the McKinley Tariff Act. *See id.* at 650. They sought to throw the Act out in toto on the ground that § 3 was an unconstitutional delegation of legislative and treaty-making power. *See id.* at 651.

[125] *See id.* at 694.

[126] *See id.* The Court concluded that the President "was the mere agent of the law making department to ascertain and declare the event upon which its expressed will was to take effect." *Id.* at 693. The two concurring Justices disagreed with the Court on the legislative delegation issue but concurred on the ground that § 3 was severable. *See id.* at 700 (Lamar, J., dissenting in part, and concurring in the judgment).

[127] *Field,* 143 U.S. at 694.

[128] *See infra* notes 220, 224, 302, and accompanying text.

Justice Harlan did not approve or disapprove this initiative — for the simple reason that the case before him did not involve any such agreement.[129]

The second case that New Dealers later canonized had the merit of involving an actual executive agreement, concluded under the ex ante authorization provisions of the Dingley Tariff.[130] The Secretary had negotiated the agreement with France[131] and an importer challenged the Collector of Customs's interpretation of its provisions. The question in *B. Altman & Co. v. United States*[132] was whether the Supreme Court could take jurisdiction of an appeal. Because the jurisdictional statute referred only to "treaties," the United States urged a narrow construction, hoping to insulate the circuit court's interpretation of executive agreements from Supreme Court review.

The Court disagreed and read the jurisdictional term broadly:

> While it may be true that this commercial agreement . . . was not a treaty possessing the dignity of one requiring ratification by the Senate of the United States, it was an international compact, negotiated between the representatives of two sovereign nations, and made in the name and on behalf of the contracting countries, and dealing with important commercial relations between the two countries . . . .[133]

As a consequence, the Court construed the word "treaty" in the jurisdictional statute to include executive agreements authorized by Congress.

This approach was entirely sensible, but it did not constitute — as later commentators asserted[134] — an effort to make substantive law and vindicate the constitutional interchangeability of treaties and congressional-executive agreements. To the contrary, the Court expressly indicated that the Secretary's agreement with France lacked "the dignity" of a treaty.[135] Indeed, France had already learned three years earlier just how undignified it might be to rely on the Secretary's

---

[129] By the time of the argument, Blaine had already concluded three agreements. *See* Francis B. Sayre, *The Constitutionality of the Trade Agreements Act*, 39 COLUM. L. REV. 751, 757 (1939). But Justice Harlan made no mention of that fact.

In any event, Justice Harlan did not intimate that such an agreement could constitutionally impose a binding international obligation on the United States, and he was not so understood by his contemporaries. Only two years later, Secretary Gresham would insist in his note to Brazil that agreements under the very proclamation provision before the Court were radically inferior to treaties. *See supra* pp. 823–24. Quincy Wright, moreover, had no trouble citing *Field* for the proposition that congressionally authorized arrangements are *not* internationally binding. *See* WRIGHT, *supra* note 49, § 159, at 233 & n.14; *see also id.* at 236 (asserting that such agreements are not binding under international law and citing *Field* in the next sentence for the proposition that they are nevertheless binding on the courts as domestic law).

[130] *See supra* notes 92–93 and accompanying text.

[131] *See* 1 MALLOY, *supra* note 58, at 542; *supra* note 95.

[132] 224 U.S. 583 (1912).

[133] *Id.* at 601.

[134] *See* McDougal & Lans (pt. 1), *supra* note 16, at 273–77; *infra* note 241.

[135] *B. Altman & Co.*, 224 U.S. at 601.

word. It was precisely the agreement before the Court that had been terminated by Congress in 1909, forcing the Secretary to deny that France could treat executive agreements as if they were interchangeable with treaties.[136]

Courts, then, were no different from anybody else. Although they took occasional notice of embryonic forms of congressional-executive collaboration, they did not put them on the same constitutional level as formal treaties.

D. *Legislative Unilateralism*

Collaboration between Congress, the President, and the courts developed deeper roots in the years ahead. Before moving further into the twentieth century, however, we should take a final look back at the nineteenth. We have not yet discussed two precedents that loom large in the New Deal myth of continuity. Compared to the executive agreements we have been considering, they are even further removed from the modern practice. Nonetheless, given their prominence, we should explain why it is anachronistic to view them as precedents.

These cases involve the American acquisitions of Texas[137] and Hawaii.[138] Their use as precedent is puzzling because they involved neither treaties *nor* executive agreements. Both transactions were accomplished entirely through the enactment of ordinary legislation[139] — and thus were merely cases of "legislative unilateralism."[140] This simple point is obscured in the standard accounts because Presidents first tried to annex these territories by negotiating treaties with the independent republics of Texas[141] and Hawaii.[142] But the Senate re-

---

[136] *See supra* p. 825. Indeed, Justice Day, who authored the Court's opinion, had been Secretary of State in 1898 when the original agreement with France had been concluded. *See* 1 MALLOY, *supra* note 58, at viii; 2 *id.* at 542. He was no doubt aware of the limitations the State Department had observed in entering agreements of this kind.

[137] *See* Joint Resolution of Mar. 1, 1845, 5 Stat. 797; Joint Resolution of Dec. 29, 1845, 9 Stat. 108; *see also* CRANDALL, TREATIES 2D, *supra* note 49, § 67, at 135–36 (describing acquisition of Texas); 4 MILLER, *supra* note 53, at 689–740 (same).

[138] *See* Joint Resolution of July 7, 1898, 30 Stat. 750, 750–51; CRANDALL, TREATIES 2D, *supra* note 49, §67, at 138.

[139] Congress used the joint resolution form in both cases.

[140] Although no agreements were involved, the annexations were closest in form to presidential agreements made under proclamation statutes. The only difference was that Congress reduced the President's formal role to the vanishing point. Rather than authorizing him to bring the legislation into effect upon finding specified facts, Congress passed the necessary legislation on its own. *See* 2 BUTLER, *supra* note 49, § 463, at 372–73 n.2 (describing the annexations as examples of "reciprocal legislation").

[141] The Senate rejected a proposed treaty on June 8, 1844, by a vote of 35 to 16. *See* 6 SEN. EXEC. J. 311–12 (1844); 4 MILLER, *supra* note 53, at 699. Earlier efforts had also been defeated. *See id.* at 737–38.

[142] President Cleveland withdrew a proposed treaty when opposition developed. *See* 28 SEN. EXEC. J. 397–98 (1893) (President's message to Senate submitting treaty); 2 JOHN W. FOSTER, DIPLOMATIC MEMOIRS 168 (1909). President McKinley's subsequent attempt met with the same

jected the treaties, leading partisans to search for a constitutional alternative that did not require a two-thirds majority.[143]

In the case of Texas, proponents of annexation pointed to an express constitutional provision: "New states may be admitted by the Congress into this Union."[144] On their view, this meant that Congress could use a joint resolution stipulating the conditions under which it was willing to admit Texas as a state.[145] Majorities in both Houses agreed and instructed President Tyler, and his successor Polk, to communicate Congress's "overture" to Texas.[146] When Texas complied with Congress's terms, President Polk's role was limited to informing Congress of this fact.[147] At that point, Congress enacted a second

---

fate. *See* 31 SEN. EXEC. J. 169–70 (1897) (President's message to Senate submitting treaty); HOLT, *supra* note 67, at 163–64.

[143] *See* HOLT, *supra* note 67, at 164. Opponents of the Texas treaty argued that annexation would amount to a declaration of war against Mexico, because Mexico, still refusing to recognize Texan independence, had announced that it would view annexation as an act of war. The power to declare war, opponents contended, rested exclusively with Congress and was beyond the scope of the treaty power. *See, e.g.,* 6 SEN. EXEC. J. 274, 277, 279 (1844); CRANDALL, TREATIES 2D, *supra* note 49, §67, at 135–36.

[144] U.S. CONST. art. IV, § 3, cl. 1; *see also* sources cited *infra* note 149.

[145] Even before the Senate rejected the treaty, Senator Henderson introduced a resolution declaring that Congress could admit Texas directly as a new state. *See* 6 SEN. EXEC. J. 311 (1844); CRANDALL, TREATIES 2D, *supra* note 49, § 67, at 136. Immediately afterwards, Senator McDuffie introduced a joint resolution, *see* CONG. GLOBE, 28th Cong., 2d Sess. 16 (1845), and President Tyler submitted the rejected treaty and all of the relevant correspondence to Congress. *See* Message of June 10, 1844, *in* 4 PRESIDENTIAL COMPILATION, *supra* note 40, at 323. On June 18, 1844, Secretary of State Calhoun affirmed the joint resolution as an alternative to the treaty, stating that "[t]his mode of effecting it will have the advantage of requiring only a majority of the two houses, instead of two thirds of the Senate." 4 MILLER, *supra* note 53, at 703. McDougal and Lans treated this statement as an early affirmation, by a noted "strict constructionist," of the modern interchangeability doctrine. They failed, however, to note the absence of any form of executive agreement, let alone any indication that Calhoun supposed he was endorsing an all-purpose alternative to senatorial "advice and consent." *See* McDougal & Lans (pt. 1), *supra* note 16, at 263–64.

[146] The joint resolution provided that Texas could become a state on certain specified conditions. *See* Joint Resolution of Mar. 1, 1845, 5 Stat. 797, 797. In accordance with an amendment added by the Senate — and apparently designed to mollify those who opposed the procedure — Congress gave the President another alternative. Section 3 authorized the President to negotiate terms of admission with the Republic. The resulting agreement could then be approved "either by treaty to be submitted to the Senate, or by articles to be submitted to the two houses of Congress, as the President may direct." *Id.* at 798. As one of his last acts in office, President Tyler rejected this option because any agreement reached through negotiation would, he believed, have to be submitted to the Senate as a treaty. *See* Letter from Mr. Calhoun, Secretary of State of the United States, to Mr. Andrew J. Donelson, Chargé d'Affaires to Texas (Mar. 3, 1845), *reprinted in* 4 MILLER, *supra* note 53, at 707–08. While adopting Tyler's decision, President Polk disagreed on the legal point, though he was "sensible that many of the sincere friends of Texas may entertain this opinion." Letter from Mr. Buchanan, Secretary of State of the United States, to Mr. Andrew J. Donelson, Chargé d'Affaires to Texas (Mar. 10, 1845), *reprinted in* 4 MILLER, *supra* note 53, at 708–10.

[147] *See* Joint Resolution of Mar. 1, 1845, 5 Stat. 797, 797. He did so on December 2, 1845.

joint resolution formally admitting Texas as a state.[148]

To be sure, this shift from treaty to statute generated enormous constitutional controversy. But it was not a debate about the use of executive agreements. Senators propounded numerous theories, including, on the one hand, the "exclusivity" of Congress's power to admit new states and, on the other, the "exclusivity" of the treaty power over the annexation of territory.[149] In retrospect, it is a little hard to understand what was motivating the constitutional objections of the opponents to the joint resolution[150] — other than hostility to the admission of new slave states.[151] There would have been a need for a treaty of

---

See Annual Message to Congress, *in* 4 PRESIDENTIAL COMPILATION, *supra* note 40, at 386.

[148] *See* Joint Resolution of Dec. 29, 1845, 9 Stat. 108.

[149] Proponents of the joint resolution in the Senate relied most heavily on Congress's express power to admit new states. *See, e.g.,* CONG. GLOBE, 28th Cong., 2d Sess. 296–98 (1845) (summary of remarks of Sen. Woodbury); *id.* at 315 (summary of remarks of Sen. Colquitt); *id.* at 321–22 (summary of remarks of Sen. Merrick); *id.* at 344 (summary of remarks of Sen. Walker); *id.* at 351–52 (summary of remarks of Sen. Bagby). Some seemed to think this an exclusive power that trumped the treaty power. *See, e.g., id.* at 298 (summary of remarks of Sen. Woodbury); *id.* at 315 (summary of remarks of Sen. Colquitt); *id.* at 321–23 (summary of remarks of Sen. Merrick). The rejected treaty of annexation would have been constitutional, they argued, only because it provided for the annexation of Texas as a territory, not its admission as a state. *See, e.g., id.* at 297 (summary of remarks of Sen. Woodbury). Others viewed the admission power as concurrent, shared with the treaty-making power. *See, e.g., id.* at 344 (summary of remarks of Sen. Walker).

Opponents generally followed the lead of the Senate Foreign Relations Committee, whose elaborate report argued that the joint resolution procedure was unconstitutional. *See* S. REP. NO. 79, 28th Cong., 2d Sess. (1845), *reprinted in* COMPILATION OF REPORTS OF COMMITTEE ON FOREIGN RELATIONS, U.S. SENATE, 1789–1901, S. DOC. NO. 231, 56th Cong., 2d Sess., pt. 6, at 78–99 (1901). The Committee argued that Congress's power to admit new states was inapplicable because it was limited to the admission of states carved out of territory already belonging to the United States. *See id., reprinted in* S. DOC. NO. 231, *supra*, pt. 6, at 95–99. Consensual acquisition of territory, in contrast to admission, could be accomplished only by treaty because the Treaty Clause required all agreements with foreign countries to be in the form of treaties. *See id.;* *see also* CONG. GLOBE, 28th Cong., 2d Sess. 280–82 (1845) (remarks of Sen. Morehead); *id.* at 292 (summary of remarks of Sen. Rives).

[150] Opposition seems to have been rooted in a sweeping vision of the treaty power that did not survive Versailles. According to this view, all compacts reached through negotiation had to be concluded as treaties, even if they imposed no binding international obligations. *See, e.g.,* S. REP. NO. 79, *supra* note 149, *reprinted in* S. DOC. NO. 231, *supra* note 149, pt. 6, at 82; 4 MILLER, *supra* note 53, at 707 (reporting President Tyler's view). The constitutional debate was complicated by the presence of two presently uncontroversial questions: whether the Constitution permits the acquisition of new territory and whether new states can be formed out of territory not part of the United States at the time of their admission. For moderns, the Louisiana Purchase answered the first, *see* S. REP. NO. 79, *supra* note 149, *reprinted in* S. DOC. NO. 231, *supra* note 149, pt. 6, at 79–80, 92–96, and Texas v. White, 74 U.S. (7 Wall.) 700, 719–26 (1868), resolved the second.

[151] This hostility was reflected in the contradictory positions that some opponents took on the issue, arguing in opposition to the treaty that Congress's power was exclusive and in opposition to the joint resolution that the treaty method was exclusive. The irony was not lost on proponents. *See, e.g.,* CONG. GLOBE APP., 28th Cong., 2d Sess. 124 (1845) (remarks of Rep. Bayly).

cession had Texas been a part of Mexico.[152] But because Texas was an independent state,[153] what would have been the point of a treaty with a country that was immediately going out of existence when the agreement was executed? As was noted at the time, Texas's rights would be determined by domestic law as soon as it had been admitted into the Union. Any promises made in a treaty would have immediately lost their international character.[154] Given this fact, a decision to use the treaty power would have ousted the House from its role in the admission of new states even though the treaty would not have generated binding international obligations.

In any event, one thing should be clear: it is wrong to view the admission of Texas as if it involved a congressional-executive agreement. While many have made this mistake,[155] their non sequitur is easy to spot. Simply because the annexation was not approved as a treaty, it does not follow that Congress achieved its goal by approving an executive agreement negotiated with President Sam Houston of Texas. Rather than creating a new legal form, Congress achieved its aim through ordinary domestic legislation.[156]

The same is true of Hawaii. In 1893 the native monarchy was overthrown and the new republic agreed to a treaty of annexation. When opposition developed in the Senate, President Cleveland withdrew the treaty, and the Republic of Hawaii survived until 1897, when another treaty was negotiated and again withdrawn.[157] The outbreak of the Spanish-American War, however, made the islands strategically important.[158] Rather than renewing a fight in the Senate, the McKinley Administration cited the precedent of Texas and urged both Houses to approve a joint resolution accepting the annexation offer by the Republic.[159]

---

[152] Even then a treaty might not have been necessary if the agreement had not imposed any continuing obligations on the United States. Mexico would not have had any rights against the United States under international law, and Texas's rights would have been purely a matter of American domestic law.

[153] Texan independence had been recognized internationally despite Mexico's fierce opposition. *See* 4 MILLER, *supra* note 53, at 728–30.

[154] *See* 14 CONG. GLOBE APP., 28th Cong., 2d Sess. 124 (1845) (reporting Rep. Bayly's endorsement of the position argued previously by Sen. Choate).

[155] *See, e.g.,* McCLURE, *supra* note 16, at 62–67. Some New Deal scholars simply failed to mention that the acquisition of Texas did not itself involve an executive agreement, citing it nonetheless as a decisive precedent. *See, e.g.,* Garner, *supra* note 101, at 485–86; McDougal & Lans (pt. 1), *supra* note 16, at 263–64; Wright, *supra* note 16, at 342 n.4.1, 343.

[156] This point was recognized by most early scholars. *See, e.g.,* 2 BUTLER, *supra* note 49, § 463, at 372–73 n.2; CRANDALL, TREATIES 2D, *supra* note 49, § 67, at 135–38; 1 WILLOUGHBY, *supra* note 51, §§ 154, 155, at 344–49; WRIGHT, *supra* note 49, § 199, at 275.

[157] *See* McDougal & Lans (pt. 1), *supra* note 16, at 266.

[158] *See, e.g.,* S. REP. NO. 681, 55th Cong., 2d Sess. 60 (1898); McCLURE, *supra* note 16, at 68.

[159] *See* 2 FOSTER, *supra* note 142, at 174.

This proposal provoked a replay of the Texas debate.[160] Advocates of the treaty approach claimed that territory must be acquired through a formal agreement approved in the traditional way;[161] proponents of the joint resolution insisted that a treaty was unnecessary when one sovereign completely swallowed up the other.[162] Once again, the transaction did not involve an executive agreement and it is anachronistic to cite it as a precedent for a modern practice it did not anticipate.[163]

E. The Constitutional Consensus

Our conclusion, it is true, runs against the grain of the modern myth of continuity. But so much the worse for the modern myth. As a final test of the rival accounts, we turn to the standard legal commentaries of the early twentieth century. If a new form of congressional-executive agreement had arisen, surely the scholars would have noticed it. This was the heyday of writing on the Treaty Clause. Large tomes and many excellent articles were devoted to the subject.[164] But none can be found that contemplates the modern doctrine, much less endorses it.

Scholars recognized that the President sometimes made agreements under the authority of proclamation or authorization statutes.[165] But

---

[160] The issue was debated throughout June 1898. *See* 31 CONG. REC. 5770–6712 (1898). The Senate Foreign Relations Committee supported the constitutionality of the procedure on the strength of the Texas precedent. *See* S. REP. NO. 681, *supra* note 158, at 1–2, 45–46. On July 7, 1898, the joint resolution was enacted. *See* Joint Resolution of July 7, 1898, 30 Stat. 750.

[161] Annexation opponents distinguished the Texas precedent on the ground that Hawaii, unlike Texas, was not being admitted as a state, noting the proponents' heavy reliance on this point during the Texas debate. *See, e.g.*, 31 CONG. REC. 6154 (1898) (remarks of Sen. Bacon); *see also supra* note 149.

Even some leading proponents of annexation had serious misgivings about the constitutionality of the joint resolution procedure. *See* McDougal & Lans (pt. 1), *supra* note 16, at 267. Secretary of State Foster himself viewed the procedure as unconstitutional. *See* 2 FOSTER, *supra* note 142, at 174. He justified it as an emergency measure necessitated by war, implying strongly that this was the view of leading Senators as well. *See id.*

[162] Most proponents of the resolution remained silent, content simply to wait out the opposition. But Senator Foraker provided the missing rationale, arguing that there was a critical distinction between a partial cession of territory and a merger of one sovereign into another. *See* 31 CONG. REC. 6152, 6332–39 (1898). Where one party to the contract ceased to exist at the moment of execution, there was no mutuality of obligation, no contract and, therefore, no need to employ the treaty procedure. *See id.* at 6333–34.

[163] The New Deal scholars usually cited Hawaii and Texas in the same breath — and in the same misleading fashion. *See, e.g.*, MCCLURE, *supra* note 16, at 67–68 (citing Hawaii and Texas as examples of the interchangeability of treaties and congressional-executive or unilateral executive agreements); Garner, *supra* note 101, at 485–86 (same); McDougal & Lans (pt. 1), *supra* note 16, at 265–66 (same); Wright, *supra* note 16, at 343 (same).

[164] Among these are Butler's two-volume treatise, both editions of Crandall's treatise, Wright's 1922 classic, the first edition of Hyde's treatise, and Moore's 1905 article, all of which are cited above in note 49.

[165] *See supra* notes 72, 76, 78, 89, 92, 95, and accompanying text.

they treated this subject as a relatively minor matter, not to be confused with treaty-making.[166] Moreover, there was a clear consensus on the inferiority of these executive agreements.[167] To quote Quincy Wright: "Such agreements appear to be dependent for their effectiveness upon the authorizing legislation, and are terminable, both nationally and *internationally*, at the discretion of Congress."[168] Even writers with connections to the State Department, who might be expected to be supporters of presidential authority, seemed to accept this view.[169]

II. THE TWENTIES

A. *The Great War and Its Aftermath*

It is unsurprising, then, that Woodrow Wilson returned in triumph from Versailles with an agreement he called a "treaty." It would require another world war, and much else, before a President would seriously consider any alternative.

The defeat of the Versailles Treaty, however, did not free the United States from legal entanglement. Because the treaty had been rejected, the country was legally at war and so was obliged to extricate itself from this embarrassment. Once again, it turned to legislative unilateralism. Congress, by joint resolution, declared an end to the state of war with Germany, Austria, and Hungary in 1921,[170]

---

[166] *See, e.g.*, 2 BUTLER, *supra* note 49, § 463, at 372 n.2; CRANDALL, TREATIES 2D, *supra* note 49, §§ 62–67, at 121–40; 1 WILLOUGHBY, *supra* note 51, § 204, at 476–78; WRIGHT, *supra* note 49, § 61, at 105–06, 235–36; Moore, *supra* note 49, at 392–96.

[167] Butler, for example, declared that arrangements reached through reciprocal legislation were not binding on either country. *See* 2 BUTLER, *supra* note 49, § 463, at 372 n.2. Similarly, Hyde wrote in 1905 that agreements under the 1890 and 1897 acts, "although expressed in the form of contract, imposed no restriction on the United States or other parties thereto to alter their tariff schedules and thus terminate their obligations." Hyde, *supra* note 49, at 229; *see also* WRIGHT, *supra* note 49, § 162, at 236 (stating that Congress may freely terminate agreements concluded under congressional authority); Edward S. Corwin, *The Power of Congress to Declare Peace*, 18 MICH. L. REV. 669, 673–74 (1920) (making the same point by implication). Similarly, John Bassett Moore quoted the entire text of Secretary Gresham's 1894 three-and-a-half page note to Brazil with apparent approval in volume five of his DIGEST OF INTERNATIONAL LAW, cited above in note 54, § 774, at 359–63. Some writers failed to consider the issue directly, but their general view that only treaties could bind the nation, expressed in the context of unilateral executive agreements, provides grounds for inferring their assent on this point as well. *See, e.g.*, 1 WILLOUGHBY, *supra* note 51, § 200, at 469; Baldwin, *Exchange*, *supra* note 49, at 464. Others simply did not address the issue at all — a surprising omission if something so momentous as interchangeability was in the works. *See, e.g.*, CRANDALL, TREATIES 2D, *supra* note 49, §§ 62–67, at 121–40.

[168] WRIGHT, *supra* note 49, § 162, at 236 (emphasis added); *see also id.* § 158, at 233 (to the same effect).

[169] *See, e.g.*, 2 BUTLER, *supra* note 49, § 463, at 372 n.2; 5 MOORE, *supra* note 54, § 774, at 359–63 (reprinting Secretary of State Gresham's letter); Moore, *supra* note 49, at 393.

[170] *See* Joint Resolution of July 2, 1921, ch. 40, 42 Stat. 105. In 1920, Congress had passed a similar joint resolution, but President Wilson, still holding out for Versailles, vetoed it. *See* Chandler P. Anderson, *United States Congressional Peace Resolution*, 14 AM. J. INT'L L. 384, 385

without any further effort at international agreement.[171] Formal treaties followed in the same year.[172]

More interesting developments arose out of the management of the massive war debt with the Europeans. So far as the Germans and other enemies were concerned, Presidents settled claims by unilateral executive agreements, without participation by the Senate or the Congress. Settlement of private claims by executive agreement was a well established power of the President.[173] Wilson and his successors did not provoke substantial controversy as they expanded these precedents to allow unilateral executive settlement of public claims of the United States.[174]

When the President turned to the Allied war debt, he faced a more serious problem. America's friends owed money because Congress had authorized the purchase of foreign bonds in a series of Liberty Bond Acts.[175] It became immediately apparent, however, that the Allies were in no condition to repay their American debts under Liberty

---

(1920). Both resolutions engendered a good deal of controversy over whether Congress had the power to terminate war. *See* 1 WILLOUGHBY, *supra* note 63, § 292, at 535–36; Anderson, *supra*, at 384–85; Corwin, *supra* note 167, at 669; John M. Mathews, *The Termination of War*, 19 MICH. L. REV. 819, 827–33 (1921).

[171] Once again, its action became an important precedent in the myth of continuity. *See* MCCLURE, *supra* note 16, at 10–11, 112; Garner, *supra* note 101, at 487; Wright, *supra* note 16, at 347 & n.27. But the debate over the peace resolution had nothing to do with the legitimacy of the congressional-executive agreement. Reminiscent of the Texas and Hawaii debates, the opponents' central claim was that the only constitutional method for establishing peace was the treaty. This was met by the rejoinder that Congress may repeal any measure it had power to adopt in the first instance. *See* Corwin, *supra* note 167, at 673. This included a declaration of war. In so doing, Congress did not create a new form of binding international agreement. It simply ended the *domestic* legal consequences that followed from the state of war. *See* 1 WILLOUGHBY, *supra* note 63, § 292, at 535–36. Corwin's position in 1920 contrasts with his later reliance on the peace resolution. *See* CORWIN, WORLD ORGANIZATION, *supra* note 16, at 46.

[172] There were separate treaties with Austria, Hungary, and Germany. *See* 3 MALLOY, *supra* note 58, at 2493 (Austria); *id.* at 2693 (Hungary); *id.* at 2596 (Germany).

[173] *See supra* note 58 and accompanying text.

[174] *See* MCCLURE, *supra* note 16, at 115–16; *see also* 5 HACKWORTH, *supra* note 69, at 393. Secretary of State Hughes cited the indemnity provisions of the Boxer Protocol of 1901, *see* 2 MALLOY, *supra* note 58, at 2006, 2008–09, as a precedent. But that settlement was controversial and was justified largely by the need for urgent action. *See supra* note 64 and accompanying text. In 1910, Willoughby claimed that the President had never, "by executive action, attempted the settlement of claims set up by the United States in its own behalf." 1 WILLOUGHBY, *supra* note 51, § 199, at 469. Nevertheless, Hughes's extension of the traditional exception did not provoke serious debate. The primary concern in this area has always been whether the President has the power to settle claims *against* the United States, not whether he may settle claims when the country is a creditor. *See, e.g., id.*

[175] *See* Victory Liberty Loan Act, ch. 100, § 7, 40 Stat. 1309, 1312–13 (1919); Fourth Liberty Bond Act, ch. 142, § 2, 40 Stat. 844, 844 (1918); Third Liberty Bond Act, ch. 44, § 2, 40 Stat. 502, 504 (1918); Second Liberty Bond Act, ch. 56, §§ 2–3, 40 Stat. 288, 288–90 (1917); First Liberty Bond Act, ch. 4, § 2, 40 Stat. 35, 35 (1917). The acts extended credits by floating United States government bonds and authorizing the use of the proceeds for the purchase of bonds issued by Allied governments. The foreign bonds were to bear the same interest rates and other terms as the United States bonds. For a description of the acts and ensuing loans see Maxwell S. Stewart,

Bond terms.[176] Shortly after the war's conclusion, President Wilson acted unilaterally to allow the short-term postponement of scheduled payments.[177] But this caused a furor in Congress,[178] which turned to the problem after the Senate rejected the Versailles Treaty.[179]

Its initial response was a 1922 statute establishing a World War Foreign Debt Commission charged with renegotiating the Allied debt within strict congressional guidelines.[180] Once these terms were approved by the President, no further action by Congress was required.[181]

As initially enacted, this statute fell within traditional understandings. There was no need for a treaty because the country was not assuming any new international obligations. Congress was simply acting under its constitutional power to dispose of property belonging to the United States — in this case, interest payments due on the Allied debt.[182] Moreover, the President and the Debt Commission were supposed to function in the same way that the President traditionally operated under proclamation statutes. That is, they were to apply statutory standards to the facts of individual cases and explain to foreign governments what they had to do to qualify for a congressionally defined benefit. Given the traditional character of the statute, neither

---

The Inter-Allied Debt, 8 FOREIGN POL'Y REP. 172, 172–75 (1932). More than 10 billion dollars were provided under these and related acts. *See id.* at 173.

[176] *See* 2 RAY S. BAKER, WOODROW WILSON AND WORLD SETTLEMENT 328–34 (1923).

[177] *See* H.R. REP. NO. 421, 67th Cong., 1st Sess. 8–10 (1921); S. REP. NO. 264, 67th Cong., 1st Sess. 8–9 (1921).

[178] *See* H.R. REP. NO. 421, *supra* note 177, at 8–10; S. REP. NO. 264, *supra* note 177, at 8–9; 62 CONG. REC. 1573, 1627, 1761, 1881, 1884, 1892–94 (1922).

[179] Even at Versailles, President Wilson and his advisers assumed that any final settlement of the inter-Allied debt problem would require congressional action. *See* Letter of Bernard M. Baruch to Woodrow Wilson, President of the United States (May 7, 1919), *reprinted in* 3 BAKER, *supra* note 176, at 347, 348–49; Memorandum from Norman H. Davis and Thomas W. Lamont to Woodrow Wilson, President of the United States (May 15, 1919), *reprinted in* 3 BAKER, *supra* note 176, at 352, 359–61.

[180] *See* Act of Feb. 9, 1922, ch. 47, 42 Stat. 363.

[181] *See id.* The Act authorized the Commission "to refund or convert, and to extend the time of payment of the principal" and interest on the foreign government bonds on such terms as were in "the best interests of the United States." *Id.* § 2, 42 Stat. at 363. Congress refused, however, to permit the Commission to lower the interest rate below four-and-one-half percent or to extend the time of maturity beyond a period of 25 years, *see id.*, and it was emphatic that the act did not "authorize . . . cancellation of any part of such indebtedness." *Id.* § 3, 42 Stat. at 363.

[182] *See* U.S. CONST. art. IV, § 3, cl. 2. Although the statute did not permit outright cancellation of debt, the rescheduling of payments at lower interest rates amounted to a disposal of property in a constitutional sense.

To be sure, there was an important difference between the debt settlements and earlier precedents. Congress clearly contemplated that the settlements would impose binding obligations both on the debtors and on the United States. But this did not involve an expansion of Congress's agreement-making powers. It merely reflected the nature of the power to dispose of property. While Congress could always change tariff rates set by presidential agreement, once the President, by agreement made under congressional authority, had disposed of property, the result was irrevocable.

the President nor the Senate Finance Committee considered the applicability of the Treaty Clause to the problem — until Senator Walsh, and a few others, raised the issue on the floor of the Senate.[183]

Walsh's objections were overwhelmed in a heated debate in which the Act gained Senate approval after proponents made the obvious points we have just sketched.[184] Indeed, Walsh's defeat was so decisive that he did not bring up the matter again when events took a different turn from the course envisioned by the statute. It became clear within a year that the congressional parameters were unrealistically strict. Rather than giving up, the Commission returned to Congress with a tentative agreement with Great Britain, the largest Allied debtor, that was more generous than the statute allowed.[185]

Congress responded by approving the agreement and by authorizing a similar procedure for other debtors.[186] As in the British case, neither the President nor the Commission could make settlements unilaterally. Instead, Congress specified that it would give ex post approval to each executive agreement.[187]

And so the participants stumbled upon a device that serves as the first genuine precedent for modern practice. Congress rather than the Senate exercised ex post review of deals negotiated by the executive and approved them by simple majority vote. Behold, the modern congressional-executive agreement!

While the settlement with Britain and other debtor nations seems important in retrospect, the participants did not find it remarkable.

---

[183] *See, e.g.,* 62 CONG. REC. 1677–81, 1801–04 (1922) (remarks of Sen. Walsh); *id.* at 1638 (remarks of Sen. Simmons). According to Senator Walsh, the settlements would be contracts between nations and therefore had to be approved through the treaty procedure. *See id.* at 1681. Despite his learned arguments, he was unable to persuade even the great isolationist Senator Borah, who remained undecided about the constitutional issue at debate's end. *See id.* at 1889.

[184] *See, e.g., id.* at 1677–78, 1686, 1855–56 (remarks of Sen. McCumber); *id.* at 1677–80, 1850–52 (remarks of Sen. Poindexter); *id.* at 1801 (remarks of Sen. Williams); *id.* at 1798–1801 (remarks of Sen. Lenroot). Senator McCumber's coup de grace was to recall Congress's earlier decision to forgive China's debt under the Boxer Protocol. If Congress could exercise its legislative authority over the Chinese debt, he asked, "why can we not do the same thing with reference to the obligations of these other countries?" *Id.* at 1856.

In the heat of debate, some Senators, perhaps caught off-guard by Walsh's eleventh-hour challenge, made expansive remarks that would later be cited by the myth-makers as support for interchangeability. *See* CORWIN, THE PRESIDENT, *supra* note 16, at 236 n.91. When their remarks are read in context, however, it is clear that these Senators had a much more modest intent — to establish that the 1922 Act was well within the traditional precedents.

[185] *See* McCLURE, *supra* note 16, at 117–18; Stewart, *supra* note 175, at 175–76.

[186] *See* Act of Feb. 28, 1923, ch. 146, 42 Stat. 1325.

[187] Settlements were to be made upon terms the Commission "may believe to be just, subject to the approval of the Congress." *Id.* at 1326. In subsequent years, Congress approved agreements with virtually all of the debtors. *See, e.g.,* Act of Dec. 22, 1924, ch. 14, 43 Stat. 719 (Lithuania); Act of May 23, 1924, ch. 167, 43 Stat. 136 (Hungary); Act of Mar. 12, 1924, ch. 52, 43 Stat. 20 (Finland); *see also* Stewart, *supra* note 175, at 176–78.

Not even Senator Walsh raised a constitutional objection.[188] The silence is unsurprising, because Congress did not suppose that it was creating a broad new substitute for senatorial "advice and consent." Instead, it was invoking its explicit, but narrow, power to dispose of American property.[189] Because the congressional action fit within a narrow traditional rubric, it was not a self-conscious affirmation of the modern doctrine of interchangeability, which insists that the two-House procedure can substitute for treaty-making across the full range of Congress's legislative power. The real birth of the modern doctrine would take place only after the specter of Versailles began to haunt Americans in the 1940s.[190]

International debt management was the most important issue emerging from the Versailles debacle. But a secondary matter later played a significant part in our story. While President Wilson was in Europe, he committed the United States to host the initial session of a new International Labor Organization (ILO) established within the Versailles framework. As opposition to the Treaty grew, this invitation became a source of embarrassment: the President had offered to play host to an organization in which the country was not — and might never be — a member.

To avoid awkwardness, the Secretary of Labor gained congressional consent under a 1913 statute requiring the President to obtain congressional approval before extending "any invitation to participate in any international congress, conference, or like event."[191] This allowed the Administration to host the ILO without prejudice to the question of membership in the organization.[192]

---

[188] No discussion of the issue appears in the Finance Committee's report, *see* S. REP. NO. 1130, 67th Cong., 4th Sess. (1923), and our research reveals no pertinent discussion in the committee hearings, *see Refunding of Obligations of Foreign Governments: Hearings on S. 2135 Before the Senate Comm. on Finance*, 67th Cong., 1st Sess. (1921), or in the floor debate in the Senate.

[189] *See* U.S. CONST. art. IV, § 3, cl. 2.

[190] During the 1920s, the Allied debtors could make payments due under their settlement agreements only because they were receiving even larger reparations from Germany. *See* Stewart, *supra* note 175, at 178–79. By 1931, with the deepening world financial crisis, Germany could no longer make its payments. *See id.* at 179. To avert the impending world financial collapse, on June 20, 1931, President Hoover proposed a one-year moratorium on all inter-Allied debt payments, and a majority of debtor nations quickly accepted. *See id.* Hoover felt bound, however, to obtain congressional authorization even for such a modus vivendi. On December 23, 1931, Congress obliged, passing a joint resolution authorizing the President to make agreements postponing debt payments for one year. *See* Joint Resolution of Dec. 23, 1931, ch. 5, § 1, 47 Stat. 3, 3.

[191] *Treaty of Peace with Germany: Hearings Before the Senate Comm. on Foreign Relations*, 66th Cong., 1st Sess. 32–33 (1919) (quoting Act of Mar. 4, 1913, ch. 149, 37 Stat. 912). Part XIII of the Treaty of Versailles (articles 387 to 427) had called for the establishment of the International Labor Organization. *See* Treaty of Peace with Germany, June 28, 1919, pt. XIII, arts. 387–427, 2 Bevans 43.

[192] *See* Joint Resolution of Aug. 15, 1919, ch. 48, 41 Stat. 279.

The question of America's relationship to the ILO returned when the Senate debated the Versailles treaty. It did not reject the ILO outright. Instead, it treated the matter in the same way as it did many others — by attaching a crippling reservation that rendered ratification meaningless. The reservation refused to authorize immediate American entry into the ILO but provided that Congress could reverse this decision later by joint resolution.[193]

In leaving this later decision up to both Houses of Congress, the Senate did not break new constitutional ground. The Senate has often assigned both Congress and the President key functions in implementing treaties. When these institutions later play the roles marked out by the Senate, they do not challenge its treaty-making monopoly, but confirm it. If, then, the Versailles Treaty had passed with the ILO reservation, any subsequent joint resolution would have been incidental to the Senate's treaty-making function.

All this might have seemed academic once the Senate rejected Versailles. However, the Senate's reference to a joint resolution, coupled with Congress's actual use of this device in connection with the ILO's first conference in Washington, was stored in long-term institutional memory. When membership in the ILO was raised once again by the Roosevelt Administration, these memories would play a surprising role in later developments. But so far as the 1920s were concerned, the ILO was just another casualty of the battle surrounding the League of Nations.

B.   Court Decisions

Putting the Great War and its consequences to one side, the Twenties saw a "return to normalcy" in the practice of executive agreements. While executive action proceeded on a broad front, there was no qualitative change in pre-war understandings.[194] By contrast, judi-

---

[193] *See* 58 CONG. REC. 8699, 8730 (1919); DENNA F. FLEMING, THE UNITED STATES AND THE LEAGUE OF NATIONS, 1918–1920, at 431 (1932).

[194] *See* Harry S. Todd, *The President's Power to Make International Agreements*, 11 CONST. REV. 160, 166–67 (1927) (treating as uncontroversial the proposition that post-Versailles executive agreements authorized by statute do not bind the country). Indeed, the President was careful to make clear to foreign countries that executive agreements were not binding on the Congress. A common provision explicitly asserted that the agreement would lapse in the event of inconsistent legislation. These clauses were typically included, for example, in agreements concluded under the Tariff Act of 1922, ch. 356, 42 Stat. 858, *see, e.g.*, Agreement According Mutual Unconditional Most-Favored-Nation Treatment in Customs Matters, May 2, 1925, U.S.-Fin., T.S. No. 715, at 2, 3–4; Agreement According Mutual Unconditional Most-Favored-Nation Treatment in Customs Matters, Dec. 2, 1924, U.S.-Greece, T.S. No. 706, at 2, 4, and agreements concluded under the Air Commerce Act of 1926, ch. 344, 44 Stat. 568 (repealed 1958), *see, e.g.*, Arrangement for the Reciprocal Recognition of Certificates of Airworthiness for Imported Aircraft, Sept. 8–9, 1933, U.S.-Swed., art. 4, E.A.S. No. 49, at 2; Arrangement on Air Navigation, May 27–31, 1932, U.S.-Germany, art. 19, E.A.S. No. 38, at 5; *see also* Letter from Secretary of State Hull to Secretary of Labor Perkins (Mar. 6, 1939) (affirming that agreements with lapse clauses are not binding under international law), *reprinted in* 5 HACKWORTH, *supra* note 68, at 398–99. McDougal and Lans

cial opinions did significantly change the legal context — though, iron-ically, the single most important decision made the creation of the modern congressional-executive agreement seem less, not more, likely.

1. Domestic Law. — The key case was *Missouri v. Holland*[195] and it concerned the federal government's effort to control the killing of migratory birds. Lower federal courts had declared unconstitutional a federal statute dealing with the problem. While birds certainly trav-eled across state boundaries, judges had trouble interpreting their free flight as "commerce."[196] The government responded with a Migratory Bird Treaty with Canada and an implementing statute.[197]

This second-round response engendered Justice Holmes's famous opinion for a seven-to-two majority. The Court refused to determine whether the lower courts were right about the Commerce Clause. Conceding arguendo that a bare statute might be unconstitutional, Holmes saved the second-round by asserting that a treaty made the crucial difference. On his view, the treaty-making powers of the Sen-ate and the President were not limited by the Constitution's explicit grants of statute-making power to Congress: "It is obvious that there may be matters of the sharpest exigency for the national well-being that an act of Congress could not deal with but that a treaty followed by such an act could . . . ."[198] Once a valid treaty occupied an area, the Necessary and Proper Clause gave Congress the authority to pass

---

explained these provisions as efforts by Presidents to prevent "the possibility of a situation in which the Executive would be forced through act of Congress to commit international delinquen-cies by unilaterally terminating international engagements." McDougal & Lans (pt. 1), *supra* note 16, at 350. Rather than reflecting a pervasive mistrust of congressional good faith, it seems far more realistic to conclude that these provisions expressed the executive branch's continuing re-spect for traditional constitutional limitations.

When an explicit lapse clause was absent, the President usually telegraphed the limited nature of the agreement in some other way — most frequently by informing the foreign country that he was seeking not to establish a new legal relationship, but only to ensure that the other country's laws fell within the parameters established by Congress. Under this very common mode, the State Department presented itself as engaged in a fact-finding mission under a proclamation stat-ute. *See, e.g.,* Arrangement for Reciprocal Recognition of Load-Line Certificates, Jan. 16, 1932, U.S.-Den., E.A.S. No. 29, at 3; Agreement for Reciprocal Recognition of Certificates of Inspection of Vessels Assigned to the Transportation of Passengers, June 1–Aug. 17, 1931, U.S.-Italy, E.A.S. No. 23, at 1; Arrangement for Relief for Double Income Tax on Shipping Profits, Mar. 31–June 8, 1926, U.S.-Japan, E.A.S. No. 3, at 2. When neither of the two standard methods was used, agreements frequently contained provisions allowing for termination on very short notice, *see, e.g.,* Provisional Agreement on Commercial Relations, Sept. 28, 1931, U.S.-Chile, E.A.S. No. 26, at 3, or were otherwise justifiable as modi vivendi, pending the conclusion of a general convention or bilateral treaty on the subject, *see, e.g.,* Arrangement for Reciprocal Recognition of Load-Line Certificates, Feb. 13–Sept. 7, 1931, U.S.-Japan, E.A.S. No. 25, at 1.

[195] 252 U.S. 416 (1920).
[196] *See* United States v. McCullagh, 221 F. 288, 290–92 (D. Kan. 1915); United States v. Shau-ver, 214 F. 154, 160–61 (D. Ark. 1914).
[197] *See* Migratory Bird Treaty Act, ch. 128, 40 Stat. 755 (1918).
[198] *Holland*, 252 U.S. at 433.

implementing legislation which otherwise might offend the Tenth Amendment.[199]

In vindicating this two-step procedure — treaty first, statute second — Holmes was not dealing with a case that involved novel kinds of congressional-executive collaboration. Nonetheless, his opinion created a less hospitable environment for the emergence of the modern doctrine. Given *Missouri*, proponents of interchangeability would have a new problem to solve: how could congressional-executive agreements overcome the powers reserved to the states by the Tenth Amendment?

By relying so heavily on the treaty form as a unique law-making instrument, Holmes made it implausible to suggest that innovative forms of congressional-executive agreement could trump the reserved powers of the states. And if this were so, it seemed obvious that these new-fangled congressional-executive agreements were constitutionally inferior to treaties.

As we shall see, the 1930s provided constitutional lawyers with new materials that allowed them to avoid *Missouri* and construct a case for interchangeability of a kind they could not anticipate in the 1920s. But it is important to restrain the inclination to read history backwards.

2. *International Law*. — Similar caution is required when viewing the development of international law during the 1920s. Increasingly, foreign courts and international tribunals were ruling that nations could not avoid obligations under international law by pleading that their undertakings lacked the formality of a treaty.[200] While none of these decisions involved the United States, a gap was opening between American constitutional understandings and emerging international norms. On the one hand, the constitutional consensus was still clear: except under narrow conditions, the President needed the advice and consent of the Senate to obligate the country internationally. On the other hand, international law was increasingly receptive to the claim that foreign countries had a right to rely on an executive's apparent authority without troubling themselves over domestic constitutional questions.

Although this gap began to emerge in the 1920s, it would be anachronistic to overemphasize it. The degree to which international law gave foreign countries the right to rely on the President's apparent

---

[199] *See id.* at 432–33.

[200] *See, e.g.*, Legal Status of Eastern Greenland, 1933 P.C.I.J. (ser. A/B) No. 53, at 71 (Apr. 5); Interpretation of the Statute of the Memel Territory, 1932 P.C.I.J. (ser. A/B) No. 49, at 300 (Aug. 11); Paris Agreement, 105 Entscheidungen des Reichsgerichts in Zivilsachen [RGZ] 156 (Germany) (June 22, 1922), *reprinted in* ANNUAL DIGEST OF PUBLIC INTERNATIONAL LAW CASES: 1919–1922, at 313–14 (John F. Williams & H. Lauterpacht eds., 1932); *see also* McDougal & Lans (pt. 1), *supra* note 16, at 321–23 (discussing these legal developments).

authority remained controversial for decades, and has not been fully resolved even today.[201] When viewed without the advantage of a crystal ball, the 1920s have much more in common with the world we have lost than with the constitutional world we take for granted today.

III. THE NEW DEAL ABROAD

The 1930s was a time of constitutional transformation. But because the New Deal revolution was principally concerned with domestic matters, we will be hitting it on a tangent. We will show how the doctrinal changes of the 1930s facilitated the future development of the modern congressional-executive agreement. Once the national government was conceded broad authority to manage the economy at home, it became plausible to suppose that analogous authority was appropriate in the international arena. This Part sketches the rippling effects on the conduct of foreign policy, but also marks their limits. While Congress granted Franklin Roosevelt new power to commit the nation in international economic affairs, New Deal practice fell far short of modern notions of interchangeability.

But the foundation for deeper changes was being laid in the larger constitutional culture. Legal intellectuals began to frame visionary proposals for fundamental revision. New judicial dicta made modern notions of interchangeability thinkable, if not yet doable. When war came, lawyers would have new intellectual tools to meet wide-ranging demands for thoroughgoing reform.

A. At Home Abroad

The New Deal could not succeed at home without revolutionizing economic policy-making abroad.[202] The new Administration wasted no time implementing an expanded conception of executive authority to make binding international commitments in the name of the United States. Within a few months, President Roosevelt sent his Secretary of

---

[201] As early as 1920, Oppenheim denied that there was any international law significance to the American distinction between executive agreements and treaties. 1 LASSA L.F. OPPENHEIM, INTERNATIONAL LAW 665–66 (Ronald F. Roxburgh ed., 3d ed. 1920). Despite Oppenheim's confidence, this question was still open to serious debate 15 years later. *See Harvard Research Draft on the Law of Treaties*, 29 AM. J. INT'L L. 657, 992–1002 (Supp. 1935). And 10 years after that, McDougal and Lans were still treating the issue as very much alive. *See* McDougal & Lans (pt. 1), *supra* note 16, at 323–31. For more recent developments, see note 464 below.

[202] Revitalization of the national economy depended on the stabilization of the international financial system, the establishment of cooperative international commodity arrangements, and the reversal of global protectionist trade policies. Three early New Deal Acts dealt with these problems in revolutionary ways. *See* Reciprocal Trade Agreements Act of 1934, ch. 474, 48 Stat. 943 (amending the Tariff Act of 1930); Gold Reserve Act of 1934, ch. 6, 48 Stat. 337; Agricultural Adjustment Act of 1933, ch. 25, 48 Stat. 31; *see also* Silver Purchase Act of 1934, ch. 674, 48 Stat. 1178.

State to the World Monetary and Economic Conference in London. The Conference was a failure,[203] but it did produce two multilateral agreements: the Silver Agreement of 1933[204] and the Wheat Agreement of 1933,[205] both designed to stabilize world prices. Although these agreements imposed binding international obligations, they fell outside the traditional rubrics of unilateral presidential authority. Nevertheless, the President did not submit them to the Senate. Acting under an expansive interpretation of the Agricultural Adjustment Act of 1933, he concluded both as executive agreements.[206] Similar developments followed under the Gold Reserve Act, enacted the next year.[207]

---

[203] *See* McClure, *supra* note 16, at 161–64.

[204] *See* Memorandum of Agreement Between the United States of America, Australia, Canada, China, India, Mexico, Peru, and Spain on Silver, July 22, 1933, E.A.S. No. 63.

[205] *See* Final Act of the Conference of Wheat Exporting and Importing Countries, Aug. 25, 1933, 141 L.N.T.S. 71; *see also* McClure, *supra* note 16, at 161–63 (describing the circumstances).

[206] President Roosevelt proclaimed the Silver Agreement on December 21, 1933, *see* Proclamation of Dec. 21, 1933, 48 Stat. 1723 (1933), citing § 43(b)(2) of the Act. *See* Agricultural Adjustment Act of 1933, ch. 25, § 43, 48 Stat. 31, 51–54; 5 Hackworth, *supra* note 69, at 401–02. That section authorized him to protect American commerce "against the adverse effect of depreciated foreign currencies." Agricultural Adjustment Act § 43(b)(2), 48 Stat. at 52. Under § 43(b)(2) the President could fix the weights of both the gold and silver dollars. The statute added:

> [I]n case the Government of the United States enters into an agreement with any government or governments under the terms of which the ratio between the value of gold and other currency issued by the United States and by any such government or governments is established, the President may fix the weight of the gold dollar in accordance with the ratio so agreed upon . . . .

Id. at 52–53. While this plainly authorizes certain gold agreements, it is stretching things to say, with Roosevelt, that the statutory language provides "clear authority" for his executive deal on silver.

The statutory basis for the Wheat Agreement was less substantial. The President apparently found authority in general provisions authorizing the Secretary of Agriculture to enter into agreements with producers "engaged in the handling, in the current of interstate or foreign commerce of any agricultural commodity." *Id.* § 8, 48 Stat. at 34.

[207] *See* Gold Reserve Act of 1934, ch. 6, 48 Stat. 337. With the collapse of the gold standard, Congress gave the President authority, through the Secretary of the Treasury, to deal in gold and foreign exchange through a two billion dollar currency stabilization fund. *See id.* § 10, 48 Stat. at 341–42. Although the Act said nothing about his entering into international agreements, the President again took a broad view. Congress did not seem to mind, extending the statutory authorization after learning of his interpretation. *See* Act of July 6, 1939, ch. 260, 53 Stat. 998; Act of Jan. 23, 1937, ch. 5, 50 Stat. 4. The Gold Reserve Act led to a series of currency "stabilization agreements," which began with the celebrated Tripartite Declaration of September 1936 by the United States, Great Britain, and France designed to calm currency markets during a long overdue devaluation of the franc. *See Review of the Month*, 22 Fed. Reserve Bull. 759, 759 (1936). It was followed by a further agreement under which the three powers made gold available for purchase by one another from their respective stabilization funds. *See* McClure, *supra* note 16, at 170–71; *Treasury Announcements Regarding Sale of Gold for Export*, 22 Fed. Reserve Bull. 852 (1936) [hereinafter *Treasury Announcements*]. In the following years, the United States entered other stabilization agreements. *See, e.g.*, 1938 Ann. Rep. of the Secretary of the Treasury on State of the Fin. 21, 268 (Brazil); 1941 Ann. Rep. of the Secretary of the Treasury on State of the Fin. 52, 358 (China); 1942 Ann. Rep. of the Secretary of the Treasury on State of the Fin. 42, 291–92 (Mexico, Ecuador, and Iceland). It is not clear

None of these emergency measures generated much constitutional controversy. But the Senate did begin to take notice during its debate on the pathbreaking Reciprocal Trade Agreements Act of 1934.[208] While representing a new departure in trade policy,[209] the Act was part of a larger reorientation in public philosophy. Consider the President's message introducing his trade initiative:

> Other governments are to an ever increasing extent winning their share of international trade by negotiated, reciprocal trade agreements. If American agricultural and industrial interests are to retain their deserved place in this trade, the American Government must be in a position to bargain for that place with other governments . . . .
>
> If the American Government is not in a position to make fair offers for fair opportunities, its trade will be superseded. If it is not in a position at a given moment rapidly to alter the terms on which it is willing to deal with other countries, it cannot adequately protect its trade against discriminations and against bargains injurious to its interests. Furthermore, a promise to which prompt effect cannot be given is not an inducement which can pass current at par in commercial negotiations.
>
> For this reason any smaller degree of authority in the hands of the Executive would be ineffective. The executive branches of virtually all other important trading countries already possess some such power.[210]

---

whether these agreements were actually intended to be binding. The Tripartite Declaration seemed to be stating only the intentions of the three powers, and the subsequent agreement for exchanging gold reserves was expressly made terminable on 24 hours notice. *See Treasury Announcements, supra,* at 852.

[208] Act of June 12, 1934, ch. 474, 48 Stat. 943; *see also infra* notes 219–23 and accompanying text (reporting the Senate debates). During the following decades, Congress refused to extend the Act's broad delegation of authority to the President for longer than three years at a time. But each time the President's authority was set to expire, Congress renewed its authorization. *See, e.g.,* Act of June 7, 1943, ch. 118, 57 Stat. 125; Act of Apr. 12, 1940, ch. 96, 54 Stat. 107; Act of Mar. 1, 1937, ch. 22, 50 Stat. 24; *see also* Harold H. Koh, *Congressional Controls on Presidential Trade Policymaking After* I.N.S. v. Chadha, 18 N.Y.U. J. INT'L L. & POL. 1191, 1195 n.14 (1986) (describing the periodic renewals).

[209] Not only was the 1934 Act the first statute since 1897 in which Congress had expressly authorized the President to enter into trade agreements, but it also granted him unprecedented discretionary powers to modify tariff rates on all products through executive agreement-making. The Tariff Act of 1909 did not include even the limited authorization of the Dingley Act of 1897, *see supra* note 93 and accompanying text, although in a small number of cases the President construed it to authorize modest agreements. *See* Sayre, *supra* note 129, at 751, 773. The 1922 Tariff Act included a proclamation provision, but it severely limited the President's discretion, only permitting him to impose penalty tariffs against countries discriminating against American commerce, but denying him any right to change ordinary tariffs. *See* Tariff Act of 1922, ch. 356, 42 Stat. 858, 944–45. Under this provision, the President entered into a series of most-favored-nation agreements. *See* sources cited *supra* note 194.

[210] FRANKLIN D. ROOSEVELT, MESSAGE FROM THE PRESIDENT OF THE UNITED STATES TRANSMITTING A REQUEST TO AUTHORIZE THE EXECUTIVE TO ENTER INTO EXECUTIVE COMMERCIAL AGREEMENTS WITH FOREIGN NATIONS, H.R. DOC. NO. 273, 73d Cong., 2d Sess. 2 (1934), *quoted in* S. REP. NO. 871, 73d Cong., 2d Sess. 8 (1934). Armed with economic analyses, statistics, and legal memoranda, Secretary of State Hull and Assistant Secretary Francis Sayre presented the Administration's case to Congress. *See 1934 Senate Hearings, supra* note 73, at

While this message had an international twist, it proceeded from the standard New Deal constitutional diagnosis. The existing law-making system was too slow and cumbersome to meet the economic challenges of the time. Americans would betray the interests of farmers and workers if they allowed their governmental system to paralyze them against the threat of unregulated competition.[211]

The country's chief economic rivals were constitutionally equipped for rapid action. Their chief executives could act promptly, while America's could only hope its promises would be ratified at home. Such promises could no longer "pass current at par in commercial negotiations." It followed that Congress must empower the executive branch to move decisively to make the most of the nation's economic opportunities. In the domestic arena, this meant delegation of law-making authority to expert administrative agencies under presidential control. Internationally, it meant the same thing. The executive must be authorized to enter into legally binding agreements: "any smaller degree of authority . . . would be ineffective."

The New Deal Congress gave the President what he wanted.[212] Not only did Roosevelt win unprecedented flexibility in changing tariff rates established by statute,[213] but presidential agreements would bind

---

4–25, 36–50. Since 1933, they asserted, other countries had rapidly entered into a large number of reciprocal trade agreements lowering the skyrocketing tariffs that had contributed heavily to the worldwide depression. *See id.* at 16, 48–49, 117–18. Most other countries, they emphasized, granted their executives authority to put tariff agreements into effect at once. *See id.* at 49–56. If the President was not given comparable authority, other countries would be unwilling to deal with the United States. *See id.* at 7, 16, 118. Moreover, the Senate simply could not be trusted with reciprocity agreements. This had been demonstrated 30 years earlier by the Senate's failure to approve the Kasson Treaties, negotiated under § 4 of the Dingley Tariff Act of 1897. *See 1934 Senate Hearings, supra* note 73, at 60 (testimony of Assistant Secretary Sayre); *see also* 78 CONG. REC. 10,080 (1934) (remarks of Sen. Pope, quoting Secretary Hull); *supra* note 97. The Senate and House were convinced, adopting the Administration's arguments, even on the Kasson Treaties, point for point. *See* S. REP. NO. 871, *supra*, at 5–18.

[211] *See, e.g.,* Franklin D. Roosevelt, A Recommendation to the Congress to Enact the National Industrial Recovery Act to Put People to Work (May 17, 1933), *in* 2 THE PUBLIC PAPERS AND ADDRESSES OF FRANKLIN D. ROOSEVELT 202–05 (Samuel I. Rosenman ed., 1938).

[212] Whenever the President found "that any existing duties or other import restrictions . . . are unduly burdening and restricting the foreign trade of the United States," he could "enter into foreign trade agreements" and "proclaim such modifications of existing duties and other import restrictions . . . as are required or appropriate" to implement his agreements. Act of June 12, 1934, ch. 474, § 350(a), 48 Stat. 943, 943. Although modified from time to time, this basic authorization remained in effect until 1962. *See* Trade Expansion Act of 1962, Pub. L. No. 87-794, 76 Stat. 872.

[213] In contrast to the Tariff Acts of 1890 and 1897, the 1934 Act gave the President authority to raise and lower existing rates. *See* Act of June 12, 1934, ch. 474, § 350(a)(2), 48 Stat. 943, 943–44; *supra* notes 77, 93, 209, and accompanying text. While the 1934 Act marked the first time Congress had given the President discretion to set tariffs by entering into trade agreements, it was not the first time it had delegated him authority to set rates. The flexible tariff provision of the 1922 Act required the President to raise or lower tariffs to equalize the costs of production of articles produced in the United States and in competing countries. *See* Tariff Act of 1922, ch. 356, § 315(a), 42 Stat. 858, 941–42.

the country for three years even if Congress changed the underlying statute.[214] No longer did foreigners need to fear a replay of the Secretary of State's cavalier dismissal of Brazil and France. They could treat our promises "at par" with those made by America's commercial rivals.

While so much was clear from the face of the statute, constitutional justifications for these departures evolved more slowly. Traditionalist critics attacked on two fronts. Their first target was the grant of authority to make executive agreements that increased or reduced rates by as much as fifty percent — depending on whether the President believed existing rates were "unduly burdening and restricting the foreign trade of the United States."[215] This expansive formula lacked an "intelligible principle,"[216] according to critics, and represented an unconstitutional delegation of legislative authority.[217]

There was nothing special about this complaint. Conservatives were making it against innumerable New Deal innovations in domestic policy.[218] The critics' second challenge was more distinctive. This was the problem raised by the treaty power: how could Congress authorize the President to make internationally binding trade agreements without the advice and consent of the Senate?

In 1934, the friends of the Administration were better prepared to confront the first challenge than the second. They simply denied that there was a serious problem posed by the broad grant of presidential authority and treated earlier Supreme Court cases as a complete answer to their critics' complaints.[219] In contrast, the Administration's

---

[214] *See* Act of June 12, 1934, ch. 474, § 2(b), 48 Stat. 943, 944. That Congress was authorizing the President to enter into binding international agreements was clear from the language of this provision, the statements of the Administration, *see, e.g.*, *1934 Senate Hearings*, *supra* note 73, at 116–18 (testimony of Assistant Secretary Sayre), and the loud complaints of opponents. As Senator Austin put it: "These agreements contemplated by the pending bill may endure for 3 years . . . . Congress may come and go and do what it pleases, but it cannot change that obligation during the period of the contract." 78 CONG. REC. 10,211 (1934); *see also id.* at 9007–08 (remarks of Sen. Borah); *id.* at 9014–15 (remarks of Sen. Long); *id.* at 9685, 10,211–14 (remarks of Sen. Austin). For commentary by leading State Department officials, see Sayre, cited above in note 129, at 755, and Green H. Hackworth, *Legal Aspects of the Trade Agreements Act of 1934*, 21 A.B.A. J. 570, 571 (1935).

[215] Act of June 12, 1934, ch. 474, § 350(a)(2), 48 Stat. 943, 943–44.

[216] J.W. Hampton, Jr. & Co. v. United States, 276 U.S. 394, 409 (1928) (rejecting a delegation doctrine challenge to the flexible tariff provision of the 1922 Tariff Act).

[217] *See* 78 CONG. REC. 9008–11 (1934) (remarks of Sen. Borah); *id.* at 9014 (remarks of Sen. Long); *id.* at 9683–84 (remarks of Sen. Austin).

[218] And they were achieving dramatic successes in the Supreme Court. *See, e.g.*, A.L.A. Schechter Poultry Corp. v. United States, 295 U.S. 495 (1935) (striking down a provision of the National Industrial Recovery Act on delegation grounds); Panama Refining Co. v. Ryan, 293 U.S. 388, 433 (1935) (same).

[219] *See, e.g.*, *1934 Senate Hearings*, *supra* note 73, at 57–70 (testimony of Assistant Secretary Sayre); *id.* at 82–98 (reprinting a State Department memorandum supporting constitutionality); 78 CONG. REC. 10,072–78 (1934) (remarks of Sen. George); *id.* at 10,192–93 (remarks of Sen. Robinson); Hackworth, *supra* note 214, at 571–73, 578; Sayre, *supra* note 129, at 759–70.

defenders were rather tongue-tied on the distinctive treaty issue, confusing it with the more familiar delegation problem.[220] While moments of clarity emerged during floor debate,[221] the congressional committee reports of 1934 did not even address the issue,[222] relying on the Democrats' voting majorities to overwhelm their critics.[223]

When the Act came up for triennial renewal in 1937, the New Dealers had begun to frame a two-part response to the Treaty Clause issue. The first part involved a relatively primitive myth of continuity. Court cases, like *Field v. Clark*, that did not even involve congressional-executive agreements were suddenly transformed into ringing declarations of their constitutionality.[224] Executive agreements reached under the McKinley and Dingley Tariffs were cited as precedents,[225]

---

[220] *See, e.g., 1934 Senate Hearings, supra* note 73, at 58–61 (testimony of Assistant Secretary Sayre); 78 CONG. REC. 10,072–73 (remarks of Sen. George); *id.* at 10,192–93 (remarks of Sen. Robinson). The tendency to conflate the two issues is, perhaps, not surprising because Field v. Clark, 143 U.S. 649 (1892), read anachronistically, easily lends itself to this misunderstanding. *See supra* notes 124–29 and accompanying text. Even in 1934, the Administration put forward *Field*'s one-line dismissal of the Treaty Clause claim as a conclusive answer to the opponents' objections. *See 1934 Senate Hearings, supra* note 73, at 60, 89–90.

[221] As opponents developed their Treaty Clause critique, Senator George began to offer a more serious response, asserting that the two-thirds rule was meant as a check not upon the Congress but upon the President. He also noted that Congress had frequently authorized the President in advance to conclude international agreements. *See* 78 CONG. REC. 10,072 (1934). The State Department took a similar line. *See* 5 HACKWORTH, *supra* note 69, at 425–26 (quoting the Department of State's Current Information Series No. 1 of July 3, 1934). Senator George's statement can be read as an early affirmation of the interchangeability doctrine, although, in the context of a confused debate, it appears more modestly as one of many attempts to come to terms with new realities.

It also took some time for the Administration's opponents to hone their constitutional critique. But by the debate's end Senator Austin had achieved clarity, insisting that the Act impermissibly proposed to authorize the President, without senatorial advice and consent, to bind the country. *See* 78 CONG. REC. 10,214 (1934); *see also id.* at 9007–08 (remarks of Sen. Borah).

[222] *See* S. REP. NO. 871, *supra* note 210; H.R. REP. NO. 1000, 73d Cong., 2d Sess. (1934). Nor did the Administration mention the issue, except in offhand comments. *See 1934 Senate Hearings, supra* note 73, at 60 (testimony of Assistant Secretary Sayre); *id.* at 90 (State Department memorandum). After adoption of the Act, the debate came alive in the law journals. *See, e.g.,* Henry S. Fraser, *The Constitutionality of the Trade Agreements Act of 1934,* 31 PROC. AM. SOC'Y INT'L L. 55, 58–67 (1937); Charles C. Hyde, *Constitutional Procedures for International Agreement by the United States,* 31 PROC. AM. SOC'Y INT'L L. 45, 45–46, 50–51 (1937); Sayre, *supra* note 129, at 753–58.

[223] The Act passed by a vote of 57 to 33, with six not voting. *See* 78 CONG. REC. 10,395 (1934).

[224] The centerpiece of the State Department's argument to Congress was *Field*'s one-liner. *See Extending Reciprocal Trade Agreement Act: Hearings Before the Senate Finance Comm.,* 75th Cong., 1st Sess. 75 (1937) [hereinafter *1937 Senate Hearings*]; *supra* notes 127–29 and accompanying text. This time the committee reports did address the constitutional issue but their approach was entirely derived from the State Department's argument. *See* S. REP. NO. 111, 75th Cong., 1st Sess. 19–20 (1937); H.R. REP. NO. 166, 75th Cong., 1st Sess. 14–15 (1937).

[225] *See 1937 Senate Hearings, supra* note 224, at 75. The State Department also relied on claims settlements and agreements under a host of other proclamation statutes and cited Taft's 1890 opinion on postal conventions. *See id.* (citing 19 Op. Att'y Gen. 513, 520 (1890)); *see also* S.

while the embarrassing episodes with Brazil and France were forgotten.

But there was more to 1937 than mythic history. We are now at the flood-tide of the New Deal, with seventy-five Democrats in the Senate and eighty-nine Republicans in the House.[226] Both Senate and House committee reports were unembarrassed by the need for innovation. In a remarkable act of self-denial, the Senate Report asserted that "[t]rade agreements should not be subjected to the cumbrous treaty-making procedure."[227] The House supplied some hard-headed policy arguments:

> The Senate and the House of Representatives are in session for only part of the year and in recent years the demands upon their time when in session have been enormous. Were either senatorial or congressional ratification to be required, the inevitable delay and the further uncertainty as to ultimate ratification would go far toward destroying the incentive of foreign countries to enter into any trade negotiations at all.[228]

By 1937 Congress was not only supporting the President when he created international obligations in the name of the United States;[229] it was self-consciously justifying this move by a constitutional rhetoric that contained a distinctive New Deal mix of mythic history and institutional realism.

B. The Limits of the New Deal Transformation

This was a genuine breakthrough, but it should not be confused with the modern congressional-executive agreement. Two large steps remained — and it is too deterministic to assert that they were inevitably implied by the New Deal transformation. The first involved the scope of activities for which presidential commitments were constitutionally legitimate. Trade Act agreements, as well as those made under other New Deal legislation, were concerned with the management of the international economy. It was a large step to move beyond this single area and proclaim that the President could make an

---

REP. NO. 111, *supra* note 224, at 19–20 (listing a variety of similar international agreements as precedents for the Trade Act).

[226] *See* CONGRESSIONAL QUARTERLY SERV., CONGRESSIONAL QUARTERLY GUIDE TO CONGRESS 96-A (4th ed. 1991).

[227] S. REP. NO. 111, *supra* note 224, at 3.

[228] H.R. REP. NO. 166, *supra* note 224, at 14. The Senate made similar points, adopting a distinctively new language familiar to modern lawyers. Were the Senate to insist upon approving trade agreements as treaties, the result would be "inevitable disastrous delay . . . . A proposal which, upon alleged grounds of furthering important legislative functions, renders those very legislative powers futile is so patently self-contradictory that all serious considerations of public policy call for its unqualified rejection." S. REP. NO. 111, *supra* note 224, at 4.

[229] The Administration was careful to leave no doubt that Secretary Hull's trade agreements were binding international obligations. *See, e.g., 1937 Senate Hearings, supra* note 224, at 38–39 (testimony of Assistant Secretary Sayre); *id.* at 57–60 (reprinting a State Department memorandum in support of extending the Act).

end run around senatorial prerogatives in other fields. The policy arguments presented in 1937 did not go that far. They relied on special institutional difficulties: presidentially managed international trade threatened to inundate the Senate with a stream of technical agreements that would overwhelm its time and energy. It was therefore counterproductive to deny the President the power to impose binding commitments on the nation.

This functional argument did not extend to the full range of international diplomacy. In particular, the Senate would not be overwhelmed if it retained its prerogative to consider the merits of political and military alliances or solemn commitments to a new world order of the Versailles type. Nor did diplomacy in these areas require speedy commitments beyond the capacity of a legislative body. It was one thing to authorize New Deal modes of economic management abroad; it was quite another to accept the modern doctrine of interchangeability.

Especially when a second step remained. This involved the crucial question of timing. The Senate reviewed classical treaties after they were negotiated. When it gave its consent, the country knew what it was consenting to. Trade Act agreements never returned to the legislature for ex post scrutiny. The last point at which Congress gave its consent was in the framing of ex ante standards. This gap between ex ante and ex post might be tolerable in matters of trade policy. But the New Deal Congress was unprepared to give the President similar leeway in entering military alliances or large-scale political commitments.[230] To the contrary, it responded to the rise of Nazism by passing Neutrality Acts in 1935, 1936, and 1937.[231] If the congressional-executive agreement were to become an all-purpose alternative to the classical treaty, the Senate would have to cede its monopoly over the ex post review of presidential agreements.

This was not going to be easy. Not only would it strike at the heart of the textual commitment to the Senate; it would also offend many powerful Senators. During the 1930s, the Roosevelt Administra-

---

[230] Indeed, it had been reluctant to do so even with regard to trade agreements. In 1937 the Administration had to struggle against efforts to amend the Act to require ex post review by Congress. *See, e.g.,* *1937 Senate Hearings, supra* note 224, at 33–34 (colloquy between Sen. Connally and Assistant Secretary Sayre in which Sen. Connally argued for ratification by Congress); *id.* at 57–60 (reprinting a State Department memorandum arguing against legislative ratification). This problem reappeared in 1940 and 1943 when the Act came up for triennial review. *See* S. REP. NO. 258, 78th Cong., 1st Sess. 46–54 (1943); S. REP. NO. 1297, 76th Cong., 3d Sess. 5–8 (1940).

[231] *See* Neutrality Act of 1935, ch. 837, 49 Stat. 1081; Neutrality Act of 1936, ch. 1, 50 Stat. 3 (1937); Neutrality Act of 1937, ch. 146, 50 Stat. 121. Combining the provisions of the 1935 and 1936 Acts, the 1937 Act imposed an evenhanded arms embargo on all countries involved in belligerency or civil strife, severely tying Roosevelt's hands in dealing with the deteriorating situation in Europe. It was not until all-out war broke out that Congress repealed the arms embargo provision. *See* Neutrality Act of 1939, ch. 2, 54 Stat. 4.

tion had better things to do than provoke a bitter senatorial struggle. Nonetheless, changes in the legal culture made it easier for the Administration to make these moves aggressively in the 1940s.

C. *Questioning the Ex Post Barrier*

Recall that the ex post barrier had already been breached in 1923 in dealing with the Allied debt.[232] But Congress had approved the terms for debt repayment in response to a rapidly changing crisis and so did not give the matter much constitutional thought.

A decade later, however, a minor event in Washington precipitated the first sweeping scholarly reappraisal of the Senate's monopoly on ex post review. In 1934, the Administration sought to join the International Labor Organization.[233] A joint resolution emphasized the innocuous character of its request: "membership of the United States would not impose *or be deemed to impose* any obligation or agreement upon the United States to accept the proposals of [the ILO] as involving anything more than recommendations for its consideration."[234] The ILO was simply a place where American representatives of labor, management, and government would talk, study, and propose. Given the press of congressional business in 1934, this matter breezed through the Senate on a voice vote without debate and without any committee report.[235] The floor debate in the House was cursory as well, and the resolution passed without anybody suggesting that a constitutional revolution was at hand.[236]

Nonetheless, this was precisely the verdict reached by Professor James Garner, Reporter for the *Harvard Research Draft on the Law of Treaties*. His brief essay of 1935 poured profound meaning into Congress's casual action of the preceding year.[237] Garner argued that the joint resolution did indeed impose obligations on the United States. He pointed out that the ILO's constitution involved much more than consultation, requiring its members to submit to the compulsory jurisdiction of the World Court in certain cases.[238] This meant that the joint resolution was an epochal event: in approving the ILO, two

---

[232] *See supra* 840–41.

[233] For a discussion of the previous effort, see above notes 191–93 and accompanying text.

[234] Joint Resolution of June 19, 1934, ch. 676, 48 Stat. 1182 (emphasis added).

[235] *See* 78 CONG. REC. 11,343 (1934).

[236] There was a committee report in the House, *see* H.R. REP. NO. 2006, 73d Cong., 2d Sess. (1934), and a brief debate, *see* 78 CONG. REC. 12,238–40 (1934). The vote was 233 in favor, 109 opposed, with 88 abstentions. *See id.* at 12,241. In the next session of Congress, Representative Tinkham of Massachusetts, an ardent isolationist, went on the offensive, proposing that the President rescind American membership. He also argued that the two-House procedure for approving adherence to the ILO was an unconstitutional invasion of the Senate's treaty-making prerogative. *See* 79 CONG. REC. 1493, 1494 (1935). Nobody seemed particularly impressed.

[237] *See* Garner, *supra* note 101, at 484.

[238] The obligations Garner mentioned were quite attenuated, even as he described them. *See id.*

Houses of Congress had substituted themselves for the Senate in giving their advice and consent to a presidential effort to bind the United States to solemn international obligations.

Garner did not mention the explicit provision in the joint resolution ostentatiously contradicting his conclusion; nor did he reflect on the surprising unanimity with which the Senate had surrendered its long-standing objections to the compulsory jurisdiction of the World Court.[239] Instead, he expanded upon his misinterpretation of the ILO resolution by asserting that it allowed Congress to join the World Court by joint resolution — an especially provocative remark in 1935, because the Senate had only recently rejected an Administration effort to obtain approval for World Court membership.[240]

But this was only the beginning of Garner's six-page essay. It then sketched the myth of continuity that lies at the foundation of now-conventional wisdom, citing the annexations of Texas and Hawaii, the Allied war debt, the Trade Agreement Act of 1934, and other cases we have analyzed.[241] This discussion led to the triumphant assertion of the modern interchangeability doctrine. Garner even suggested that America might now enter the League of Nations through a congressional-executive agreement.[242] However fanciful its construction of the ILO Resolution, this essay — by an important scholar in the leading American journal of international law — broke the scholarly consensus, which had not taken interchangeability seriously.[243]

---

[239] For the long, tortured history, see, for example, DENNA F. FLEMING, THE TREATY VETO OF THE AMERICAN SENATE 168–250 (1930) [hereinafter FLEMING, TREATY VETO]; DENNA F. FLEMING, THE UNITED STATES AND THE WORLD COURT *passim* (1945) [hereinafter FLEMING, WORLD COURT]; and McDougal & Lans (pt. 2), cited above in note 16, at 567–68.

[240] The vote was 52 in favor, 36 opposed. *See* 79 CONG. REC. 1146–47 (1935). Garner also made a narrower argument, invoking the established practice regarding international organizations: membership in the court did not require the United States to accept the compulsory jurisdiction of the court; it only required the country to pay a share of the common expenses for the court's maintenance. *See* Garner, *supra* note 101, at 483; *see also supra* notes 115–18 and accompanying text.

[241] These included Taft's 1911 tariff reciprocity agreement with Canada, the Dingley Tariff Act of 1897 and the agreements reached under it (Garner cited the *Altman* case as establishing "[t]heir constitutional validity"!), postal conventions and Taft's 1890 opinion regarding their constitutionality, and the 1921 peace resolution ending World War I for purposes of domestic law. Garner, *supra* note 101, at 485–87.

[242] *See id.* at 487–88.

[243] The first argument for interchangeability we have found, and from which Garner quite likely drew, appeared in a House report in 1925. *See* H.R. REP. NO. 1569, 68th Cong., 2d Sess. 16 (1925). Growing weary of the Senate's endless delays in approving American adherence to the World Court treaty, and citing many of the precedents on which Garner later relied, the House Foreign Affairs Committee asserted "that, by a resolution originating in the House, adherence to the World Court could be secured by legislation." *Id.* at 9, 16. On March 3, 1925, by a vote of 303 to 28, the House adopted a resolution urging Senate action, but failed to act on the Committee's radical suggestion. *See* 66 CONG. REC. 5413–14 (1925); *see also* Bertram D. Hulen, *New Methods Sought to Ratify Treaties*, N.Y. TIMES, Feb. 17, 1935, at E7 (citing same precedents).

It took some time for the rest of the scholarly world to catch up.[244] Francis Sayre and Charles Cheney Hyde, both leaders in the field, recognized that the Trade Agreements Acts of 1934 and 1937 had authorized the President to make binding international obligations without the consent of the Senate.[245] But they explicitly rejected grand claims of interchangeability, asserting that many matters could be handled only by treaty.[246] As to the ILO matter, neither Sayre nor Hyde glimpsed its revolutionary potential.

Garner's sweeping reevaluation was even more distant from the practice of the late 1930s. President Roosevelt invariably went to the Senate, not Congress, when he wanted ex post approval of interna-

---

[244] Compare, for example, Professor Manley Hudson's tame response to the ILO resolution. *See* Manley O. Hudson, *The Membership of the United States in the International Labor Organization*, 28 AM. J. INT'L L. 669, 675 (1934). Still, Garner was not entirely alone. In 1938, Professor John Mathews wrote a brief article in the *American Journal of International Law* expressing ambivalent support for Garner's radical proposal. *See* John M. Mathews, *The Joint Resolution Method*, 32 AM. J. INT'L L. 349, 351 (1938). Even in 1935, there were already Senators and Congressmen who shared Garner's agenda. *See, e.g.*, H.R. 4668, 74th Cong., 1st Sess. (1935) (approving membership in the World Court); S.J. Res. 119, 74th Cong., 1st Sess. (1935) (approving membership in the League of Nations); S.J. Res. 51, 74th Cong., 1st Sess. (1935) (proposing an amendment providing for two-House majority approval of treaties); *see also* Hulen, *supra* note 243, at E7 (describing these legislative efforts). None of these initiatives made it out of committee.

[245] *See* Hyde, *supra* note 222, at 50; Sayre, *supra* note 129, at 755. Sayre was Assistant Secretary of State and Hyde had been the State Department's Solicitor. Even after the Trade Agreements Act, however, there were a number of writers who clung to the traditional view that the President and Congress could not constitutionally make binding international agreements. *See, e.g.*, FRANCIS O. WILCOX, THE RATIFICATION OF INTERNATIONAL CONVENTIONS: A STUDY OF THE RELATIONSHIP OF THE RATIFICATION PROCESS TO THE DEVELOPMENT OF INTERNATIONAL LEGISLATION 231 (1935); William H. Simpson, *Legal Aspects of Executive Agreements*, 24 IOWA L. REV. 67, 71–73 (1938). Simpson quoted a 1934 letter from the State Department that seems, at least arguably, to have taken the same view. *See id.* at 86.

[246] *See* Hyde, *supra* note 222, at 46. Hyde continued to hold this view as late as 1945. *See* 2 HYDE, *supra* note 17, § 509A, at 1416–18; *see also* Sayre, *supra* note 129, at 755 (analyzing the similarities and differences between treaties and executive agreements).

Sayre rested the distinction between executive agreements and treaties on two grounds. First, he noted that in concluding treaties Presidents may depart from established national policies and law, but their adventurous innovations must pass the check of the Senate's power of ex post review. In contrast, in making executive agreements, the President had to "act scrupulously within the laws and conform to the policies already established by the Congress." *Id.*

Sayre's second point loosely invoked Vattel's distinction, revived 30 years earlier by. Simeon Baldwin, between ongoing obligations and one-time deals:

International agreements involving political issues or changes of national policy and those involving international arrangements of a permanent character usually take the form of treaties. But international agreements embodying adjustments of detail carrying out well-established national policies and traditions and those involving arrangements of a more or less temporary nature usually take the form of executive agreements.

Id.

Hyde took a slightly different approach, identifying specific subject areas that were traditionally understood to be the preserve of the treaty power. These included, inter alia, extradition, naturalization, guarantees of neutrality and of independence, succession to immovable property, the restoration of friendly relations after a war, and the adjustment of claims against the United States. According to Hyde, "[s]uch a practice speaks for itself." Hyde, *supra* note 222, at 46–47.

tional agreements. As late as 1940, the executive continued to speak respectfully of the Senate monopoly. Robert Jackson, then Attorney General, was asked by the President to pass judgment on Roosevelt's response to the British defeat at Dunkirk. The President was torn between Churchill's desperate appeals for aid and Congress's insistence on American neutrality.[247] He responded by making an executive agreement with Churchill trading fifty "over-aged" destroyers for long-term leases on naval bases in British colonies.[248] He then asked Jackson to clear a passage through the legal minefield.

Jackson's formal opinion is revealing for the way it framed the legal question: "whether such an agreement can be concluded under Presidential authority or whether it must await ratification by a two-thirds vote of the United States Senate."[249] To nobody's surprise, Jackson concluded that presidential authority would suffice.[250] For our purposes, the striking characteristic of Jackson's opinion is its silence on the option of ex post approval by both Houses of Congress.[251]

Yet even as Jackson was writing his opinion, the State Department was preparing an initial assault on the Senate's monopoly.[252] The time was coming when Garner's essay would no longer be an academic exercise in hyperactive legal imagination. It would become a visionary statement of a constitutional agenda for a White House mobilizing itself for war.

D. *Judicial Opinions*

Judicial opinion shifted even more radically than academic discussion. As the decade began, *Missouri v. Holland* remained an insur-

---

[247] *See, e.g.,* ARTHUR M. SCHLESINGER, JR., THE IMPERIAL PRESIDENCY 105–09 (1973).

[248] The agreement is reprinted in MCCLURE, cited above in note 16, at 391–93.

[249] 39 Op. Att'y Gen. 484, 486 (1940).

[250] Jackson invoked the Vattel theme, *see supra* note 59, arguing that a treaty was necessary only for agreements involving "commitments as to the future which would carry an obligation to exercise powers vested in the Congress." 39 Op. Att'y Gen. at 487. He denied that the destroyers deal was such an agreement and went on to construe statutes Congress had passed to limit presidential authority as empowering him to implement the agreement. *See id.* at 489–94.

[251] The Destroyers for Bases Agreement was among the most controversial executive agreements ever concluded, provoking a sharp debate. *Compare* Quincy Wright, *The Transfer of Destroyers to Great Britain,* 34 AM. J. INT'L L. 680, 681 (1940) (supporting the agreement) *with* Herbert W. Briggs, *Neglected Aspects of the Destroyer Deal,* 34 AM. J. INT'L L. 569, 584–87 (1940) (attacking Jackson's opinion) *and* Edwin Borchard, *The Attorney General's Opinion on the Exchange of Destroyers for Naval Bases,* 34 AM. J. INT'L L. 690, 690 (1940) (same). Corwin vigorously disputed Jackson's exercise in statutory interpretation. *See* Edward S. Corwin, *Executive Authority Held Exceeded in Destroyer Deal,* N.Y. TIMES, Oct. 13, 1940, at 6. Even in the 1970s, Senators Church and Fulbright were attacking the deal as a usurpation of the Senate's constitutional prerogatives. *See* 117 CONG. REC. 10,355 (1971) (reprinting address by Sen. Fulbright); 116 CONG. REC. 13,563 (1970) (remarks of Sen. Church).

[252] See the discussion of the St. Lawrence Seaway Agreement, below at notes 340–45 and accompanying text. On March 19, 1941, Jackson would himself sign a memorandum affirming the constitutionality of the interchangeability doctrine. *See infra* note 342.

mountable obstacle to the claim that congressional-executive agreements had the same dignity as treaties. By decade's end, *Missouri* had been reduced to an historical footnote and new landmarks had transformed the legal landscape in ways that made novel forms of interbranch collaboration legally plausible — though not inevitable.

Begin with the way in which the New Deal revolution overwhelmed *Missouri*. When Justice Holmes wrote in 1920, the federal government confronted very real limits upon its power to invade areas traditionally reserved to the states under the Tenth Amendment. The migratory birds in *Missouri* served as a metaphor for a vast array of problems that eluded effective statutory control on both national and state levels.[253] By allowing the federal government to use treaties to overcome the "invisible radiation[s] from the general terms of the 10th Amendment,"[254] Justice Holmes endowed the treaty form with truly remarkable constitutional potency.

By the early 1940s, the New Deal revolution had swept away the principles of limited government that made *Missouri* seem important. It suddenly became obvious that the birds and the bees were flying in interstate commerce,[255] and that a treaty was no longer a necessary predicate for federal regulation. *Missouri*'s enhancement of the Treaty Clause had become practically irrelevant. If and when the congressional-executive agreement became an institutional reality, there would never be a real-world case in which it would be inferior to a treaty on *Missouri* grounds. After all, a congressional-executive agreement generally takes the form of a joint resolution of both Houses, which is then signed by the President. It therefore meets all the tests of a federal statute — and hence will almost always trump state law in a post-New Deal world in which the powers of Congress are virtually plenary.[256]

But it was one thing for the New Deal Court to make *Missouri* irrelevant, and quite another for the Justices to build new landmarks that would positively facilitate innovation. Here is where the (in)famous *Curtiss-Wright* decision became important.[257] The case did not directly address the legitimacy of the congressional-executive

---

[253] *See supra* note 198 and accompanying text.

[254] Missouri v. Holland, 252 U.S. 416, 434 (1920).

[255] In Wickard v. Filburn, 317 U.S. 111, 125 (1942), which construed Congress's commerce powers as virtually unlimited, the Supreme Court decisively rejected the pre-New Deal restrictive reading of the Commerce Clause, as symbolized by Hammer v. Dagenhart, 247 U.S. 251, 272 (1918), which elaborated the pre-New Deal view.

[256] *See* HENKIN, *supra* note 12, at 70, 76 (resting Congress's plenary powers on both the Commerce Clause and Congress's implied foreign affairs powers); Louis Henkin, *The Treaty Makers and the Law Makers: The Law of the Land and Foreign Relations*, 107 U. PA. L. REV. 903, 920–30 (1959) (same). The new conceptions of the Commerce Clause did, however, confront resistance in the area of race relations. See our discussion of the Bricker Amendment controversy below at notes 445–51 and accompanying text.

[257] *See* United States v. Curtiss-Wright Export Corp., 299 U.S. 304 (1936).

agreement. Indeed, it did not involve any international agreement, but arose under a proclamation statute empowering President Roosevelt to impose an arms embargo on the participants in the Chaco War in South America.[258] The problem with the statute, according to appellees, was the vagueness with which it delegated the proclamation power to the President.

This was a serious charge in 1935, because the Supreme Court had just struck down the National Industrial Recovery Act on delegation grounds.[259] Speaking for the *Curtiss-Wright* Court, Justice Sutherland assumed, but did not decide, that the statute might have been unconstitutionally vague had it involved a domestic matter.[260] But the foreign affairs power was different, and broad delegations were constitutionally acceptable.[261]

The holding was of direct importance for the New Deal's Trade Agreements Acts, silencing the conservatives' charge that they too were unconstitutional delegations of legislative power.[262] But Sutherland's opinion also made an indirect contribution to the coming challenge to the Senate's treaty-making prerogative, asserting that the foreign affairs power "did not depend upon the affirmative grants of the Constitution."[263] On Sutherland's view of this "vast, external realm, . . . the President alone has the power to speak or listen as a representative of the nation."[264]

All of this, it should be remembered, was said in an uncontroversial context. It would be a sad state of affairs to bar the President from proclaiming an embargo during a war in which the United States was neutral. Nonetheless, Sutherland's emphasis on the non-textual foundations of the foreign affairs power would shift the ground of future battles over the Treaty Clause. It was no longer enough for defenders of the Senate's prerogative to fend off claims that Article I provided Congress with an independent basis of power to enter into binding international agreements; they would also be obliged to con-

---

[258] *See* Joint Resolution of May 28, 1934, ch. 365, 48 Stat. 811; *see also* Proclamation of May 28, 1934, 48 Stat. 1744, 1744–45 (making a proclamation pursuant to the joint resolution).

[259] *See* A.L.A. Schechter Poultry Corp. v. United States, 295 U.S. 495, 528–29 (1935); Panama Refining Co. v. Ryan, 293 U.S. 388, 420–21 (1934).

[260] *See Curtiss-Wright*, 299 U.S. at 315.

[261] *See id.* at 315–29.

[262] *See supra* notes 216–19 and accompanying text. The Administration relied on *Curtiss-Wright* when the 1934 Act came up for triennial renewal in 1937. *See, e.g., 1937 Senate Hearings, supra* note 224, at 75.

[263] *Curtiss-Wright*, 299 U.S. at 318.

[264] *Id.* at 319. Sutherland's historical account and presidentialist bias have been the subject of penetrating criticism. *See, e.g.*, HENKIN, *supra* note 12, at 23–26; HAROLD H. KOH, THE NATIONAL SECURITY CONSTITUTION 94 (1990).

front Sutherland's suggestion that the exercise of foreign affairs powers could proceed without any basis in the text whatsoever.[265]

What is more, in listing examples of unenumerated powers, Sutherland mentioned "the power to make such international agreements as do not constitute treaties in the constitutional sense (*Altman & Co. v. United States*)."[266] As we have seen, *Altman* did not remotely suggest judicial support of the modern interchangeability doctrine.[267] But such subtleties would soon be erased by the myth of continuity.[268]

A similar atmospheric effect was created by two cases arising out of Roosevelt's decision to recognize the Soviet Union: the *Belmont*[269] and *Pink*[270] decisions of 1937 and 1942. In contrast to *Curtiss-Wright*, these cases were based on an executive agreement, but one in which Congress played no role. The question of compensation to American creditors had poisoned relations with the Soviets during the Twenties. Roosevelt thought it imperative to obtain some form of compensation, and the Soviets obliged with the Litvinov Assignment. Part of a larger executive agreement, the Assignment permitted the American government to collect all of the Soviets' outstanding claims in the United States, and to use the proceeds to compensate Americans for the Bolshevik expropriations.[271]

Belmont and *Pink* considered the Assignment's relationship to New York state law. Both opinions, and especially the war-time decision in *Pink*, enthusiastically embraced the agreement. Technically, the question was whether an executive agreement, unaided by Congress, trumped inconsistent state law. Justice Douglas answered with a resounding yes: "A treaty is a 'Law of the Land' under the Supremacy Clause of the Constitution. Such international compacts

---

[265] *See, e.g., 1937 Senate Hearings, supra* note 224, at 75; McDougal & Lans (pt. 1), *supra* note 16, at 255–56.

[266] *Curtiss-Wright*, 299 U.S. at 318.

[267] *See supra* notes 132–36 and accompanying text.

[268] The Administration immediately transformed Sutherland's brief reference into a definitive Supreme Court endorsement of innovative forms of congressional-executive agreement-making. *See, e.g., 1937 Senate Hearings, supra* note 224, at 75. This expansive interpretation was not compelled by the text of the opinion. It was also directly contradicted by Sutherland's 1919 book, *Constitutional Power and World Affairs*, which confined executive agreements to arrangements that "affect administrative matters, as distinguished from policies, and those which are of only individual concern, or limited scope and duration, as distinguished from those of general consequence and permanent character." SUTHERLAND, *supra* note 70, at 121. Because this book developed the controversial historical and theoretical arguments that were the basis of *Curtiss-Wright*, *see id.* at 24–47, it seems unlikely that Sutherland had, sub silentio, radically revised his views about executive agreements at the time he wrote the opinion.

[269] United States v. Belmont, 301 U.S. 324, 330–32 (1937).

[270] United States v. Pink, 315 U.S. 203, 229–30 (1942).

[271] The text of the agreement is set forth in *Pink. See id.* at 212–13; *see also* 1 HACKWORTH, *supra* note 69, at 302–05 (detailing correspondence of Presidents Coolidge and Roosevelt with Soviet diplomats regarding improvement of relations between the two countries).

and agreements as the Litvinov Assignment have a similar dignity."[272] This was a strong statement, because the Supremacy Clause failed to mention any such legal animal, and the Court was endorsing the subordination of the states to a unilateral executive decision.[273] Like *Curtiss-Wright*, it provided significant legitimation for the transformation we shall be describing. Nonetheless, our problem is quite different from the one raised by the Litvinov Assignment. We are not asking whether a unilateral executive agreement can trump state law; we are asking whether the House of Representatives can trump one sixth of the Senate.

Nonetheless, the judiciary's refusal to limit the Supremacy Clause to treaties undoubtedly made formal criteria seem less constitutionally significant. The days of *Missouri v. Holland*, when the treaty form possessed special constitutional potency, were past.

E. Summing Up the New Deal

But the future remained uncertain. Taken for all it was worth, the practice of the 1930s could have been assimilated within a traditional framework. As we have seen, the President always had the power to bind the country in limited categories of cases dealing with military matters and the settlement of claims. It was a stretch to add a broad new category to this list and assert that he could also, with the prior authorization of Congress, make binding agreements in economic affairs. Yet this is precisely the direction in which most leading commentators, with the exception of Garner, were moving in the late 1930s.

Even in the trade area, one should avoid exaggerating New Deal innovation. If NAFTA had been negotiated in 1937, Roosevelt would have submitted it as a treaty to the Senate without recognizing that he had a choice in the matter. While the Trade Acts had given him ex

---

[272] *Pink*, 315 U.S. at 230 (citation omitted). Still, neither *Belmont* nor *Pink* suggested that the Court would validate executive agreements on subjects ranging far outside the traditional doctrinal categories. Citing Moore's 1906 *Digest of International Law*, *Belmont* described the field of unilateral action in the restrictive language of the traditional categories: "an international compact, as this was, is not always a treaty which requires the participation of the Senate. There are many such compacts, of which a protocol, a modus vivendi, a postal convention, and agreements like that now under consideration are illustrations." *Belmont*, 301 U.S. at 330–31; *see also Pink*, 315 U.S. at 229 (quoting *Belmont*).

[273] Justice Douglas arguably went even further, indirectly suggesting that unilateral executive agreements might be constitutionally equivalent to acts of Congress: "All constitutional acts of power, whether in the executive or in the judicial department, have as much legal validity and obligation as if they proceeded from the legislature . . . ." *Pink*, 315 U.S. at 230 (internal quotation marks omitted) (quoting THE FEDERALIST No. 64, at 394 (John Jay) (Clinton Rossiter ed., 1961)). This claim remains controversial and is contrary to the prevailing view. *See, e.g.*, HENKIN, *supra* note 12, at 184–87; *see also* United States v. Guy W. Capps, Inc., 204 F.2d 655, 658 (4th Cir. 1953) (voiding an executive agreement on the grounds that it was in conflict with a congressional statute), *aff'd on other grounds*, 348 U.S. 296 (1955).

ante authorization to bind the country within fixed congressional parameters, it was still a big step to challenge the Senate on its home
turf and deny its traditional right to give ex post "advice and consent"
to major international agreements.

A change in legal atmosphere is one thing; a decisive and self-conscious transformation in constitutional practice quite another. While
the senatorial monopoly over treaty-making might have been shaken a
bit in the minds of a small legal elite, the role of the Senate had not
been seriously questioned by the American people during the 1930s. It
was only the searing experience of world war that transformed a bit of
legal esoterica into the stuff of a constitutional revolution.

IV. THE GREAT TRANSFORMATION

A. *The Triumph of Interchangeability*

The American Constitution is unthinkable without war. The original document is born of revolution; and then there are the Civil War
Amendments. War leads to sacrifice, to a grim determination that this
carnage shall not have been in vain, to solemn steps to avoid its repetition. This is the dynamic at work in the story that follows.

During the 1930s, the Senate's rejection of the League of Nations
had taken on a new meaning. Hitler's rise was accompanied by a
flood of agonizing reappraisals of the Senate's historical performance
of its treaty-making powers.[274] When war struck, the Senate's rejection of the League of Nations became a symbol of isolationist irresponsibility.[275] Nor could the Constitution escape a heavy share of the
blame. A majority of the Senate had supported the Treaty of Versailles by a vote of forty-nine to thirty-five.[276] It was the Constitution

---

[274] Major works published in the early 1930s include: ROYDEN J. DANGERFIELD, IN DEFENSE
OF THE SENATE: A STUDY IN TREATY MAKING (1933); FLEMING, cited above in note 193; FLEM-
ING, TREATY VETO, cited above in note 239; and HOLT, cited above in note 67.

[275] *See, e.g.*, PAUL BIRDSALL, VERSAILLES TWENTY YEARS AFTER 296–97 (1941); FLEMING,
WORLD COURT, *supra* note 239, at 164. It was not unusual for internationalists to blame the war
on the Senate. *See, e.g., Amendment to Constitution Relative to the Making of Treaties: Hearings
Before the Subcomm. of the House Comm. on the Judiciary*, 78th Cong., 2d Sess. 7 (1944) [herein-
after *House Judiciary Committee Hearings*] (testimony of Rep. J. Percy Priest) (recalling the
"tragic circumstances along the treacherous trail that led from that vote in the Senate through the
next two decades — a trail that led through Manchuria and Ethiopia to Munich, Pearl Harbor,
Italy, and Tarawa"); SUMNER WELLES, THE TIME FOR DECISION 397 (1944); Charles Seymour,
Versailles in Perspective, 19 VA. Q. REV. 481, 483 (1943).

[276] *See* 59 CONG. REC. 4599 (1920). Wilson had opposed this resolution because he viewed the
Senate's 15 reservations as unacceptable. But the votes tell only a small part of the tortured
history. *See generally* FLEMING, *supra* note 193, at 474–500 (recounting Senator Lodge's brilliant
manipulation of Senate procedural rules, supported by Senate "irreconcilables" and "reservation-
ists"); HOLT, *supra* note 67, at 249–307 (same). In a famous confession, Lodge's point-man in the
Senate, Senator Watson, reported that Lodge intended not only to defeat the Versailles Treaty
despite its support by 80% of the country, but to throw the onus for its defeat onto President
Wilson. *See* JAMES E. WATSON, AS I KNEW THEM 190–91 (1936).

that allowed a "recalcitrant one-third plus one"[277] to set the stage for the rise of Hitler and the resumption of world carnage.

Not, mind you, that this revisionist interpretation of Versailles had swept the field of American public opinion.[278] Isolationists had held their own during the 1930s, winning important victories like the Neutrality Act of 1937[279] — until the outbreak of war. At that point, isolationism was thrown onto the defensive,[280] and the rising death tolls brought a growing public determination to avoid the mistakes of the past. The Senate could not be permitted to reenact the tragedy of Versailles and prepare the way for World War Three. The Constitution's "fatal defect"[281] had to be corrected before it was too late.[282]

As the tides of war began to shift in 1943, the need to secure the peace became a national preoccupation.[283] By October 1943, Gallup was already obtaining surprising responses when he asked about the Constitution's two-thirds rule.[284] Only 14% had no opinion; 25% were in favor of the traditional rule, while 54% thought that a majority in

---

[277] CORWIN, WORLD ORGANIZATION, *supra* note 16, at 38 (internal quotation marks omitted) (quoting Secretary of State John Hay).

[278] Borchard, for instance, blamed the defeat of Versailles on Wilson and viewed the Treaty not as "a treaty of peace but a declaration of war." Borchard, *Shall the Executive Agreement, supra* note 17, at 665.

[279] *See* Neutrality Act of 1937, ch. 146, 50 Stat. 121.

[280] Even as late as July 18, 1939, Senator Borah, a leading isolationist, had publicly challenged the President's claim that a general war was imminent. Borah claimed that his own independent sources, which he believed were superior to Roosevelt's, had assured him there would be no war. *See* FLEMING, WORLD COURT, *supra* note 239, at 142. When Hitler invaded Poland less than three months later, Borah was still claiming it was a "phony war." *Id.* at 143. At this point, however, isolationists could no longer defeat amendments to the Neutrality Act when the President called Congress back for a special session. *See supra* note 231.

[281] FLEMING, WORLD COURT, *supra* note 239, at 156.

[282] As Fleming put it:

> Every government in the world doubts the ability of the United States to help organize the coming victory, because all know that the Constitution of the United States contains a fatal defect. They know that, so far as constructive effort to build a better world goes, our government is permanently deadlocked within itself by a division of the power to make and execute foreign policy between the President and the Senate. They must calculate that the constructive plans of the executive are always at the mercy of a self-assertive minority in the Senate.

Id.

[283] Public opinion polls revealed large, and growing, support for a post-war international organization to maintain the peace. In July 1942, the Gallup poll showed 59% in favor of participation in a post-war organization, with 22% opposed and 19% undecided. By December 1942, Gallup was reporting 73% in favor, with 27% opposed. In June 1943, Gallup found 78% in favor, with only 13% opposed and 9% undecided. *See* KENNETH COLEGROVE, THE AMERICAN SENATE AND WORLD PEACE 117–18 (1944). Other polls corroborated this rapid decline in isolationist sentiment. *See id.* at 38–39. Reflecting this massive shift, state legislatures began adopting resolutions supporting a world organization and in some cases calling for a world federation. *See id.* at 119–20.

[284] Gallup surveyed public opinion on the issue in October 1943, May 1944, and February 1945. Respondents were asked:

> *Which one of these three ways would you, personally, favor as the best way to have peace treaties approved?*

both Houses should replace two-thirds of the Senate.[285] By May 1944, the margin had become more lop-sided — 60% were in favor of a two-House procedure, only 19% remained traditionalist.[286] Constitutional change became a staple of editorial writers, pundits, and politicians. By 1943 the *New York Times* began editorializing on behalf of a constitutional amendment,[287] and other leading newspapers[288] soon fol-

---

The three alternatives given voters are: (1) Approval by the President only, (2) Approval by the President and a majority of the whole Congress, (3) Approval by the President and two-thirds of the Senate — the present method.

George Gallup, *Public Favors House Voice in Ratifying of Treaties*, WASH. POST, June 16, 1945, at 7; *see also Ratification of Peace Treaties*, OPINION NEWS (Nat'l Opinion Res. Center, Denver, Colo.), Feb. 6, 1945, at 3 (reporting results of October 1943, May 1944, and Febrary 1945 polls).

[285] *See Peace Treaties and the Senate Two-Thirds Rule*, OPINION NEWS (Nat'l Opinion Res. Center, Denver, Colo.), Nov. 8, 1943, at 3. Seven percent favored a unilateral presidential procedure. *See id.*

[286] *See Congressional Ratification of Treaties*, OPINION NEWS (Nat'l Opinion Res. Center, Denver, Colo.), May 30, 1944, at 2. Support for presidential unilateralism remained at 7%. The numbers remained stable in the February 1945 survey, with 58% supporting the two-House method, 22% the traditional system, 8% presidential unilateralism, and 12% without opinion. *See* Gallup, *supra* note 284, at 7; *Ratification of Peace Treaties*, *supra* note 284, at 3.

[287] *See America's Treaty Making*, N.Y. TIMES, Aug. 19, 1943, at 18. During the next two years, the *Times* ran at least five more editorials supporting an amendment. *See Approval of Treaties*, N.Y. TIMES, Apr. 17, 1944, at 22; *Approval of Treaties*, N.Y. TIMES, May 22, 1944, at 18; *The Senate's Treaty Power*, N.Y. TIMES, Sept. 5, 1944, at 18; *The Approval of Treaties*, N.Y. TIMES, Nov. 29, 1944, at 22; *The Treaty-Making Power*, N.Y. TIMES, May 3, 1945, at 22. As early as 1943, the *Times* was confident that overwhelming public support would ensure quick approval by the states. *See America's Treaty Making*, *supra*, at 18. It only became more confident as time passed: the polls "indicate not only that a heavy majority of the voters is in favor of changing the system of treaty ratification but that this majority has become greater as the question has been more discussed and better understood." *Approval of Treaties*, N.Y. TIMES, May 22, 1944, at 18. Even as the *Times* warned the Senate of the dangerous course it was traveling, it rebuked those who contended that a formal amendment was unnecessary, saying: "This is merely to argue that we can get around the Constitution by conspiring with each other to call a spade by another name." *Approval of Treaties*, N.Y. TIMES, Apr. 17, 1944, at 22.

[288] In less than a year, the *Washington Post* ran no fewer than seven editorials advocating an amendment and calling for an all-out national campaign to oust the Senate of its monopoly. *See Approval of Treaties*, WASH. POST, Aug. 27, 1944, at 4B; *Two-Thirds Rule*, WASH. POST, Oct. 21, 1944, at 6 [hereinafter *Two-Thirds Rule Oct. 21, 1944*]; *Two-Thirds Rule Repeal*, WASH. POST, Feb. 26, 1945, at 8; *Signal to the House*, WASH. POST, Feb. 28, 1945 at 8; *A National Necessity*, WASH. POST, May 1, 1945, at 8 (warning that the two-thirds rule is undemocratic and retaining it after the war would be "a bid for national suicide"); *Two-Thirds Rule*, WASH. POST, May 3, 1945, at 10 ("The House will be asked to do nothing more, when it votes today, than to recognize and act upon this simple, common-sense truth for the sake of preventing World War III."); *Vital to Peace*, WASH. POST, June 25, 1945, at 6. Although the initial impetus for the amendment was the concern that the Senate might repeat the Versailles experience when called upon to approve the United Nations Charter, the *Post*, realizing that the overwhelming strength of public opinion assured bipartisan senatorial support for the Charter, took a broader view as time wore on:

We cannot overlook the fact, however, that a shadow continues to hang over our entire relationship to this peace system. The shadow is the two-thirds rule for approval of treaties in the Senate. . . . But no one should be deceived by a favorable outlook for a single treaty. International dealings will probably be more numerous in the postwar era than ever before. . . . It would be self-defeating to leave in our Constitution a provision which permits a minority of one-third plus one of the Senate to sabotage international collaboration in these fields.

lowed. The call was already being taken up in the Congress.[289] By 1945, the movement was gaining steam, with more newspapers,[290] scholars,[291] national organizations,[292] political leaders,[293] opinion mak-

---

Two-Thirds Rule Oct. 21, 1944, supra, at 6; *see also* 91 CONG. REC. 4296 (1945) (quoting editorials supporting amendment in the *Free Press of Detroit* on November 27, 1944, the *Sun* of Chicago on December 3, 1944, the *Times-Dispatch* of Richmond on January 2, 1945, and the *Star Journal* of Minneapolis on November 17, 1944); *History Confounds the Senator*, NASHVILLE TENNES-SEAN, Dec. 2, 1944 (supporting an amendment), *reprinted in House Judiciary Committee Hearings, supra* note 275, at 138–39; *Majority Rule*, NASHVILLE TENNESSEAN, Nov. 25, 1944 (same), *reprinted in* 90 CONG. REC. A4588 (1944).

By no means was opinion unanimous. *See, e.g., The Senate and Peace*, N.Y. HERALD TRIB., Apr. 17, 1944, at 14 (supporting the two-thirds rule); *Not a Question of Prestige*, SHREVEPORT TIMES, Jan. 16, 1945 (same), *reprinted in* 91 CONG. REC. A213 (1945); *Stick to First Principles*, INDIANAPOLIS STAR, Mar. 7, 1945 (same), *reprinted in* 91 CONG. REC. A1495 (1945).

[289] Six constitutional amendments were introduced in the House during the 78th Congress. *See* H.R.J. Res. 264, 78th Cong., 2d Sess. (1944); H.R.J. Res. 246, 78th Cong., 2d Sess. (1944); H.R.J. Res. 238, 78th Cong., 2d Sess. (1944); H.R.J. Res. 64, 78th Cong., 1st Sess. (1943); H.R.J. Res. 31, 78th Cong., 1st Sess. (1943); H.R.J. Res. 6, 78th Cong., 1st Sess. (1943). They were nearly identical to each other, substituting a majority vote in both Houses for the two-thirds vote mandated by the existing Treaty Clause. In the same Congress, Senator Gillette introduced in the Senate a series of amendment proposals that would have preserved the Senate's monopoly but repealed the two-thirds rule. *See* COLEGROVE, *supra* note 283, at 170.

[290] *See, e.g., Assert for the People*, NASHVILLE TENNESSEAN, May 5, 1945 ("The people are white hot for such a step."), *reprinted in* 91 CONG. REC. A2123 (1945); *By a Majority*, CHATTA-NOOGA TIMES, May 5, 1945 (noting that "this present destructive war probably would have been averted if that rule had been in effect after World War No. 1"), *reprinted in* 91 CONG. REC. A2086 (1945); *Only Way to Ensure Peace*, NEWS AND OBSERVER (Raleigh), May 5, 1945 (contending that the two-thirds rule was partly "responsible for the death and destruction in World War No. 2"), *reprinted in* 91 CONG. REC. A2093 (1945); *Opening of a Good Fight*, BIRMINGHAM NEWS, May 6, 1945, *reprinted in* 91 CONG. REC. A2171 (1945); Allen Morris, *Florida Leads Treaty Fight*, ORLANDO MORNING SENTINEL, May 7, 1945, *reprinted in* 91 CONG. REC. A2186 (1945).

[291] There were many prominent monographs and essays. *See, e.g.,* SOL BLOOM, THE TREATY-MAKING POWER, FOURTEEN POINTS SHOWING WHY THE TREATY-MAKING POWER SHOULD BE SHARED BY THE HOUSE OF REPRESENTATIVES (1944); COLEGROVE, *supra* note 283; CORWIN, WORLD ORGANIZATION, *supra* note 16; FLEMING, WORLD COURT, *supra* note 239, at 156–84; Borchard, *A Reply, supra* note 17; Borchard, *Shall the Executive Agreement, supra* note 17; Walter F. Dodd, *International Relations and the Treaty Power*, 30 A.B.A. J. 360 (1944); McDougal & Lans (pts. 1 & 2), *supra* note 16; James R. Morford, *For the Constitutional Amendment as to the Ratification of Treaties*, 30 A.B.A. J. 605 (1944); Wright, *supra* note 16; Herbert Wright, *The Two-Thirds Vote of the Senate in Treaty-Making*, 38 AM. J. INT'L L. 643 (1944). During hearings in the House, a large number of prominent scholars went on record in favor of a constitutional amendment. *See House Judiciary Committee Hearings, supra* note 275, *passim*.

[292] Active supporters included the League of Women Voters, General Federation of Women's Clubs (representing 16,000 clubs and 2,500,000 members), Young Women's Christian Association, National Women's Trade Union League, and the Council for Social Action of the Congregational Christian Churches. *See, e.g., House Judiciary Committee Hearings, supra* note 275, at 59, 75, 97, 127, 131; *Vital to Peace, supra* note 288, at 6.

[293] Proponents did their best to take their proposed amendment to the people. *See, e.g.,* 91 CONG. REC. 4297 (1945) (noting addresses by Rep. Merrow to the Foreign Policy Association in Philadelphia and Men's Club of the First Congregational Church in Toledo, Ohio); BLOOM, *supra* note 291, at 18–19 (monograph by the then-Chairman of the House Committee on Foreign Affairs, arguing in favor of an amendment); James W. Fulbright, *Treaty by Resolution*, N.Y. HERALD TRIB., Nov. 3, 1943, at 24 (editorial by then-Rep. Fulbright); Claude Pepper, *A Summons Against the 'Kiss of Death*,' N.Y. TIMES MAG., Dec. 12, 1943, at 5, 41 (article by a Senator from Florida);

ers,[294] and state legislatures[295] plunging into the debate. In May the House of Representatives formally approved a constitutional amendment ousting the Senate from its traditional prerogative. Under its proposal, a majority of both Houses would be granted the power to approve treaties.[296] The bottleneck was going to be the Senate. If it could be forced to surrender, there was broad confidence that three fourths of the states would approve the proposed amendment by the end of the war.[297]

Should Treaties Be Ratified by a Majority of Both Houses?, TOWN MEETING, Oct. 19, 1944, at 7, 16–17 (radio debate between Rep. James W. Fulbright, Rep. Estes Kefauver, Sen. Raymond E. Willis, and Dr. Edwin Borchard); Representative James C. Auchincloss, Address Before the Women's Republican Club of Monmouth County, New Jersey (Mar. 16, 1945), *reprinted in* 91 CONG. REC. A1548–49 (1945); Representative Chester E. Merrow, Remarks Before the General Court of New Hampshire (Jan. 17, 1945), *reprinted in* 91 CONG. REC. A183–85 (1945); Representative Chester E. Merrow, Radio Address from the Studios of WTOP, Washington, D.C. (Apr. 17, 1945), *reprinted in* 91 CONG. REC. A1785–86 (1945); *see also* Wendell Willkie, *Cowardice at Chicago*, COLLIER'S, Sept. 16, 1944, at 11, 77–79.

[294] Opinion pieces on both sides were omnipresent. *See, e.g.*, HUGH GIBSON, THE ROAD TO FOREIGN POLICY 179–81 (1944) (supporting the Senate's traditional treaty prerogative); Harry E. Barnes, *Globaloney Unlimited*, THE PROGRESSIVE, Mar. 20, 1944, at 10 (book review) (same); June Barrows, *Letters to the* Times: *Ratification of Treaties*, N.Y. TIMES, July 1, 1944, at 14 (same); Ira E. Bennett, *Peace by Law, Not by Treaty?*, CHRISTIAN SCIENCE MONITOR MAG., June 3, 1944, at 2 (attacking Senate's treaty role); Edward S. Corwin, *Power — Two Views — "An Out-of-Date Fifth Wheel to Governmental Coach,"* ST. LOUIS TIMES, June 16, 1944 (same), *reprinted in House Judiciary Committee Hearings, supra* note 275, at 135–37; Ralph W. Page, *Senate Two-Thirds Rule Faces Show-Down*, PHILA. BULL., Nov. 25, 1944 (favoring amendment), *reprinted in* 90 CONG. REC. A4588 (1944); Jack H. Pollack, THIS MONTH, Mar. 1945 (same), *reprinted in* 91 CONG. REC. A1445–46 (1945); Merlo Pusey, *Treaty Power: Road to Abolition of Two-Thirds Rule*, WASH. POST, Nov. 29, 1944, at 11 (favoring amendment); Helen D. Reid, J. AM. ASS'N U. WOMEN, Winter 1945 (same), *reprinted in* 91 CONG. REC. A974 (1945).

[295] Connecticut, New Hampshire, and North Carolina passed resolutions urging Congress to send an amendment to the states. *See Vital to Peace, supra* note 288, at 6; *see also* 91 CONG. REC. 1543 (1945) (reporting the North Carolina resolution). Florida invoked the alternative Article V procedure, formally applying to Congress to convene a Constitutional Convention. *See Vital to Peace, supra* note 288, at 6; *see also* 91 CONG. REC. 4965–66 (1945) (discussing the Florida resolution).

[296] The final version insisted on absolute majorities in both Houses, not simply a majority of those present. *See* 91 CONG. REC. 4343 (1945) (amendment by Rep. Schwabe). The vote was 288 to 88, with 56 abstentions. *See id.* at 4367.

[297] Two things were generally conceded: that the states would rapidly approve an amendment if given the chance and that the Senate would resist. Nevertheless, many thought the Senate's resistance could be overcome by a sufficient show of support in the House. Editorial writers prodded the Senate to take the high road of statesmanship, warning that anything less would be disastrous both for the Senate and for the country. *See, e.g.*, *The Senate's Treaty Power, supra* note 287, at 18; *Two-Thirds Rule Oct. 21, 1944, supra* note 288, at 6; *Two-Thirds Rule Repeal, supra* note 288, at 8; *A National Necessity, supra* note 288, at 8.

But in February 1945, the Senate Judiciary Committee announced that it would not consider any constitutional amendments until after the end of the war, allowing the soldiers to return home and participate in the national debate. In response, the *Post* declared that "the Senate will have to be blasted out of its foxhole of entrenched power." *Signal to the House, supra* note 288, at 8.

But this was not the New Deal way. An Administration campaign for a constitutional amendment threatened to fracture the fragile bipartisan coalition that Roosevelt had been building for a new internationalist foreign policy. Even if Roosevelt had gained the necessary two-thirds majority, the bitter battle might have alienated key Republican supporters of the emerging internationalist consensus. Instead of sacrificing policy substance for constitutional form, the Administration gained its constitutional triumph through more informal, but equally effective, means.

By the time the war ended, the Administration had laid the legal foundation for a new constitutional compromise: while the Senate might retain its traditional powers over treaty-making, the President would gain the constitutional authority to call upon Congress, instead of the Senate, to approve pending international obligations. Our task is to see how the terms of this compromise were fashioned in the cauldron of war — to the point where it could be used as a bipartisan alternative to a formal amendment in the post-war years.

B. The Role of Legal Intellectuals

Along with the outbreak of war in Europe came a new wave of legal scholarship — two waves in fact. The authors who published in 1940 and 1941 extended trends already visible in the 1930s. The second wave hit in 1944 and thematized the constitutional consciousness emerging out of the war effort.

The implications of New Deal theory and practice were canonized in Edward Corwin's 1940 classic *The President: Office and Powers*, which attempted a comprehensive analysis of the Presidency. As part of this effort, Corwin examined the relationship between the treaty power and the developing practice of executive agreement.[298] Picking up the standard internationalist line, Corwin viewed the Treaty Clause as a "mistake[ ] that . . . must be chalked up against the Framers."[299] Worse yet, there was not "the least likelihood in the world of its ever being corrected by the method indicated by the Framers for such cases — that of constitutional amendment. When two thirds of the Senate consent to relax any of that body's powers something like the millennium will have dawned."[300]

But Corwin did not despair: "such is the 'infinite variety' of the Constitution that less formal means have been discovered for mitigating 'the mistake' — [whose] full potentialities had not yet been fully

---

[298] *See* CORWIN, THE PRESIDENT, *supra* note 16, at 232–40.

[299] *Id.* at 234–35.

[300] *Id.* at 235.

realized."[301] Touching on some of the familiar precedents,[302] Corwin argued that the Senate should not be conceded a constitutional monopoly on international agreements.[303] But he had not yet worked out a full-fledged account of the modern alternative.[304]

It fell to Wallace McClure to take this next step in *International Executive Agreements*. Previously, the best defense of interchangeability was Garner's six-page essay of 1935.[305] McClure now devoted 400 pages to a comprehensive defense that touched all potential precedents. McClure had worked in the State Department, and his book discussed many agreements that were only available in the Department's archives.[306] Its publication in 1941 transformed the legal debate. A marginal (if growing) practice on the fringe of treaty law was now presented as central to American diplomacy since the Founding.[307]

Just in the nick of time. Like Corwin, McClure could not anticipate how the Second World War would transform his subject. His book was the work of a loyal New Dealer whose principal client was Franklin Roosevelt. His presidentialist bias led him to advocate an extreme form of interchangeability. He was not content to establish that both Houses of Congress could substitute for the Senate in ratifying presidential initiatives.[308] He contended that the President could

---

[301] *Id.*

[302] *See id.* at 235–39 & n.90. These included postal conventions; the 1934 Trade Agreements Act; the annexations of Texas and Hawaii; the peace resolution of 1921 (about which he had written in a different vein in 1920, *see* Corwin, *supra* note 167, at 674–75); the World War I debt settlements; the International Labor Organization; a host of unilateral executive agreements, such as the Rush-Bagot Agreement of 1817, the Boxer Protocol of 1901, the Santo Domingo affair of 1905, and the Lansing-Ishii Agreement of 1917; and the Supreme Court decisions in United States v. Belmont, 301 U.S. 324 (1937), Altman & Co. v. United States, 224 U.S. 583 (1912), and Field v. Clark, 143 U.S. 649 (1892).

[303] Without even referring to his earlier views on the "durability" of executive agreements, *see supra* notes 70 & 167, Corwin denied the contention that they are binding only on the administration entering into them, claiming that this view had been "refuted by history." CORWIN, THE PRESIDENT, *supra* note 16, at 238.

[304] Corwin argued that the precedents had established the power of Congress "to legislate generally concerning external affairs." CORWIN, THE PRESIDENT, *supra* note 16, at 235. But he did not spell out precisely what this meant, suggesting only that there was "no easily statable limit" to congressional power under Article I, "however 'the recalcitrant third plus one man' of the Senate may feel about the matter." *Id.* at 236.

[305] *See* Garner, *supra* note 101. Professor David Levitan wrote an article in 1940 that foreshadowed McClure's argument but was far more cautious in its conclusions. *See* David M. Levitan, *Executive Agreements: A Study of the Executive in the Control of the Foreign Relations of the United States*, 35 ILL. L. REV. 365, 371, 395 (1940). Levitan denied that Congress had the power to authorize the President to enter into binding agreements. *See id.* at 371 (relying upon an oft-quoted remark of John Bassett Moore).

[306] *See, e.g.*, MCCLURE, *supra* note 16, at 57 n.24, 67 nn.64–65.

[307] *See id.* at 189–90, 368.

[308] To be sure, McClure did extol the democratic superiority of a two-House approval procedure over the two-thirds rule and even over presidential unilateralism. *See id.* at 367–74. But he insisted that the Constitution itself did not tie the President's hands, and he defended that free-

bind the nation unilaterally on any matter, "regardless of congressional approval or at least if Congress does not by law dissent."[309] This was a very radical proposal: rather than requiring the President to obtain majorities in both Houses, McClure would allow the President to win so long as one third of either House could be induced to support his veto of dissenting legislation.[310]

Paradoxically, this extreme claim simplified McClure's scholarly task. He presented all executive agreements — whether unilateral, congressionally authorized or approved, or ancillary to treaties — as if they were essentially the same. He could therefore rely on the sheer number of agreements to reject the claim that the Senate held a monopoly on agreement-making.[311] He made no serious effort to demonstrate that the traditional typologies were inadequate to explain historical practice.[312] Nonetheless, his relentless enumeration of agreement after agreement gave internationalists a new legal weapon as the country began to confront the specter of Versailles.

It took some time for other legal scholars to integrate McClure's contribution into their own thinking. But as Allied victories began to focus the nation's consciousness on the problem of "building the peace," other writers followed McClure's lead. The years 1944 and 1945 witnessed a brilliant burst of revisionist writing. Three major

---

dom of action as necessary given the disorderly state of international relations. *See id.* at 370–80. He also warned against exaggerating the democratic deficit in unilateral executive agreements because the President is "the uniquely responsible . . . representative of all the people" and in his hands "the maximum of flexibility, wieldiness, and centralization are combined with the maximum of security against anti-democratic employment of power." *Id.* at 375; *see also id.* at 372–73 ("[N]o President has to any considerable extent misused his power thus to deal with governments other than his own.").

[309] *Id.* at 363.

[310] Indeed, McClure went further, arguing that the President could enter into binding agreements on any subject matter and that Congress was powerless to stop him. *See id.* at 332–43. The difficult question, he thought, was whether for *domestic* purposes an executive agreement, like a treaty, would supersede not only any inconsistent state law (as in United States v. Belmont, 301 U.S. 324, 331–32 (1937)) but also any inconsistent act of Congress. In his view, there were strong grounds for so believing, but he nevertheless reached the contrary conclusion based on "the entire tenor" of the Constitution. MCCLURE, *supra* note 16, at 343.

[311] For example, he put a special twist on the many cases in which the President had acted under the authority of a congressional statute. Rather than emphasizing the ways in which these precedents remained distant cousins of the modern congressional-executive agreement, he used them to support his brief for presidential unilateralism: not only had the President acted unilaterally from the earliest days of the Republic, but Congress had also passed statutes on many occasions in support of presidential power. *See* MCCLURE, *supra* note 16, at 331.

Conversely, at the time he was writing, American history yielded only one important case in which Congress, rather than the Senate, engaged in ex post review of binding international agreements negotiated by the President. This was the case of the Allied debt settlements, and they had been understood at the time as a special application of Congress's narrow power to dispose of property. *See supra* notes 180–89 and accompanying text. This fact did not trouble McClure. *See* MCCLURE, *supra* note 16, at 324–35. Given his bias toward presidential unilateralism, it made sense for him to weave this single case into a much larger tapestry.

[312] *See supra* notes 49–70 and accompanying text.

legal scholars — Edward Corwin,[313] Myres McDougal,[314] and Quincy Wright[315] — wrote powerful manifestos for interchangeability.[316] But Corwin and McDougal meant something different from McClure. For them, the principal alternative to the traditional Senate role was not presidential unilateralism, but the ex post review of executive agreements by both Houses of Congress.[317] This made their appeal to precedent more difficult, but it did not stop them — and many others — from elaborating on McClure's myth of continuity.

For a leading scholar like Quincy Wright, McClure's appeal to an ongoing pattern of constitutional usage justified a high-visibility shift in his previously published views. We last saw him in 1922 emphasizing that executive agreements entered pursuant to statute were "terminable, both nationally and *internationally*, at the discretion of Congress."[318] But in 1944 Wright switched,[319] citing "the development of Congressional and executive practice, and of judicial opinion, as well as historical research."[320]

For revisionists like Corwin and McDougal, this appeal to precedent was only part of a broader argument containing three other elements. The first was an historical critique of senatorial treaty-making. Whatever the abstract merit of the Founders' initial decision, it was a failure in practice. The Founders imagined that the Senate, by virtue of its small size and stable composition, might provide confidential ad-

---

[313] *See* CORWIN, WORLD ORGANIZATION, *supra* note 16.

[314] *See* McDougal & Lans (pts. 1 & 2), *supra* note 16.

[315] *See* Wright, *supra* note 16.

[316] In the same period, major scholars also published books advocating a constitutional amendment to achieve a similar result. *See, e.g.,* COLEGROVE, *supra* note 283, at 166; FLEMING, WORLD COURT, *supra* note 239, at 164–70. Colegrove rejected the new doctrine of interchangeability as "a palpable evasion of the fundamental law," COLEGROVE, *supra* note 283, at 110, and urged a formal amendment as the only acceptable solution. Fleming's view was less rigid. Although the constitutional amendment was the preferred method, *see* FLEMING, WORLD COURT, *supra* note 239, at 164–70, the Senate's monopoly had to be defeated at all costs, *see id.* at 156–87. If senatorial obstruction precluded that option, then either the joint resolution method or McClure's unilateralism would win the day. *See id.* at 177–83.

[317] Their emphasis on the role of the Congress was in some tension with their devotion to New Deal presidentialism. McDougal and Lans, for example, argued that the President has a very wide area of exclusive independent authority, but fell back upon the requirement of congressional approval to eliminate the need to mark these boundaries precisely. *See* McDougal & Lans (pts. 1 & 2), *supra* note 16, at 244–55, 535–36.

[318] WRIGHT, *supra* note 49, § 162, at 236 (emphasis added). Wright had also taken a traditional view of the President's unilateral authority to bind the country. *See id.* §§ 161, 165–166, 169, at 235, 238, 240, 243; *see also supra* notes 49, 52, 57, 58, 64, 70, and accompanying text (describing Wright's views).

[319] Wright's revised view was quite similar to McClure's. He argued that the President has authority to enter into international agreements "limited only by the qualification that he ought not to engage the good faith of the United States to something which may not be carried out." Wright, *supra* note 16, at 348.

[320] *Id.* at 354 n.62. In 1922, Wright had advocated the substitution of majorities in both Houses for two thirds in the Senate, noting that "[t]his change . . . would, of course, require a constitutional amendment." WRIGHT, *supra* note 49, § 266, at 368 n.26.

vice to the President on treaty negotiation.[321] But even George Washington found the Senators unwilling to play their part when he visited them to discuss the first federal treaty, that with the Creek Indians. Washington left in a huff, and no future President returned.[322] In any event, the Senate had become far too large to play the Founding role.[323] Rather than serving as select guardians of the national interest, the Senators treated treaties as just another occasion for partisan politics.[324]

But the Senate's special role was not only a practical failure; it could no longer be defended in principle. Revisionists doubted whether the Founders' decision was anything more than a horse-traders' compromise.[325] In any event, times had changed, and the grant of a senatorial monopoly was premised upon an outdated notion of states' rights. In the modern age of total war, the national interest was paramount in forming foreign policy and should never be subordinated to considerations of state and regional advantage. Yet the Senate monopoly, when married to the two-thirds rule, was a standing invitation for sectional interests to blackmail the majority in an effort to gain selfish privileges.[326] Nor could the classical system be plausibly defended by invoking a principled preference for non-involvement in world affairs: "however wise the Fathers' original desires 'to live alone and like it' may have been in 1789, in the age of the robot bomb and world economic interdependence, isolationism is bankrupt as a guide to policy."[327]

Instead of tolerating an anachronistic foreign policy, Americans should confront the blatantly undemocratic character of the status quo. Senators representing a tiny fraction of the population could veto

---

[321] *See* CORWIN, WORLD ORGANIZATION, *supra* note 16, at 32–33; McDougal & Lans (pt. 2), *supra* note 16, at 539–40.

[322] *See* CORWIN, WORLD ORGANIZATION, *supra* note 16, at 33; McDougal & Lans (pt. 1), *supra* note 16, at 207 n.56.

[323] *See* CORWIN, WORLD ORGANIZATION, *supra* note 16, at 34; McDougal & Lans (pt. 2), *supra* note 16, at 545–46.

[324] Following the examples of Fleming, Holt, and others, *see supra* note 274 and accompanying text, McDougal and Lans launched a scathing attack on the Senate's history of obstructionism. *See* McDougal & Lans (pt. 2), *supra* note 16, at 553–73. Corwin relied on a more nuanced structural analysis. In his view, the Versailles debacle primarily resulted from the impossibility of realizing the Founders' original design. Once the Senate had rejected its role as presidential advisor, it inevitably began to view its function as independent, and even antagonistic, to the presidential negotiation function, leaving the foreign policy process hopelessly in conflict. *See* CORWIN, WORLD ORGANIZATION, *supra* note 16, at 32–36.

[325] *See* McDougal & Lans (pt. 2), *supra* note 16, at 541–43. McDougal and Lans relied on the historical work of Charles Warren, cited above in note 31, at 272, who viewed the Founding decision as based entirely on the narrow economic interests of southerners in maintaining navigational rights on the Mississippi.

[326] *See* CORWIN, WORLD ORGANIZATION, *supra* note 16, at 33, 53–54; McDougal & Lans (pt. 2), *supra* note 16, at 546–49.

[327] McDougal & Lans (pt. 2), *supra* note 16, at 551.

initiatives that gained the assent of a popularly elected President and majorities in both Houses.[328] This antidemocratic bias was especially intolerable in a world in which the line between foreign and domestic policy-making had become arbitrary. If a two-House procedure was good enough for the resolution of fundamental questions at home, why not for those that had implications overseas?[329]

Having demonstrated to their satisfaction that the senatorial prerogative was bankrupt in theory and practice, the revisionists developed a third prong of their argument — advancing a sophisticated theory of constitutional change. There was no need to wait for the "millennium"[330] when the Senate would repent and accept an Article V amendment repudiating its prerogative. The fate of the Electoral College suggested an alternative scenario. In this case, a sustained pattern of usage had successfully eroded the dysfunctional and antidemocratic aspects of the Founding text,[331] and the revisionists' relentless construction of the myth of continuity was an effort to provide a similar basis in usage for their attack on the Treaty Clause.[332]

But the revisionists did not rest their cause on the slow accretion of precedents. They also emphasized the need for constitutional law to keep up with the self-conscious decisions of the American people. This is how Myres McDougal and Ascher Lans opened their extremely influential work of 1945:

> The people have made up their minds as to the general kind of foreign policy they want. In elections and by-elections extending over a period of five years, in Congressional resolutions, and in the platforms and speeches of party candidates, a line of policy has been laid down as precisely as the processes of voting and popular expression permit. Firmly, deliberately, and in large majority, the people have said that they want a foreign policy which continues our war-time alliances and which seeks to create upon that foundation both a new general security organization . . . and all the other supporting institutions.[333]

---

[328] *See* CORWIN, WORLD ORGANIZATION, *supra* note 16, at 47–50, 53; McDougal & Lans (pt. 2), *supra* note 16, at 574–82.

[329] *See* McDougal & Lans (pt. 2), *supra* note 16, at 547–48.

[330] *See* CORWIN, THE PRESIDENT, *supra* note 16, at 235.

[331] *See* CORWIN, WORLD ORGANIZATION, *supra* note 16, at 37; McDougal & Lans (pt. 1), *supra* note 16, at 296–98. Corwin also cited, as examples of the *"working* constitution," the development of the President's cabinet and the transformation of the Senate's treaty-making role from that of executive council to legislative critic. CORWIN, WORLD ORGANIZATION, *supra* note 16, at 37. He was disposed to believe that *"the most beneficial type of constitutional change is that which issues gradually from, and so has been thoroughly tested by, successful practice." Id.* at 41. McDougal and Lans devoted an entire chapter of their opus to developing a theory of constitutional change through usage and offered a long list of examples. *See* McDougal & Lans (pt. 1), *supra* note 16, at 290–306.

[332] *See* CORWIN, WORLD ORGANIZATION, *supra* note 16, at 37–38; McDougal & Lans (pt. 1), *supra* note 16, at 290.

[333] McDougal & Lans (pt. 1), *supra* note 16, at 181–83 (footnotes omitted).

Corwin, and many others, agreed that a minority of Senators — potentially representing an even smaller minority of the population — should be prevented from using an obsolete constitutional form to frustrate this considered judgment of the American people.[334] It would be especially wrong to allow the Senate to take advantage of an empty formalism when the congressional-executive agreement provided an intrinsically superior way for a modern democratic state to enter into decisive international commitments.

Needless to say, this brand of progressive constitutionalism provoked a strong response. On the intellectual front, the counterattack was led by Professor Edwin Borchard.[335] His sharp polemics parried his opponents' claims at every point. In his view, the revisionists' portrayal of historical usage ignored an obvious distinction between the trivial and the important:

> The 'Founding Fathers' formulated this distinction in terms of 'important' matters, which were to be the subject only of formal federal treaties — known to the Founders as 'treaties of peace, of amity and commerce, consular conventions, treaties of navigation' — and 'routine' or unimportant questions. . . . [Executive] agreements in the past have dealt either with routine questions, within the President's admitted constitutional powers, or have related to matters which the Senate deemed too unimportant for formal treaty procedure.[336]

He vigorously disputed his opponents' history, charging that they had concealed their radical break with a constitutional tradition that had served the nation well. He also disputed their political science and democratic theory. In his view, the revisionists were wrong to suppose that the Senate's rejection of the League of Nations played a crucial role in the genesis of the Second World War.[337] They were even wronger to suppose that the values underlying the classical system were obsolete. The fact that treaties might, under twentieth-century

---

[334] According to Corwin, the Senate's prerogative was "a fifth wheel to the governmental coach, and a fifth wheel of a very cumbrous and out-of-date model when we consider the Senate's characteristic methods of transacting business." CORWIN, WORLD ORGANIZATION, *supra* note 16, at 54.

[335] Borchard's vigorous efforts included not only his numerous articles, but also town hall debates, testimony before Congress, and the preparation of legal memoranda for submission to Congress. See note 17 above for citations to his many articles on the subject, and notes 405 & 429 below for citations to his congressional testimony and memoranda. Other friends of the Senate's prerogative included Herbert Briggs and Herbert Wright. *See* Briggs, *The UNRRA Agreement*, *supra* note 17, at 650; Wright, *supra* note 291, at 644.

[336] Borchard, *Shall the Executive Agreement*, *supra* note 17, at 669–70 (footnotes omitted). Like Baldwin 30 years before, *see supra* notes 58–59, Borchard was loosely invoking the Vattel-inspired distinction between treaties and agreements.

[337] *See, e.g.*, Borchard, *Shall the Executive Agreement*, *supra* note 17, at 665; *cf.* Edwin S. Borchard, *Flaws in Post-War Peace Plans*, 38 AM. J. INT'L L. 284, 286 (1944) (viewing collective security arrangements, such as the League of Nations and the anticipated post-World War II successor, as undesirable).

conditions, commit the nation to wage total war did not somehow make the Senate's role anachronistic.

To the contrary, with the stakes so high, it was perfectly appropriate to continue the Founders' insistence that important commitments be approved by two thirds of the Senate. Rather than giving too much weight to minority interests, the classical system was based on a superior understanding of democracy, preventing the President from using patronage and partisan appeals to win narrow victories that might do long-run damage.[338] Borchard acknowledged that New Deal practice had begun to erode the Senate's monopoly: "Since 1933 there has been a considerable extension in the use of the executive agreement . . . . But these examples of [its] expanded employment . . . are not evidence of approved practice but of the encroachment of the Executive on the Senate prerogative. They are not 'usage,' but 'abuse of power.'"[339]

This sharp and continuing counterattack by conservative intellectuals provided a crucial dimension to the ongoing process of transformation. At every point along the way, Borchard and other conservatives shored up resistance in the Senate and the country to the revisionist critique. Despite revisionist talk of anachronism, the conservatives demonstrated that the country *had a choice* about the changes being proposed, and that it was not too late to reaffirm the values of federalism and caution expressed by the older constitutional tradition.

C. The Anatomy of a Constitutional Moment

The interaction of all-out war, popular anxiety about the peace, and escalating constitutional debate provided the heady environment for an intensive reexamination of senatorial prerogatives under the Treaty Clause. The modern congressional-executive agreement emerged out of a complex institutional struggle that unfolded during the third and fourth terms of the Roosevelt(-Truman) Administration. During the first phase, the President and his State Department went on the constitutional offensive. The Senate reacted with alarm, but sensing the profound change of war-time public opinion, did not launch an all-out struggle in defense of its prerogative. As the tide of war shifted in 1943, the Senate reached a series of ad hoc accommodations with the President and the House of Representatives. During this early period, Senators would constantly rise on the floor to explain why the Senate's decision to join with the House to approve particular executive agreements should not be construed as a general capitulation of its sole prerogative to give "advice and consent." Nonetheless, the cases began to add up by a process we call "piecemeal precedentialism." The particular casuistries presented by particular Senators on

---

[338] *See* Borchard, *A Reply, supra* note 17, at 660–63.

[339] *Id.* at 649.

particular occasions were easily lost in the mists of time while the hard fact of Senate acquiescence remained in plain view. By 1944, the outlines of a new constitutional procedure were visible to the players in Congress, the White House, and the State Department.

But they had not yet been worked up into a widely recognized and popularly understood alternative to the treaty-making process. Instead, these rough sketches served as a proposal for future constitutional development: if President, Senate, and House cooperated with one another to develop recent precedents, they could create a more internationalist alternative to the classical procedure that had brought about the tragedy of Versailles.

This emerging alternative provided part of the background for the elections of 1944, which triggered a more intensive and self-conscious exploration of constitutional alternatives. After the defeat of Dewey and an array of isolationist Senators, the House of Representatives immediately began to consider a constitutional amendment formally stripping the Senate of its treaty-making monopoly. As Allied armies triumphed in Europe, two thirds of the House supported a formal amendment providing for the ratification of treaties by majorities in both Houses.

While the President had no role to play under Article V, this did not mean that Roosevelt lapsed into inactivity. Rather than throwing its public support behind the House initiative, the Administration pushed forward with a constitutional compromise that would make an Article V amendment unnecessary. On the one hand, Roosevelt placated the Senate's sense of prerogative by offering it the United Nations Charter as a treaty. But on the other hand, the Administration aggressively elaborated the existing stock of piecemeal precedents by processing other crucial elements of the post-war order as congressional-executive agreements.

The ball was in the Senate's court: would it accept the President's compromise or insist on its traditional monopoly, and engage in a bitter-end struggle for its prerogative? The Senate's answer came loud and clear: compromise was better than conflict. Throughout 1945 and 1946, the Senate approved a series of congressional-executive agreements that it would have peremptorily rejected a couple of years before. As before, voices were heard on the Senate floor raising the constitutional battle-cry; but the Senate as a whole rejected these traditionalists and took a new view of its powers, as part of Congress, to authorize binding agreements under Article I. With the Senate joining the House and the President in approving one agreement after another, the constitutional question soon dropped from Senate committee reports, leaving only an occasional Senator to grumble about the newly established doctrine.

So much for the anatomy of the constitutional transformation: War → Constitutional Proposal → Triggering Election → Constitutional Solution by the Unanimous Consent of Senate, House, and President. Our next task is to put some flesh on these bare bones.

D. *The Proposal Phase: 1941–1943*

The State Department was already experimenting with the congressional-executive agreement before Pearl Harbor. The fate of this experiment suggests that, without the war-time transformation of public opinion, this innovation would have gone nowhere.

The story behind the initial experiment begins in 1934, when the Senate turned down, by a vote of forty-six to forty-two, a treaty with Canada proposing the construction of the St. Lawrence Seaway.[340] Given the strong regional opposition to the Seaway, the project was unlikely to get the necessary support of two thirds of the Senate. The years that followed the Senate's action, however, were marked by intellectual ferment amongst the legal elite. Not only was Garner challenging the Senate's treaty-making monopoly in scholarly circles but Wallace McClure, a long-time official in the State Department, was hard at work on his pathbreaking book. With nothing to lose, and a Seaway to gain, this was the perfect context for innovation — especially because Roosevelt was a strong supporter of the project.

In 1939, the State Department's Legal Adviser approved the use of an executive agreement with Canada — so long as it was followed by the ex post approval of both Houses.[341] After the Seaway Agreement was signed in 1941, it was passed on to Congress with a misleading citation to the annexations of Texas and Hawaii.[342] In defending the Administration's initiative, Assistant Secretary of State Berle added some principles to the Legal Adviser's precedents:

---

[340] *See Great Lakes–St. Lawrence Basin: Hearings on S. 1385 Before a Subcomm. of the Senate Comm. on Commerce*, 78th Cong., 2d Sess. 281 (1944) [hereinafter *Commerce Committee Hearings*].

[341] *See* 4 DEP'T ST. BULL. 364, 365 (1941) (reprinting a March 13, 1941 memorandum from the Legal Adviser, referring to a February 10, 1939 memorandum), *reprinted in Commerce Committee Hearings, supra* note 340, at 279.

[342] The Canadians were understandably concerned about the use of the joint resolution form. The Prime Minister signed the agreement only after the United States placed on the formal record opinions of the American Legal Adviser and the Attorney General affirming that the agreement would be binding. These formal affirmations permitted the Canadian Legal Adviser to conclude that the United States could not subsequently deny the validity of the agreement. *See Commerce Committee Hearings, supra* note 340, at 277.

The Legal Adviser to the State Department prepared the legal memorandum citing the precedents of Texas and Hawaii, along with legislation authorizing the building of bridges over the Niagara River and a subway under the Detroit River. He then affirmed the legitimacy of the two-House procedure as an alternative to the classical method. *See* 4 DEP'T ST. BULL. 364, 365–66 (1941), *reprinted in Commerce Committee Hearings, supra* note 340, at 280. Attorney General Jackson wrote a letter concurring in the Legal Adviser's view. *See id.*

[I]n an issue of this size and of this importance, it was hardly fair to place in the hands of the minority of one house the ultimate decision on a measure of very great importance to the entire country. For that reason the agreement form was selected, and it is in that form that it is here.[343]

Such an aggressive presentation provoked predictable senatorial resistance,[344] and the Administration withdrew the entire proposal after the Japanese struck at Pearl Harbor.[345]

As the war intensified, the State Department returned to the offensive, with better results. The first piecemeal precedent was generated by an agreement in which the American government forgave Panama some of its debts and ceded it some property in exchange for the lease of sites for military bases.[346] This context was more favorable to legal innovation for two reasons. First, unlike the Seaway, it did not engage conflicting economic interests of regional dimension. Second, it could be tightly linked to the war effort.

Nonetheless, the State Department proceeded cautiously. It treated Panama's grant of military leases as if it had no legal relationship to the deal.[347] The Department simply sought a joint congressional resolution ceding the property and forgiving the debts.[348] This initiative

---

[343] *Great Lakes–St. Lawrence Basin: Hearings on H.R. 4927 Before the House Comm. on Rivers and Harbors*, 77th Cong., 1st Sess., pt. 1, at 45 (1941) (statement of Adolf A. Berle, Assistant Secretary of State).

[344] After President Roosevelt submitted the agreement to Congress, *see* 87 CONG. REC. 2521 (1941), Senator Clark expressed his doubts, *see id.* at 2522. The Administration, however, already had supporters. *See id.* (remarks of Sen. Barkley).

[345] The official reason for the Administration's withdrawal of the agreement was the "necessity for conserving materials for the war effort." S. REP. No. 1499, 79th Cong., 2d Sess. 19 (1946).

[346] The State Department divided the deal into two agreements, both of which were concluded on the same day. In the first, the Panamanian government made a large number of military sites available without compensation. In the second, the United States ceded certain properties and forgave outstanding debts. The President only went to Congress to obtain approval of the second agreement. *See* S. REP. No. 1720, 77th Cong., 2d Sess. 2–4 (1942) (reprinting the President's message to Congress describing the arrangements); Briggs, *Panama Joint Resolution, supra* note 17, at 687. He could conclude the first agreement unilaterally, he thought, under his powers as Commander-in-Chief.

[347] According to the Administration, the two agreements were entirely separate. Congress's approval of the President's largesse was not a condition to the effectiveness of the bases agreement. *See, e.g.,* 89 CONG. REC. 3326 (1943) (remarks of Rep. Bloom); 88 CONG. REC. 9282, 9284 (1942) (remarks of Sen. Connally, Chairman of the Senate Foreign Relations Committee). These official pretenses were belied by the fact that Panama was holding up ratification of the military sites agreement until Congress approved the transfer of properties and forgiveness of the debt. *See, e.g.,* Briggs, *Panama Joint Resolution, supra* note 17, at 691.

[348] By characterizing the property transfer agreement as independent of the military sites agreement, the Administration made its case much easier: all that was involved was an exercise by Congress of its express power to dispose of property of the United States. *See* U.S. CONST. art. IV, § 3, cl. 2. The proposed joint resolution did not need to mention, let alone "approve," any executive agreement. *See* S. REP. No. 1720, *supra* note 346, at 4, 6–7; *see also* 88 CONG. REC. 9267, 9269 (1942) (remarks of Sen. Connally); *id.* at 9282 (remarks of Sen. Gillette). Professor Briggs warned ominously that if the President repeated such a deceptive practice there could be

fell short of modern practice in two respects. First, it did not expressly acknowledge that the American disposal of property was part of a larger international bargain. Second, although Congress was well aware of the President's agreement, it was not asked to approve it. It was merely asked to pass a joint resolution incorporating America's side of the bargain into law.

This seemingly minor matter was widely viewed as the opening salvo in a struggle over the ratification procedures to be used at the end of the war, and news articles predicted the fiercest senatorial debate in years.[349] During the lengthy argument on the floor,[350] Senators continually referred to the high stakes:

> [Senator Taft:] I have a book by Mr. Wallace McClure written apparently for the purpose of maintaining that anything that can be done by treaty can be done by executive agreement. It seems to me that this is an extremely dangerous doctrine and one to which the Senate should give no support.[351]

Despite Taft's plea, the Senate did support the joint resolution approving the President's cession of property.[352] The debate was full of confused efforts by individual Senators seeking to reassure themselves about the Senate's traditional prerogative. And if the agreement with Panama had stood alone, surely its constitutional significance would have long since been forgotten.

But even as the debate on Panama proceeded, Secretary of State Cordell Hull was planning more aggressive confrontations. By the summer of 1943, Hull was questioning the need to end the war with a comprehensive treaty of the Versailles type. Instead, he began a series of piecemeal negotiations through which the President might commit

---

"a Senatorial revolt" at the critical moment when a post-war peace treaty was before it. *See* Briggs, *Panama Joint Resolution, supra* note 17, at 691.

[349] *See, e.g.*, Arthur Krock, *Debate on Panama*, N.Y. TIMES, Dec. 2, 1942, at 23; *see also* Briggs, *Panama Joint Resolution, supra* note 17, at 686 (noting the implications for post-war settlements).

[350] *See* 88 CONG. REC. 9266–87 (1942).

[351] *Id.* at 9276; *see also id.* at 9270–71 (remarks of Sen. Connally) (denouncing McClure). Both proponents and opponents were at pains to assure themselves of their steadfast opposition to any further expansion in the use of executive agreements, pledging to defend the Senate's prerogatives, especially its right to approve any post-war peace or economic settlements. *See id.* at 9267, 9271 (remarks of Sen. Connally); *id.* at 9267–68 (remarks of Sen. Vandenberg); *id.* at 9276–80 (remarks of Sen. Taft) (observing that "[a]s a matter of fact, no treaties of any importance have been submitted to the Senate since I have been a Member of the body"); *id.* at 9281 (remarks of Sen. Wiley); *id.* at 9282–84 (remarks of Sen. Gillette); *id.* at 9286 (remarks of Sen. Clark of Missouri). Senators also used the occasion to make yet another attempt to delineate the appropriate spheres for treaties and executive agreements. *See, e.g., id.* at 9267–68 (remarks of Sen. Vandenberg); *id.* at 9270–72 (remarks of Sen. Connally); *id.* at 9276–80 (remarks of Sen. Taft).

[352] For procedural reasons, the resolution was not finally passed until the next session. *See* Joint Resolution of May 3, 1943, ch. 92, 57 Stat. 74; S. REP. NO. 201, 78th Cong., 1st Sess. 1–2 (1943).

the country by an interlocking web of executive agreements.[353] The first of these was the United Nations Relief and Rehabilitation Administration (UNRRA) Agreement, dealing with aid for areas liberated by the Allies and signed by forty-four countries.[354]

When leading Senators got wind of Hull's plan, they reacted sharply. Arthur Vandenberg, the ranking Republican on the Foreign Relations Committee, immediately proposed a resolution insisting that the UNRRA agreement be submitted as a treaty.[355] Instead of voting on this resolution, the Committee established a special subcommittee of ranking members headed by Chairman Tom Connally to negotiate with Hull.[356]

The result was a famous blow-up, with the aristocratic Hull stomping out of the meeting. But senatorial negotiations continued with Hull underlings Frances Sayre and Dean Acheson.[357] The large stakes were widely recognized. A *New York Times* report on these discussions shared the front page with coverage of the Allied conquest of Sicily:

> The whole question of ratification of peace agreements by two thirds vote of the Senate is well on the way toward being resolved in favor of a plan by which these agreements will be approved piecemeal by majority vote of the two houses of Congress. . . . The implications were revealed in a guarded statement by Senator Vandenberg . . . :
>
> . . . .
>
> 'I am hopeful that this mutual effort may be sufficiently successful to set a pattern for other post-war problems short of the actual treaty of final peace. It ought to be possible for reasonable men to find a formula

---

[353] *See* COLEGROVE, *supra* note 283, at 92; FLEMING, WORLD COURT, *supra* note 239, at 179; *Senators May Vote Pacts by Majority Along with House*, N.Y. TIMES, Aug. 18, 1943, at 1.

[354] *See* 38 AM. J. INT'L L. 33, 33–39 (Supp. 1944). Professor McDougal, who would soon write the leading essay that helped legitimate the two-House procedure, was then general counsel of the Office of Foreign Relief and Rehabilitation Operations and played a major role in drafting the UNRRA agreement. *See To Enable the United States to Participate in the Work of the United Nations Relief and Rehabilitation Administration: Hearings on H.J. Res. 192 Before the House Comm. on Foreign Affairs*, 78th Cong., 1st & 2d Sess. 159–60 (1943–1944) [hereinafter *House Hearings*].

[355] Formally, Vandenberg's resolution called for an investigation to determine whether the agreement should properly be submitted as a treaty. *See* 89 CONG. REC. 7433 (1943) (remarks of Sen. Vandenberg); DEAN ACHESON, PRESENT AT THE CREATION 71 (1969); *Urges Hull Modify World Relief Pact*, N.Y. TIMES, July 9, 1943, at 15. Comparing the new relief agency to the League of Nations, Vandenberg declared, "[n]ow is the time . . . to find out precisely what pattern of things to come we shall follow." 89 CONG. REC. 7434 (1943).

[356] The subcommittee also included Democrats Theodore Green and Elbert Thomas and Republicans Arthur Vandenberg and Robert La Follette. *See* S. REP. NO. 688, 78th Cong., 2d Sess. 4 (1944).

[357] Secretary Hull had anticipated Republican opposition, but apparently was surprised to find Connally stridently defending the Senate's prerogatives. *See* COLEGROVE, *supra* note 283, at 29; *see also* ACHESON, *supra* note 355, at 72.

which will permit the merits of these many unavoidable war liquidations to be considered without detouring primarily into procedural rows.'[358]

But it would take more than a few handshakes to legitimize the congressional-executive agreement. The Senate subcommittee's effort to agree with the State Department on general principles broke down,[359] and the Administration returned to the practice of piecemeal precedentialism. It struck an ad hoc deal with the special subcommittee to gain its consent to the two-House procedure in the case of UNRRA and allowed each side to put its own interpretation on the precedent.

To win the subcommittee's consent, the State Department renegotiated the agreement with the other forty-three countries, stripping the text of any references obligating the United States to provide funds for the new agency's programs.[360] This allowed Senator Vandenberg to go along with the Administration's innovation.[361] In his view, the removal of express American financial commitments meant that the UNRRA agreement no longer imposed binding international obligations upon the United States, and hence did not serve as a precedent eroding the Senate's treaty-making prerogative.[362] Others were not so sure.[363] Senator Theodore Green, the main Democratic negotiator for

---

[358] *Senators May Vote Pacts by Majority Along With House, supra* note 353, at 1; *see also* 90 CONG. REC. 1737–39 (1944) (remarks of Sen. Vandenberg); COLEGROVE, *supra* note 283, at 31; FLEMING, WORLD COURT, *supra* note 239, at 179.

[359] *See Plan for Majority on Pacts Limited,* N.Y. TIMES, Aug. 19, 1943, at 15. Different commentators reached different conclusions about future prospects. *Compare* FLEMING, WORLD COURT, *supra* note 239, at 179 (optimistic) *with* COLEGROVE, *supra* note 283, at 31–33 (pessimistic).

[360] The subcommittee also insisted on a number of other changes. Most of these are detailed in *United Nations Relief and Rehabilitation Organization: Hearings on H.J. Res. 192 Before the Senate Comm. on Foreign Relations,* 78th Cong., 2d Sess. 7–28 (1944) [hereinafter *Senate Hearings*] (statement of Dean Acheson, Assistant Secretary of State). Whether they were of any great significance was a subject of dispute. *Compare* ACHESON, *supra* note 355, at 72 (doubting their importance) *with Senate Hearings, supra,* at 10–14 (reporting colloquies between Acheson and Vandenberg explaining the effects of the Senate's changes).

[361] Vandenberg took the lead role in the Senate in promoting the agreement. *See* 90 CONG. REC. 1729–45 (1944). As Acheson later explained, he "was just emerging from his isolationist chrysalis." ACHESON, *supra* note 355, at 71. In presenting the joint resolution, Vandenberg mixed isolationist rhetorical flourishes with conciliatory gestures lauding the State Department for its unprecedented cooperation. *See, e.g.,* 90 CONG. REC. 1730, 1738–39 (1944). Lest it upset the apparent gains made with Vandenberg, the Administration did not contradict his account and publicly emphasized the important role he had played. *See, e.g., Senate Hearings, supra* note 360, at 10–14; *House Hearings, supra* note 354, at 158–59.

[362] Vandenberg was emphatic about this point, repeatedly framing questions to Acheson and other Administration witnesses so as to leave the clearest possible record and fortify himself against criticism by his erstwhile isolationist allies. *See Senate Hearings, supra* note 360, at 10–21, 40–45; 90 CONG. REC. 1739, 1741 (1944).

[363] Some conservative scholars reacted skeptically to Vandenberg's categorical assertions. *See, e.g.,* Briggs, *The UNRRA Agreement, supra* note 17, at 654–56. Because UNRRA's functions consisted of more than collecting and disseminating information and providing a discussion forum, it did not fit easily into the traditional model of international organizations. *See supra* notes 115–18 and accompanying text. It was certainly true, as Vandenberg emphasized, that the United

the subcommittee, probably expressed the spirit of the moment best: "he hoped that the procedure . . . would prove an abiding precedent but he could not predict that this would be so."[364]

Even when considered as a precedent, congressional action on UNRRA was some distance away from the NAFTA standard. While NAFTA begins straightforwardly with Congress expressly approving the President's agreement with Mexico and Canada, the UNRRA agreement is a formal anomaly. Part of the document was consistent with an entirely familiar congressional role: it contained an authorization of funds for the new international agency.[365] But another part consisted of the full text of the executive agreement.[366] And a third part was even more interesting. Here Congress appended "reservations" to the UNRRA text, specifying certain limiting conditions to its consent.[367] This made sense only if Congress were emulating the Senate's traditional treaty practice.

A final factor compounded the confusion. Even before Congress had given its approval, the President had signed the UNRRA agreement.[368] Under the terms of the agreement, this was sufficient, without more, to bind the United States.[369]

All this confusion should not blind us to the precedent's importance. Indeed, the Senators were perfectly aware that they were inventing something new. Senator Vandenberg emphasized that consultations with the State Department had

> produced what we both understand is to be not merely an Executive agreement, but an agreement approved by Congress. . . . [T]he theory upon which the agreement now comes to Congress is that it has ceased to be an Executive agreement alone, which in our opinion would have been a gross violation of the proprieties as well as of the law. It has

---

States was not legally obligated to furnish funds, but once funds were appropriated, the agreement created an institutional framework controlling the distribution of relief, over which the United States had limited legal influence. *See* Joint Resolution of Mar. 28, 1944, ch. 135, 58 Stat. 122, 122–25 [hereinafter Agreement for UNRRA] (including the text of the UNRRA agreement in the legislation enabling the United States to participate in the United Nations Relief and Rehabilitation Administration).

[364] *Plan for Majority on Pacts Limited*, *supra* note 359, at 15.

[365] *See* Agreement for UNRRA, *supra* note 363, at 122. Section 1 authorized the appropriation of $1,350,000,000 for the participation of the United States in the work of UNRRA. *See id.*

[366] *See id.* at 122–27. Senator Vandenberg had insisted that the text of the agreement be included verbatim in the joint resolution. *See, e.g.*, *House Hearings*, *supra* note 354, at 159. This was apparently to ensure that the agreement itself would be before Congress and would not be submitted just for its information.

[367] *See* Agreement for UNRRA, *supra* note 363, at 128.

[368] The agreement had been concluded on November 9, 1943, several months before the joint resolution came before Congress. *See, e.g.*, *id.* at 122; *House Hearings*, *supra* note 354, at 161–62.

[369] *See* Agreement for UNRRA, *supra* note 363, at 127 (reprinting Article X of the agreement). For this reason, Professor Briggs concluded that the reservations had no legal effect under international law. *See* Briggs, *The UNRRA Agreement*, *supra* note 17, at 656–57.

been submitted to Congress for congressional approval and not merely for congressional information.[370]

Senator Taft immediately picked up on this point:

I think [Sen. Vandenberg] introduces a new suggestion in constitutional law, which I hope may be the fact. The Senator says that the agreement has ceased to be an Executive agreement. Obviously, however, it has not become a treaty . . . . Apparently the Senator suggests that it is a new kind of thing, an Executive-congressional agreement, which may be entered into with foreign nations. I think it is a rather good suggestion, but it is a novel suggestion . . . . I never have seen such a field defined, and I think it will be difficult to define it. It is very difficult to define the field in which the President may operate by Executive agreement as opposed to what he may do only by treaty. But if we are now to have a third field in which he may operate by Executive agreement approved by Congress, the whole matter will be quite confused. I think it is a good idea, but it ought to be defined.[371]

We have reached a critical moment in our story — when leading members of the Republican opposition were beginning to take the constitutional proposal seriously.

A similar openness to constitutional reform emerged from the Senate's confrontation with the Connally Resolution of 1943.[372] As originally framed, the Resolution put the Senate on record as declaring "[t]hat the United States, acting through its constitutional processes" should join in the future world organization.[373] This proposal provoked a two-week long debate,[374] with many Senators rearguing the

---

[370] 90 CONG. REC. 1736 (1944).

[371] *Id.* Senator Connally added that the Foreign Relations Committee would take up the problem of defining "the boundaries of what are treaties and what are not treaties." *Id.*

[372] The Senate seems to have been pushed into action by an increasingly assertive House of Representatives. William Fulbright, then a Representative, had sought to put both Houses on record as favoring the creation of an international organization "to establish and to maintain a just and lasting peace, among the nations of the world, and as favoring participation by the United States therein through its constitutional processes." H.R. Con. Res. 25, 78th Cong., 1st Sess. (1943) (as amended); *see also* 89 CONG. REC. 7662 (1943); *id.* at 7728–29 (recording the vote). After the House passed the resolution, Senator Gillette reported that "there was some feeling in the Senate that the House had gone out of bounds." FLEMING, WORLD COURT, *supra* note 239, at 173; *see also* CORWIN, WORLD ORGANIZATION, *supra* note 16, at 34–35. It was only then that Senator Connally geared up for a unilateral Senate effort to define its position on the post-war order. Members of the House claimed that it was the Fulbright resolution that finally prodded the Senate into action. *See, e.g., House Judiciary Committee Hearings, supra* note 275, at 21 (statement of Rep. Gossett).

[373] S. REP. NO. 478, 78th Cong., 1st Sess. 1 (1943). The other two clauses provided, uncontroversially, that the war should be waged "until complete victory is achieved" and that the United States should cooperate with its allies in securing the peace. *Id.*

[374] As in the cases of Panama and UNRRA, there was a palpable sense of anxiety running through the debate. Senators repeatedly insisted that the only constitutional method for conclud-

merits of the League of Nations.[375]

For present purposes, a procedural theme is more relevant. Some Senators were concerned that the Connally Resolution might be construed as "advice and consent" of the Senate to any United Nations treaty falling within its broad parameters. To rebut this concern, Senator Connally added a clause on behalf of the Foreign Relations Committee:

> That, pursuant to the Constitution of the United States, any treaty made to effect the purposes of this resolution, on behalf of the Government of the United States with any other nation or any association of nations, shall be made only by and with the advice and consent of the Senate of the United States, provided two thirds of the Senators present concur.[376]

This sufficed to calm one set of anxieties only to stir another. Citing McClure, Senator Revercomb emphasized the danger of a presidential flanking maneuver around the senatorial prerogative. He therefore moved to add a final sentence to Connally's new provision: "That participation by the United States of America in such an organization shall be by treaty only."[377]

But the Senate refused this invitation to all-out struggle. Senator Connally denied that Revercomb's proviso was necessary because such a presidential end-run was already precluded by Connally's own amendment.[378] As Revercomb pointed out, this seemed a weak response given recent executive practice and the clear signs that it planned to avoid the Senate.[379] Nonetheless, Revercomb's effort to make the Senate's claim crystal clear was voted down overwhelmingly.[380] The Senate then moved on to adopt Connally's version by a resounding vote of eighty-five to five.[381]

---

ing the post-war settlement was by treaty. *See, e.g.,* 89 CONG. REC. 9068–69 (1943) (remarks of Sen. Austin); *id.* at 9101 (remarks of Sen. Taft) (denouncing McClure). At the same time, others voiced the fear that the Administration was planning to disregard the Senate's prerogatives. *See, e.g., id.* at 9111 (remarks of Sen. Revercomb); *id.* at 9111–12 (remarks of Sen. Danaher).

To everyone's surprise, Senator Hayden lauded McClure and Garner and made an impassioned plea for interchangeability. *See id.* at 9206–10. The Senate responded like a lynch mob, with Vandenberg declaring that any President taking Hayden's line should be impeached. *See id.* at 9209. Only one other Senator seemed remotely supportive of the new doctrine. *See id.* at 9110 (remarks of Sen. Overton).

[375] *See, e.g., id.* at 9175–84 (remarks of Sen. Shipstead).

[376] *Id.* at 9066.

[377] *Id.* at 9109.

[378] *See id.* at 9112 (remarks of Sen. Connally); *see also id.* at 9111 (remarks of Sen. Vandenberg) (agreeing with Sen. Connally); *id.* at 9113 (remarks of Sen. George) (to the same effect).

[379] *See id.* at 9112.

[380] *See id.* at 9115.

[381] *See id.* at 9221–22. Right before the final vote, the Senate also rejected by voice vote an amendment by Senator Reynolds that would have achieved Revercomb's purpose by explicitly requiring the President to submit any "agreement, pact, compact, or understanding," as well any treaty, for two-thirds approval. *Id.* at 9219.

The resulting position of the Senate, said Edward Corwin in his 1944 book, was "not unlike that of the Supreme Court following the 1936 elections."[382] Just as the Court had begun to repudiate the landmark decisions of the *Lochner* era in 1937, the Connally Resolution began a similar retreat by the Senate from its own landmark decision: the rejection of the Versailles Treaty.[383]

Not that these piecemeal decisions of 1943 added up to anything resembling a definitive constitutional solution. As Connally himself made clear, his Resolution did not legally commit a future Senate to refrain from repeating its Versailles blunder — though the vote of eighty-five to five was certainly an indication that a replay of Versailles was unlikely. Even less did it commit the Senate to cooperate in the creation of more congressional-executive agreements like Panama and UNRRA.

Yet the precedents did open up a self-conscious path of constitutional development. By the end of 1943, not only was public opinion swinging sharply against a repetition of Versailles, but leaders in the Senate, as well as in the House and the executive branch, were already seriously exploring constitutional alternatives that would crystallize this sea-change in public opinion. The ground had been prepared for an intensified dialogue — both between the different branches and between political leaders and ordinary citizens — as the nation turned to consider its choices for President and Congress in 1944.

E. The Triggering Election

As in the 1860s, America stunned the world by holding a (close) election in the midst of total war. By Election Day, the tide of popular opinion had swung decisively against isolationism.[384] Sensing this, both Roosevelt and Dewey emphatically committed themselves to an internationalist future.[385]

---

[382] CORWIN, WORLD ORGANIZATION, *supra* note 16, at 53.

[383] As Corwin put it, the Senate, increasingly caught between the legal arguments in favor of interchangeability and the rising internationalist sentiment in the country, "wisely proposes to endeavor to put its house in order betimes." *Id.* at 52–53.

[384] *See supra* notes 283–86 and accompanying text. According to opinion polls, support for American participation in a post-war international organization to keep the peace had skyrocketed from 26% in 1937 to 72% in 1944. *See* Arthur Sweetser, *The United States and World Organization in 1944,* 409 INT'L CONCILIATION 195, 197 (1945).

[385] Both emphasized their internationalist credentials from the outset of the campaign. Roosevelt devoted virtually his entire acceptance speech to this theme, deriding the Republicans for their isolationist past. *See* Franklin D. Roosevelt, The People Will Decide (June 20, 1944), *in* 10 VITAL SPEECHES OF THE DAY 610–11 (1944). Dewey endorsed virtually the same internationalist program. *See* Thomas E. Dewey, I Accept the Nomination (June 28, 1944), *in* 10 VITAL SPEECHES OF THE DAY, *supra,* at 578–79.

This same pattern repeated itself in later foreign policy addresses. Roosevelt returned to the Senate's catastrophic rejection of the League, *see* Franklin D. Roosevelt, American Foreign Policy (Oct. 21, 1944), *in* 11 VITAL SPEECHES OF THE DAY, *supra,* at 35, and warned that a Republican victory would place diehard isolationists in control of key committees. *See id.* at 35–37. Three

But there remained a difference between the parties. Despite Dewey's protestations, the Republican platform contained an important concession to the party's isolationist wing. Although it pledged support for a world organization, the platform insisted that "pursuant to the Constitution of the United States any treaty or agreement to attain such aims . . . shall be made only by and with the advice and consent of the Senate."[386] Note the way in which the congressional-executive agreement was already making headway. The Republicans were insisting on a two thirds vote, but even they recognized that the treaty form wasn't what it used to be.[387] The Democratic platform went further. It entirely avoided the "T-word" and pledged that the Administration would "make all necessary and effective agreements and arrangements" to insure that the new world organization could preserve the peace.[388]

While this is an important difference, we do not wish to present the 1944 election as if it were a European-style referendum on this key issue. The relationship between elections and constitutional transformations in America has been more subtle. Rather than relying on up-or-down votes on contested propositions, our constitutional tradition has recognized regularly scheduled elections as part of a subtler constitutional dialogue between the citizenry and the elites in Washington, D.C.[389] Thus, if Dewey had won the election, defenders of the Senate's treaty-making monopoly would have persistently recalled the Republican platform's express commitment on the subject. If the isolationist wing of the Republican Party had been reinforced in the senatorial elections, President Dewey would have faced an insurmountable obstacle in pushing forward with a two-House alternative to the classic treaty process. Under this electoral scenario, the transformative promise of the piecemeal precedents of 1943 would have been consigned to the garbage pail of history.

---

days later Dewey responded, countering Roosevelt point for point and reaffirming his support for "a world organization to prevent future wars." Thomas E. Dewey, We Must Have Unity for Peace (Oct. 24, 1944), *in* 11 VITAL SPEECHES OF THE DAY, *supra*, at 39. Turning the tables, he painted Roosevelt as the true isolationist, who had moved the country away from the League and failed to keep the nation properly defended. *See id.* at 39–41.

[386] Republican Platform for 1944, *in* NATIONAL PARTY PLATFORMS 1840–1960, at 408 (Kirk Porter & Donald Johnson eds., 1961) [hereinafter NATIONAL PARTY PLATFORMS].

[387] This plank was immediately recognized as a significant concession to the isolationist wing of the party. *See Platform Makers Shifted a Little on Foreign Policy*, N.Y. TIMES, June 28, 1944, at 1, 13. The Republican *New York Herald Tribune* viewed the plank as a "challenge to common sense," and predicted that it would "unquestionably cost the party votes." *Mr. Dewey's Opportunity*, N.Y. HERALD TRIB., June 28, 1944, at 26. Corwin also harshly criticized the plank in a letter to the *New York Times*, once again stating the interchangeability thesis. *See* Edward S. Corwin, *An Opportunity Overlooked*, N.Y. TIMES, June 30, 1944, at 20.

[388] Democratic Platform of 1944, *in* NATIONAL PARTY PLATFORMS, *supra* note 386, at 403.

[389] *See* ACKERMAN, *supra* note 8, chs. 2, 10; Ackerman & Katyal, *supra* note 33 (manuscript at 125–31).

But the election returns generated a very different momentum.[390] Not only did Roosevelt beat Dewey, but 1944 saw the defeat or departure of nine leading isolationist Senators.[391] Rather than reinforcing the constitutional status quo, the elections gave the President and Congress a fresh mandate to go further with their preliminary challenge to the Senate's prerogative. Given the overwhelming shift toward internationalism expressed by both leading candidates and the popular support given to the more internationalist slate, wouldn't the American citizenry support a much bolder challenge to the Senate monopoly?

This was not the first time in American history that a regularly scheduled election had generated momentum for constitutional reform. Similar functions were discharged by the elections of 1866 and 1936, which provided popular mandates for Reconstruction Republicans and New Deal Democrats in their struggles to transform the domestic constitution.[392] In each of these cases, the party of constitutional conservatism had been competing on relatively equal terms with the party of constitutional reform before the elections took place; afterwards, however, the party of reform returned to power with a sense of renewed popular authority and challenged the chastened conservatives to consider whether it was wiser to consider a constitutional compromise than to escalate the battle.

In calling these "triggering elections," we emphasize that they do not determine the final outcome. The ultimate constitutional solution will be shaped not only by the partisans of reform, but also by the constitutional conservatives. If the conservatives resist to the bitter end, they will be playing a high-stakes game. On the one hand, the reformers may back down; but on the other hand, resistance may provoke even greater demands for constitutional change, and the reformers may ultimately gain a popular mandate for a transformation even bolder than their original agenda. When faced with these critical choices, American conservatives have proven remarkably accommodating: rather than risk greater defeat by remaining intransigent until the next election, they have generally accepted a constitutional compromise — whose form and substance depends on particular contingencies.[393] Thus, it would be a serious mistake to suppose that triggering

---

[390] The election was widely understood as giving Roosevelt a mandate to lead the country into the United Nations. *See, e.g.*, Denna F. Fleming, "Is Isolation Dead?" Only an Alert Public Can Defend the November Verdict (Nov. 22, 1944), *in* 11 VITAL SPEECHES OF THE DAY, *supra* note 385, at 110.

[391] Senators Nye, Danaher, Gillette, and Davis were defeated. Senators Reynolds and Bone did not stand for re-election, and Holman, Clark (Missouri), and Clark (Idaho) were defeated in primaries. Senator Taft was barely re-elected. Many of these Senators were replaced by confirmed supporters of a post-war organization. *See id.*; *see also* COLEGROVE, *supra* note 283, at 202–09 (summarizing voting records of isolationist Senators).

[392] *See* ACKERMAN, *supra* note 8, ch. 2.

[393] *See* BRUCE ACKERMAN, WE THE PEOPLE: TRANSFORMATIONS chs. 5–8 (forthcoming 1996).

elections determine ultimate outcomes in some mechanistic way. They serve instead to shift the balance of perceived legitimacies — both in the country and on Capitol Hill — away from the constitutional status quo and toward the legitimation of a new question: given the constitutional reformers' success in sustaining their support among the People, what precisely should the new constitutional solution look like?

This was, in any case, the immediate consequence of the 1944 election. Despite its "lame duck" status, the House Judiciary Committee held hearings on the Treaty Clause in November[394] and reported out a simple constitutional amendment on December 4, 1944: "Hereafter treaties shall be made by the President by and with the advice and consent of both Houses of Congress."[395] The committee's report is a remarkably penetrating document.[396] Significantly, it did not indulge the myth of continuity developed by New Deal intellectuals to avoid the need for formal amendment. But it did emphasize other revisionist themes, vigorously denying that the Founders' grant of power to the Senate was consistent with modern principles of democratic accountability.[397] The report also turned a critical eye on the Senate's use of its treaty-making powers: "From the moment the United States became a world power as a result of the Spanish-American War," the Senate's performance had been "disturbingly bad."[398] Worse yet, the Senate's consistent obstructionism had led Presidents to resort to unilateral executive agreements:

> The committee does not condemn the agreements as illegal. They were for the most part necessary for the welfare of the country and have subsequently been approved by Congress, but most of them should have been submitted as treaties. This, the committee believes, would have been done if they could have been considered as other legislation [i.e. by the majority vote of both Houses].

---

[394] *See House Judiciary Committee Hearings, supra* note 275, at iii–iv.

[395] H.R.J. Res. 320, 78th Cong., 2d Sess. (1944); H.R. REP. NO. 2061, 78th Cong., 2d Sess., 1 (1944). An identical resolution was introduced in the following session. *See* H.R.J. Res. 60, 79th Cong., 1st Sess. (1945); H.R. REP. NO. 139, 79th Cong., 1st Sess. 1 (1945). There were several other proposals during the 78th and 79th Congresses, which generally differed only in wording. *See supra* note 289.

[396] *See* H.R. REP. NO. 2061, *supra* note 395; *see also* H.R. REP. NO. 139, *supra* note 395 (subsequent report in the following session).

[397] The report reasoned:

If a majority of the Members of the Senate and of the House of Representatives cannot protect the interest of the people of this Nation, then our Government, and our future is in a disastrous plight. . . . One-third plus one of the membership of the smaller House of Congress has final decision over what has become one of the paramount problems of government. It is possible that 17 Senators, representing a population of only 4,000,000 people, could thwart the will of the majority of the people and of the States.

H.R. REP. NO. 2061, *supra* note 395, at 6.

[398] *Id.* at 4. The report recalled the Senate's rejection of arbitration treaties for the peaceful settlement of disputes, the Treaty of Versailles, the League of Nations, and the World Court. *See id.* at 4–5.

This is an unhealthy tendency. It has far-reaching and disastrous pos-
sibilities. The maintenance of the two thirds rule instead of working to
maintain a great power in the Senate is actually taking that power away
from the Senate. Congress should act as a check upon the treaty-making
powers of the President, but, by maintaining a rule which prevents negotiations which the people desire, the Congress is on the road to eliminat-
ing itself from this important function of government.[399]

In short, the real alternative to the congressional-executive agreement
was the unilateral exercise of presidential power. It was only by
changing the status quo that Congress stood a chance of reining in the
ascendant executive.

Despite this profound warning, the hearings held by the committee
revealed a fascinating complexity. While an impressive array of leading commentators favored a formal amendment,[400] a number were already denying that it was a constitutional necessity. So far as they
were concerned, a formal amendment merely provided a useful clarifi-
cation of the constitutional precedents that had already established the
interchangeability of congressional-executive agreements with
treaties.[401]

A similar countercurrent emerged in a debate on the Senate floor
in December 1944. This was provoked by a special-interest effort to
take advantage of the last minute rush of business to gain a legislative
victory. The friends of the St. Lawrence Seaway had long seen their
hopes dashed on the rock of senatorial prerogative and had been exploring the alternative of a congressional-executive agreement.
Although the Administration had withdrawn its proposed executive
agreement with Canada after Pearl Harbor, proponents sensed that
the time was right and tried to tack it on to an Omnibus Rivers and
Harbors bill rolling through Congress in the last days of the session.[402]

The result was a fiasco. The Seaway's regional opponents refused
to permit such a controversial measure to be added onto a pork-barrel

---

[399] *Id.* at 8–9.

[400] *See supra* notes 291 & 316. The House report drew heavily on their testimony. *See* H.R.
REP. NO. 2061, *supra* note 395, at 3–9.

[401] *See, e.g., House Judiciary Committee Hearings, supra* note 275, at 145 (statement of Quincy
Wright); *id.* at 44–46 (testimony of Melvin D. Hildreth); *id.* at 69 (statement of Denna Fleming).
One former Representative, after surveying the authorities and precedents, argued that adoption
of the resolution proposing a constitutional amendment would be counterproductive because interchangeability was already the law. *See id.* at 114–20 (testimony of David J. Lewis). He recom-
mended that the committee instead report a resolution expressly confirming the constitutionality
of the interchangeability thesis. *See id.* at 119.

[402] In September 1943, Senator Aiken introduced a bill to approve the St. Lawrence agreement. *See* S. 1385, 78th Cong., 1st Sess. (1943). The Senate Commerce Committee held hearings
in November 1944 limited solely to the constitutional question whether the agreement should be
submitted as a treaty or as a congressional-executive agreement. *See* S. REP. NO. 1499, *supra*
note 345, at 20. Before the committee's record was closed, Senator Aiken sought to attach his bill
to the pending rivers and harbors legislation. *See id.*

measure at the last minute.[403] The Senate defeated the Seaway amendment by a vote of fifty-six to twenty-five.[404] Yet this abortive maneuver revealed how quickly the election had changed the balance of legitimacy on the constitutional question. The Seaway, after all, posed an especially sensitive issue because the Senate had already rejected it as a treaty. If this judgment could be constitutionally overruled by a two-House majority, it would be a dramatic demonstration of the Senate's repudiation of its traditional reading of the Treaty Clause.

Nevertheless, immediately after the election, the State Department used its Seaway testimony to announce full interchangeability as the Administration's official position.[405] When the question came to the floor, the proposed congressional-executive agreement was greeted with new respect.[406] Senator Aiken even lauded "Dr. McClure and all the other great authorities on constitutional law" who advocated interchangeability.[407] Never before had influential Senators uttered such heresies on the floor of the chamber. With remarkable speed, the elec-

---

[403] Opponents relied almost exclusively on the procedural point. *See* 90 CONG. REC. 9218 (1944) (remarks of Sen. Bailey); *id.* at 9216–17, 9242 (remarks of Sen. Overton). Even Senators who were favorable to, or undecided about, the project were persuaded by the procedural objection. *See, e.g.,* S. REP. NO. 1499, *supra* note 345, at 20; 90 CONG. REC. 9219–20 (1944) (remarks of Sen. Burton); *id.* at 9237 (remarks of Sen. Lucas).

[404] *See* 90 CONG. REC. 9243 (1943).

[405] Green Hackworth, the State Department's Legal Adviser, asserted that the only difference between treaties and congressional-executive agreements was the procedure by which they were approved, and that was a question, at least in the first instance, for the President to decide. *See Commerce Committee Hearings, supra* note 340, at 8–17, 23, 39, 72–75. When pressed, he acknowledged only one other difference: Congress could only authorize an agreement on a subject falling within the legislative powers granted to it by Article I. *See, e.g., id.* at 15, 93; *see also id.* at 301–08 (State Department memorandum of December 4, 1944 affirming Hackworth's testimony).

Unsurprisingly, some Senators responded testily, charging that the Administration was trying to establish a precedent that a two-House procedure could be used even for an agreement, like the Seaway, that had previously been defeated as a treaty. *See, e.g., id.* at 265–68. Although feebly denying the accusations, Hackworth did little to dispel their concerns. *See id.* He even declined to answer whether, under his theory, the United States could adhere to a post-war peace organization through the two-House procedure. *See id.* at 16, 240–41.

The only other witness to testify before the committee was Professor Borchard. *See id.* at 102–215. Borchard was so impressive that Senator Aiken thought it necessary to launch an ad hominem attack on the Senate floor, contending that Borchard was a paid agent of private utility interests opposed to the project. *See* 90 CONG. REC. 9221 (1944).

Even before Hackworth announced the Administration's official position, Secretary of State Hull, in a letter to Senator Vandenberg, had revealed its thinking, without making absolutely clear the limits of the new doctrine. *See Commerce Committee Hearings, supra* note 340, at 301–02 (reprinting Hull's letter stating that of the "two constitutional methods," the Administration had chosen the two-House procedure because the project was fundamentally domestic, not international, in nature and would involve a large appropriation of funds).

[406] *See, e.g.,* 90 CONG. REC. 9134–36 (1944) (remarks of Sen. Langer); *id.* at 9220–21 (remarks of Sen. Pepper); *id.* at 8560–63, 9221 (remarks of Sen. Aiken).

[407] *Id.* at 9221.

tion was turning the balance of legitimacy in favor of constitutional change.

F. *Constitutional Solutions*

As the new Seventy-ninth Congress began its 1945 session in January, the country was approaching a crossroads. The question was not so much whether, but how, the Senate would lose its monopoly over treaty-making. A wave of proposed constitutional amendments flooded the House,[408] and in May, the long debate culminated in decisive action.[409] By a vote of 288 to 88,[410] the House sent the Senate a variation on the Judiciary Committee's proposal.[411] Its amendment would have required both Houses to support a treaty by absolute majorities, and not merely by majorities of those voting.[412] The Administration also stood at a constitutional crossroads. With Gallup polls showing a strong majority against the Senate[413] and newspapers agitating throughout the country, the time was ripe for Administration action.[414] Should the President intervene on behalf of the House initiative?

Even before Roosevelt died in April, he had already tipped his hand against a move that threatened to lead him down the path that ruined Woodrow Wilson. It was a truism of the time that Wilson had unnecessarily alienated the Republican leadership while he was negotiating for the League in Versailles. To avoid this blunder, Roosevelt had appointed leading Republicans like Senator Vandenberg[415] to the delegation that would found the United Nations. If he had then joined a frontal attack on the Senate's prerogative, he would have provoked the partisan reflexes of Vandenberg and his fellow Republicans.[416] Even if their opposition had been overcome, winning Senate approval for the House amendment would have poisoned the atmos-

---

[408] *See supra* notes 289, 395, and accompanying text.

[409] The extraordinarily rich debate was held on May 1, 2, 7, 8, and 9 of 1945. *See* 91 CONG. REC. 4008–85, 4217–4370 (1945).

[410] *See id.* at 4367–68.

[411] The Judiciary Committee's resolution had proposed that treaties be approved by majority votes of those present in both Houses. *See supra* notes 289, 395, and accompanying text.

[412] Representative Schwabe of Missouri offered the amendment. *See* 91 CONG. REC. 4343 (1945). When the Chairman of the Judiciary Committee and author of the resolution, Hatton Sumners, agreed to Schwabe's revision, it carried the day. *See id.* at 4349–50.

[413] *See supra* notes 283–86 and accompanying text.

[414] *See supra* notes 287, 288, 290, and accompanying text.

[415] *See* CONGRESSIONAL QUARTERLY SERV., CONGRESS AND THE NATION 1945–1964, at 97 (1965).

[416] While Vandenberg had played a positive role in the development of the congressional-executive agreement, *see supra* notes 361, 362, 366, and accompanying text; *infra* note 440 and accompanying text, he had been a consistent champion of the Senate's treaty-making prerogative during his long isolationist period. *See supra* notes 351, 355–71, 374, and accompanying text.

phere, undermining the bipartisan support necessary for an internationalist foreign policy.

From the Administration's perspective, only an arid formalist would have leaped quickly onto the House's bandwagon without exploring less confrontational alternatives. Instead of insulting the Senate, the State Department took no position on the House amendment, but bided its time to await further events.[417] As it allowed this Sword of Damocles to swing gently over the Senate's head, the Administration created conditions for a constitutional compromise. On the one hand, it gratified traditionalist sensibilities by offering the United Nations Charter to the Senate as a treaty;[418] on the other hand, it aggressively presented other key elements in the emerging international system as congressional-executive agreements. This put the Senate on probation. During the rest of the Seventy-ninth Congress, it could either accept the Administration's constitutional compromise or confront the prospect of fighting a life-or-death struggle over the House amendment.

More precisely, the Senate had three options. First, it could reenact the Versailles scenario by killing the United Nations Charter, and then try to defend its monopoly by voting down the formal amendment proposed by the House. Given the isolationists' defeat in the 1944 elections, there was no chance that this would happen.[419] A second strategy was more plausible. Under this scenario, two thirds of the Senate would approve the Charter and then declare war on interchangeability by rejecting any important agreement the President tendered for majority approval by both Houses. This would have forced Americans to confront the precise issue at stake: were they prepared to trust the Senate's future good behavior, or had they concluded that, despite the Senate's approval of the United Nations Charter, it was wiser to support the House's demand to strip the Senate of its treaty-making monopoly? Or third, the Senate could decide that the time for

---

[417] Legal Adviser Hackworth was scheduled to testify on the amendment before the House Judiciary Committee on November 29, 1944. He cancelled at the last moment to testify before the Senate Commerce Committee on the St. Lawrence Seaway dispute. *See House Judiciary Committee Hearings, supra* note 275, at 37; *Commerce Committee Hearings, supra* note 340, at 217. It was on this occasion that he publicly announced the State Department's adoption of the full interchangeability doctrine. *See supra* note 405 and accompanying text. This was the first indication that the Administration was supporting a process of informal revision rather than formal amendment of the Treaty Clause. We have found no direct evidence that Roosevelt explicitly considered this matter before he died in April 1945, though we think it very likely.

[418] *See Report of President Roosevelt in Person to the Congress on the Crimea Conference,* N.Y. TIMES, Mar. 2, 1945, at 12 (announcing that the Charter would be submitted to the Senate); *see also American Nations Form an Alliance to Protect Peace,* N.Y. TIMES, Mar. 4, 1945, at 25 (stating that the Act of Chapultepec, a predecessor to the regional mutual defense pact, the Inter-American Treaty of Reciprocal Assistance (Rio Treaty), would be submitted to the Senate).

[419] The Senate approved the Charter on July 28, 1945 by a vote of 89 to 2. *See* 91 CONG. REC. 8190 (1945); *see also* Proclamation by the President of the United States of June 26, 1945, 59 Stat. 1031, 1031.

compromise had arrived. Rather than reject presidential end-runs around the Treaty Clause, it would henceforth cooperate with the President and the House in establishing an accumulating set of piece-meal precedents that would establish the congressional-executive agreement as constitutionally interchangeable with the treaty. Which, then, would it be: Fight (Strategy Two) or Switch (Strategy Three)?

The Senate's moment of truth was not long delayed. Shortly after Roosevelt presented the U.N. Charter as a treaty, and the House proposed its Senate-stripping amendment, the Administration submitted the Bretton Woods Agreements for majority approval by both Houses. The challenge could not have been clearer. In establishing the World Bank and the International Monetary Fund (IMF), Bretton Woods did nothing less than create the foundations of a new world economic order. If the Senate would not insist on its treaty-making monopoly in such a case, where would it draw the line?

Lawyers for the State Department joined with those in the Treasury to prepare an elaborate memorandum seeking to calm senatorial anxieties.[420] Indulging the myth of continuity developed by the scholars, they ransacked history for any precedent that bore the remotest resemblance to Bretton Woods. They argued that prior practice had undermined all of the principled limitations that might save some privileged place for the Treaty Clause. Thus, they rejected the idea that executive agreements could not impose legally binding obligations by pointing to the New Deal legislation of the 1930s. And they could now point to precedents in which the Senate had allowed both Houses to approve international organizations such as UNRRA;[421] indeed, at the very moment it was considering Bretton Woods, the Senate was lending its support to another congressional-executive agreement authorizing the country to join the Food and Agricultural Organization (FAO). Neither of these agencies was nearly as important as the IMF or the World Bank. But from a legal point of view, what *precisely* was the difference?

The Administration's lawyers saw no need to provoke the Senate by raising this question in so pointed a fashion. Nor did they answer it by repeating the forthright statement of interchangeability made by the State Department during the preceding year.[422] Instead they took a more lawyerly course — discussing each of the accumulating precedents and then concluding that, all things considered, a congressional-executive agreement "is in fact preferable in this case to any other

---

[420] *See Bretton Woods Agreements Act: Hearings on H.R. 3314 Before the Senate Comm. on Banking and Currency*, 79th Cong., 1st Sess. 529–62 (1945) [hereinafter *Hearings on Bretton Woods Agreements*].

[421] *See id.* at 536.

[422] *See supra* note 405 and accompanying text.

form of procedure."[423] Even such a modest conclusion would have generated an outcry before the triggering election of 1944. But the Senate now swallowed its objections and approved both Bretton Woods and the FAO during 1945.[424]

Over the next few years, the Senate's retreat turned into a rout as the Administration proposed international agreements on a proliferating range of subjects for congressional approval.[425] Although Senators first challenged the accelerating practice, this did not last long. Partisans of the Administration were ready with an increasingly impressive multi-level defense. They denied they were out to destroy the classic system, repeatedly pointing to the President's submission of the United Nations Charter as a treaty as proof. They insisted that the only question was whether a modern alternative was also constitutionally legitimate. Having narrowed the issue to interchangeability, they took a two-track approach. On the one hand, proponents emphasized the peculiar features of the particular agreement under consideration. This allowed them to search history for the precedents that most resembled their particular initiative. At the same time, they sought to undermine any principled doctrine by which defenders of the classic system could limit the scope of the congressional-executive agree-

---

[423] *Hearings on Bretton Woods Agreements, supra* note 420, at 530. The Legal Adviser thought joint action of Congress preferable, because the agreements affected "importantly powers of Congress in the field of banking and currency and commerce among others." *Id.* at 537.

[424] *See* Bretton Woods Agreements Act, ch. 339, 59 Stat. 512 (1945); Joint Resolution of July 31, 1945, ch. 342, 59 Stat. 529 (providing for U.S. membership in the United Nations Food and Agriculture Organization).

[425] In 1945, Congress also passed the United Nations Participation Act of 1945, ch. 583, 59 Stat. 619, which implemented American obligations under the United Nations Charter. The statute directed the President to submit "Article 43" agreements to Congress for approval by joint resolution or statute, not by treaty. *See id.* §6, 59 Stat. at 621. Article 43 of the Charter called upon member states to reach special agreements with the Security Council under which contingents of their armed forces would be available for use as a United Nations army. With the outbreak of the Cold War, no special agreements were ever concluded, but the issue may well arise in coming years.

In 1946, 1947, and 1948, use of the two-House procedure continued apace. Congress approved American participation in the United Nations Educational, Scientific, and Cultural Organization (UNESCO), *see* Joint Resolution of July 30, 1946, ch. 700, 60 Stat. 712; the International Refugee Organization, *see* Joint Resolution of July 1, 1947, ch. 185, 61 Stat. 214; the World Health Organization, *see* Joint Resolution of June 14, 1948, ch. 469, 62 Stat. 441; and the Caribbean Commission, *see* Joint Resolution of Mar. 4, 1948, ch. 97, 62 Stat. 65. It also approved the United Nations Headquarters Agreement, *see* Joint Resolution of Aug. 4, 1947, ch. 482, 61 Stat. 756, under which the United States agreed to provide the United Nations with the immunities and guarantees necessary to perform its functions at its New York headquarters, and it approved the trusteeship agreement for the Territory of the Pacific Islands, *see* Joint Resolution of July 18, 1947, ch. 271, 61 Stat. 397. In 1947, the President submitted the United Nations Convention on Privileges and Immunities to both Houses, *see* S. REP. No. 559, 80th Cong., 1st Sess. (1947), but Congress rejected it. For later uses of the new form, see below pp. 893–96, 900–01, 905–06, and note 441.

ment.[426] Each time the Administration convinced a majority of the Senate to join the House in support of an executive agreement, it created a new precedent for further expansion.

This process of piecemeal precedentialism transformed the constitutional status quo with remarkable speed. This became clear at the very next session, when traditional defenders of the Senate's prerogative made a last-ditch effort to stem the tide. The context was congenial to the defenders, because it arose as part of the unending saga of the St. Lawrence Seaway. As we have seen, the Seaway's advocates had lost their battle for a treaty in 1934 and for a congressional-executive agreement in 1944.[427] But they would try, and try again, until they won in 1954 — when the St. Lawrence Seaway Agreement finally gained approval through a two-House procedure.

For present purposes, the 1946 effort of the Seaway's partisans was particularly revealing. In the words of the Foreign Relations Committee, "the defeat of a treaty with Canada on the same subject . . . might at least raise an inference of avoidance by the executive of the senatorial prerogative."[428] Moreover, use of the two-House procedure was forcefully denounced on constitutional grounds by the Seaway's regional opponents, who had retained the leading academic critic, Professor Edwin Borchard, to state their case.[429]

The Senate Foreign Relations Committee was sufficiently impressed to appoint a special five-member subcommittee to consider the constitutional question. By a vote of four to one, they rejected Borchard's appeal.[430] Of the subcommittee's members, only Senator White raised his voice in opposition:

---

[426] In the early period, the State Department was careful to find some basis for claiming that the agreements did not impose binding obligations on the United States. For instance, buried deep in the Legal Adviser's lengthy memorandum on the Bretton Woods Agreements was the observation that parties could withdraw on notice. *See Hearings on Bretton Woods Agreements, supra* note 420, at 556–57; *see also* S. REP. No. 717, 79th Cong., 1st Sess. 7–8 (1945) (justifying provision for approval of Article 43 agreements by joint resolution on the ground that Article 43 agreements would be ancillary to the Charter); S. REP. No. 357, 79th Cong., 1st Sess. 10–11, 20–22 (1945) (reprinting a letter from Dean Acheson, Assistant Secretary of State, to Senator Warren R. Austin, Mar. 15, 1945, justifying the two-House procedure for adherence to FAO as in accordance with historical precedents regarding international organizations). By the time the President submitted the Headquarters and Pacific Trust Territory agreements, *see supra* note 425, which indubitably imposed binding obligations on the country, there was no longer any need to reassure the Senate.

[427] *See supra* notes 340–45, 402–04, and accompanying text.

[428] S. REP. No. 1499, *supra* note 345, at 57; *see supra* notes 340–45 and accompanying text.

[429] Professor Borchard not only testified before the Senate committee, *see Great Lakes–St. Lawrence Basin: Hearings on S.J. Res. 104 Before a Subcomm. of the Senate Comm. on Foreign Relations*, 79th Cong., 2d Sess. 399–406, 1311–21 (1946) [hereinafter *St. Lawrence Hearings*], but also submitted two lengthy memoranda on the subject. *See id.* at 407–54, 1321–30. Dean Acheson countered by submitting the most complete and impressive legal memoranda yet produced by the State Department. *See id.* at 997–1064.

[430] *See* S. REP. No. 1499, *supra* note 345, at 9–10.

Now we witness the challenge by an executive department of the constitutional right of the Senate of ratification, and in its stead, acceptance of this new theory that the President may enter into agreements of any and every nature with foreign governments and that Congress may by majority vote give its consent thereto and effectuate the same. In what is here proposed is bold evasion of constitutional procedure, and the elimination of the Senate as a part of the treaty-making power under our Constitution.[431]

But the majority repudiated this ancient senatorial creed. It explicitly rejected three basic principles that had traditionally been used to assert the superior dignity of the treaty over the modern upstart. First, it denied that only treaties could generate binding international obligations.[432] Second, it denied that the Senate's power to give "advice and consent" gave it a monopoly over the ex post review of international agreements: "The procedure in this case does not appear to be different in substance from the procedure followed in connection with UNRRA, the Food and Agriculture Organization, and the Bretton Woods legislation . . . ."[433] Yesterday's piecemeal precedents had become today's general principle.

The same fate awaited a third senatorial line of defense. Traditionalists had sought to dismiss the accumulating line of precedents by claiming that they dealt with relatively trivial matters and that the treaty-making power retained its monopoly over truly important commitments: "The committee believes that the relative importance of projects has little to do with the case and in any event there have been many occasions on which foreign agreements of at least comparable importance, including the Bretton Woods agreements, have been dealt with through legislation."[434]

After considering the majority and dissenting opinions of its special subcommittee, the Senate Foreign Relations Committee favorably reported the resolution by a vote of fourteen to eight.[435] This was, we think, a crucial turning point. The keeper of the senatorial prerogative had not only refused to defend the integrity of the Senate's earlier decision rejecting the Seaway treaty; it had self-consciously rejected the principled distinctions that would allow for a systematic defense of the senatorial monopoly. The Seaway resolution never made it to the Senate floor, and its regional opponents continued to blast away at their

---

[431] *Id.* at 96.

[432] *See id.* at 56.

[433] *Id.*

[434] *Id.* at 57. The majority report also cited our special relationship with Canada as a further justification for its decision to approve the two-House procedure. It mentioned as well that the State Department had not claimed "that any foreign negotiation can be concluded in this manner," *id.* at 58 (internal quotation marks omitted), providing wiggle room for some future Senate bent on reasserting its constitutional monopoly.

[435] *See id.* at 4.

opponents' use of the congressional-executive agreement.[436] But the damage had been done. While opponents could still muster a majority against the Seaway, they could no longer plausibly assert that proponents were required to win a super-majority.[437] Indeed, when the Seaway finally was validated through a two-House procedure in 1954, the vote in the Senate was fifty-one to thirty-three — less than two thirds.[438]

But let us return to 1946 and the Seventy-ninth Congress. Within the space of two short years, this single Congress had lived through a remarkable transformation. As it began its first session in 1945, the House of Representatives was launching an all-out campaign to strip the Senate of its monopoly on treaty-making through a formal constitutional amendment. But now, with Bretton Woods approved and the Senate subcommittee's repudiation of the traditional monopolistic reading of the Treaty Clause, the need for serious consideration of the House's constitutional amendment had passed. A bloody formalist struggle was unnecessary now that the Senate had made its switch in time.

Granted, the enactment of a formal amendment would have helped future generations of lawyers mark the precise historical spot at which the Senate lost its monopoly. But constitutional law is not created for the intellectual convenience of constitutional lawyers. It is up to lawyers to understand the Constitution as the creation of the American people and to identify the specific historical moments at which they have supported fundamental changes.

To a sensitive lawyer, an episode from the Eightieth Congress speaks louder than a formal amendment. At long last, the Republicans had triumphed in the elections of 1946 and now commanded majorities in both Houses of the Eightieth Congress. With Harry Truman on the defensive in the White House, it was still possible for the Republican Senate to take up the cudgels for its traditional treaty-making monopoly, and refuse to cooperate with any further congressional-executive agreements.

But this did not happen. Instead, the President and the State Department pronounced the new doctrine of interchangeability with in-

---

[436] *See, e.g.,* S. Rep. No. 810, 80th Cong., 2d Sess., pt. 2, at 1–2 (1948). The Seaway again went down in the Senate in 1948, by a vote of 57 to 30. *See* Borchard, *The St. Lawrence Waterway and Power Project, supra* note 17, at 413.

[437] In subsequent battles over the Seaway, the Foreign Relations Committee declined to reopen the constitutional issue. Hearings were held and reports written, but the majority simply referred back to its 1946 report. *See, e.g.,* S. Rep. No. 810, *supra* note 436, at 1–2; *see also* S. Rep. No. 1489, 82d Cong., 2d Sess. 1 (1952) (failing even to mention the constitutional issue). The minority refused to give up, but its objections were more symbolic gestures than serious challenges. *See, e.g.,* S. Rep. No. 810, *supra* note 436, at 1–2. The 1947 version of the Seaway resolution, S.J. Res. 111, 80th Cong., 1st Sess. (1947), was introduced by Senator Vandenberg himself, then Chairman of the Foreign Relations Committee.

[438] *See* 100 Cong. Rec. 525 (1954).

creasing self-confidence. Here is President Truman forwarding an executive agreement undertaking trusteeship obligations for America's Pacific Island territories:

> I have given special consideration to whether the attached trusteeship agreement should be submitted to the Congress for action by a joint resolution or by the treaty process. I am satisfied that either method is constitutionally permissible and that the agreement resulting will be of the same effect internationally and under the supremacy clause of the Constitution whether advised and consented to by the Senate or whether approval is authorized by a joint resolution. The interest of both Houses of Congress in the execution of this agreement is such, however, that I think it would be appropriate for the Congress, in this instance, to take action by a joint resolution.[439]

If Roosevelt had said this in 1945, it would have been a declaration of war on the Senate. A dozen years earlier, no President would have appealed to the putative "interest" of the House of Representatives to justify his decision. And yet, in 1947, not a murmur was reported from the upper chamber as it joined the House in approving yet another congressional-executive agreement.[440]

Interchangeability had become part of the living Constitution.[441]

---

[439] H.R. Doc. No. 378, 80th Cong., 1st Sess. 2 (1947).

[440] Indeed, the report prepared by Senator Vandenberg's Committee on Foreign Relations, *see* S. Rep. No. 471, 80th Cong., 1st Sess. (1947), never mentions the issue, except to say that the joint resolution was introduced in response to the President's message to Congress. It then simply reproduces the full text of the message "[f]or the information of the Senate." *Id.* at 3.

Similarly, the United Nations, not the Senate, apparently raised some question about the joint resolution procedure for approving the Headquarters Agreement. In response, the Attorney General prepared a formal opinion designed to set its mind at ease. *See* 40 Op. Att'y Gen. 469, 470 (1946).

[441] In subsequent years, both President Truman and President Eisenhower sought congressional, not senatorial, consent to ambitious efforts to establish a powerful organization to govern international trade. *See* HARRY S. TRUMAN, MESSAGE FROM THE PRESIDENT, S. DOC. NO. 61, 81st Cong., 1st Sess. (1949); *Extension of Reciprocal Trade Agreements Act: Hearings on H.R. 1211 Before the Senate Committee on Finance*, 81st Cong., 1st Sess., pt. 2, at 985–1039 (1949) [hereinafter *1949 Senate Hearings*] (reprinting the Charter of the proposed International Trade Organization); President's Message Requesting Legislation Authorizing United States Participation in the Organization for Trade Cooperation (Apr. 14, 1955), *reprinted in* H.R. REP. NO. 2007, 84th Cong., 2d Sess. 56–59 (1956). On both occasions, the initiatives were withdrawn when it became apparent that they could not win majority approval because of rising protectionist sentiment in the country. *See Trade Agreements Extension Act of 1951: Hearings Before the Senate Finance Comm.*, 82d Cong., 1st Sess. 10, 13 (1951) [hereinafter *1951 Senate Hearings*]; State Department Press Release (Dec. 6, 1950), *reprinted in* 23 DEP'T ST. BULL. 977 (1950); WILLIAM DIEBOLD, THE END OF THE ITO 23–24 (Princeton Essays in International Finance No. 16, 1952); John H. Jackson, *The General Agreement on Tariffs and Trade in United States Domestic Law*, 66 MICH. L. REV. 249, 252, 265–66 (1967). Scattered senatorial grumblings about the two-House procedure played no significant role. *See Trade Agreements System and Proposed International Trade Organization Charter: Hearings Before the Senate Comm. on Finance*, 80th Cong., 1st Sess. 167–69 (1947) [hereinafter *1947 Senate Hearings*] (remarks of Sen. Milliken).

With the impasse over a powerful world trade organization, the status of the General Agreement on Tariffs and Trade (GATT) became a matter of intense dispute. GATT had never been submitted by the executive either for senatorial or for congressional approval, on the ground that

V. THE ERA OF CODIFICATION

The birth of the congressional-executive agreement was a self-conscious, but ad hoc process. Over the next half-century, Congress consolidated these precedents by passing statutes that used the congressional-executive agreement as a tool for the control of foreign policy.

A. *Consolidation*

This first happened in an entirely new field. The Atomic Energy Act of 1946 included a short section on international matters, which treated the new congressional-executive agreement as interchangeable with the traditional treaty.[442] Fifteen years later, a similar move was made in the Arms Control and Disarmament Act of 1961.[443] In creating a framework for arms control, Congress did not insist that the President bring agreements back to the Senate as treaties but explicitly approved an alternative procedure involving ex post review by both Houses.[444]

---

the existing Trade Agreements Act provided the President with sufficient authority. *See, e.g.,* *1951 Senate Hearings, supra,* at 12–13; *1949 Senate Hearings, supra,* at 1050–56 (reprinting a State Department memorandum explaining the legal basis for each GATT provision); *1947 Senate Hearings, supra,* at 71–74, 173–76; Jackson, *supra,* at 257–65. With increasing vociferousness, Senators and Representatives demanded that GATT be submitted for approval — but by Congress, not the Senate. *See, e.g., 1951 Senate Hearings, supra,* at 10–13; *1947 Senate Hearings, supra,* at 174–76; H.R. REP. No. 2007, *supra,* at 47 (minority views). With Presidents resisting this demand, Congress initiated guerilla war tactics, enacting statutes undermining the U.S. commitment to GATT. *See* Jackson, *supra,* at 266–68 (describing Congress's various hostile legislative efforts). Senators recognized that the chances of ultimate victory were far greater if the House joined the Senate in insisting that GATT be brought forward for an up-or-down vote. The result of the GATT imbroglio, then, was to encourage Senators to reaffirm the constitutional legitimacy of the two-House procedure.

[442] *See* Atomic Energy Act of 1946, ch. 724, § 8, 60 Stat. 755, 765. Section 8 provided that "any treaty approved by the Senate or *international agreement thereafter approved by Congress*" would supersede inconsistent provisions of the Act. *Id.* (emphasis added). Section 124 of the Atomic Energy Act of 1954, ch. 1073, 68 Stat. 919, 939–40, expressly authorized the President to enter into multilateral agreements, either in the form of treaties or congressional-executive agreements, for cooperation in the peaceful use of atomic energy. *See id.* at 940. Both proponents and opponents assumed the interchangeability of treaties and congressional-executive agreements. *See* S. REP. No. 1699, 83d Cong., 2d Sess. 21, 103, 134–35 (1954), *reprinted in* 1954 U.S.C.C.A.N. 3456, 3476, 3495. More recently, § 123 was amended to require that certain kinds of nuclear technology agreements be approved by both Houses within 60 days of their submission by the President. *See* Export Administration Amendments Act of 1985, Pub. L. No. 99-64, sec. 301(a)(3), (b), § 123, 99 Stat. 120, 159–60.

[443] *See* Arms Control and Disarmament Act, Pub. L. No. 87-297, § 33, 75 Stat. 631, 634 (1961).

[444] Section 33 prohibits the executive from obligating the United States to disarm or reduce its armaments "except pursuant to the treaty making power of the President under the Constitution or unless authorized by further affirmative legislation by the Congress of the United States." *Id.* This provision was added on the floor of the House, *see* 107 CONG. REC. 20,308 (1961), and the Senate approved it without dissent or debate. Senator Sparkman simply indicated that the "language did not appear in the Senate bill because it was implicitly assumed that such was the case in any event." *Id.*

Consolidation of the new device also occurred the next time the Treaty Clause became a subject for wide-ranging constitutional debate. During the early 1950s, Senator Bricker led a vigorous campaign to amend the Clause.[445] His primary target was *Missouri v. Holland* and its suggestion that the Senate could ratify treaties that constitutionally trumped powers reserved to the states by the Tenth Amendment. Brickerites sought an explicit amendment overruling this decision, warning their colleagues that liberals might otherwise override racially discriminatory state laws by ratifying human rights treaties.[446]

Bricker's defense of states' rights came very close to success, failing only because of President Eisenhower's determined resistance.[447] The important point for us, however, does not deal with substance but strategy: if Bricker hoped to enact his amendment, he had to gain the consent of the House, which was unlikely to support any attempt to roll back its gains in foreign affairs. This helps explain a tell-tale transformation in the text of the "Bricker Amendment." Early versions contained a proviso that "[e]xecutive agreements could not be made in lieu of treaties."[448] In 1954, Bricker changed his tune, and

---

Congress further entrenched the two-House procedure by enacting a series of "congressional veto" statutes, asserting a correlative congressional, ¬ot senatorial, power to disapprove executive agreements before they become effective. *See, e.g.*, Atomic Energy Act of 1958, Pub. L. No. 85-479, sec. 4, § 123(d), 72 Stat. 276, 277 (requiring the President to submit agreements for military uses of atomic technology to Congress for a 60-day period, during which Congress could by concurrent resolution disapprove the agreement); Export Administration Amendments Act of 1985, Pub. L. No. 99-64, sec. 301(a)(3)–(b), § 123(d), 99 Stat. 120, 159–60 (amending § 123(d) to provide for disapproval by joint resolution); Foreign Assistance Act of 1974, Pub. L. No. 93-559, sec. 45(a)(5), § 35(b), 88 Stat. 1795, 1814 (providing Congress with the right to disapprove by concurrent resolution certain agreements to export military supplies); Arms Export Control Act, Pub. L. No. 99-247, sec. 1(a), § 3(d)(2), 100 Stat. 9 (1986) (amending same to require joint resolution); Fishery Conservation and Management Act of 1976, Pub. L. No. 94-265, § 203, 90 Stat. 331, 340 (permitting Congress to prevent any international fishery agreement from going into effect by passing a joint resolution of disapproval within 60 days after submission of the agreement to Congress). All of these provisions have now been brought into apparent compliance with the requirements of INS v. Chadha, 462 U.S. 919 (1983), by requiring two thirds of *both* Houses to override a presidential veto.

[445] There were many different versions of the Bricker Amendment. Senator Bricker began his campaign for the amendment in 1951, and was not decisively defeated until 1954. *See* DUANE TANANBAUM, THE BRICKER AMENDMENT CONTROVERSY 157–90 (1988). The controversy did not die completely until the late 1950s. *See id.* at 191–215.

[446] *See id.* at 6, 27, 54, 93. The Brickerites failed to anticipate later Supreme Court decisions holding that Congress's commerce powers provided a sufficient basis for national civil rights legislation. *See, e.g.*, Katzenbach v. McClung, 379 U.S. 294, 304 (1964); Heart of Atlanta Motel v. United States, 379 U.S. 241, 258 (1964). Given these developments, their fixation upon *Missouri v. Holland* now appears quixotic.

[447] *See* TANANBAUM, *supra* note 445, at 175–90.

[448] S.J. Res. 102, 82d Cong., 1st Sess. § 4 (1951); *see also* S.J. Res. 130, 82d Cong., 2d Sess. § 4 (1952), *reprinted in Treaties and Executive Agreements: Hearings on S.J. Res 130 Before a Subcomm. of the Senate Comm. on the Judiciary*, 82d Cong., 2d Sess. 4 (1952). Recalling earlier understandings, these versions would have operationalized this provision by defining the difference between executive agreements and treaties in terms of their duration. Executive agreements would automatically expire one year after the end of the term of the President who made the

insisted that an "international agreement shall become effective as internal law in the United States only through legislation by the Congress."[449] This represented a complete turnaround. Rather than closing off end-runs around the Senate's treaty-making power, Bricker expressly recognized the legitimacy of the congressional-executive agreement.[450] When a virtually identical proposal was defeated by only one vote in the Senate,[451] two thirds minus one of the Senate went on record recognizing the House as a legitimate player in the process of agreement-making.

During the first generation after Roosevelt, then, the Senate repeatedly recognized the legitimacy of the loss of its constitutional monopoly.[452] In the aftermath of Watergate and Vietnam, however, new

---

agreement, unless Congress and the succeeding President agreed to extend it for another term. *See id.*; *see also* S.J. Res. 102, 82d Cong., 1st Sess., § 4 (1951) (providing for automatic expiration after six months).

[449] 100 CONG. REC. 1332 (1954) (recording Bricker's proposed amendment to S.J. Res. 1, 83d Cong., 1st Sess. (1953)); *see* TANANBAUM, *supra* note 445, at 226 app. K. Bricker's first proposal in the 83d Congress provided that all executive agreements "shall be made only in the manner and to the extent to be prescribed by law." 99 CONG. REC. 160 (1953) (reprinting S.J. Res. 1, 83d Cong., 1st Sess. (1953)). As reported favorably by the Judiciary Committee, the resolution provided even more emphatically that "Congress shall have power to regulate all executive and other agreements . . . with any foreign power or international organization." S. REP. NO. 412, 83d Cong., 1st Sess. 1 (1953). The version quoted in the text was the only one actually put to a vote by the full Senate. Brickerites also introduced regular legislation that would have required the termination of executive agreements within six months after the term of the President who concluded them and would have made them subject to the legislative action of Congress. *See* S.J. Res. 2, 83d Cong., 1st Sess. (1953); S.J. Res. 122, 82d Cong., 2d Sess. (1952).

[450] Not that all Senators accepted interchangeability with equanimity. Denouncing McDougal and Lans and McClure, many struggled in vain to find a workable formula for reasserting the senatorial prerogative. *See* S. REP. NO. 412, *supra* note 449, at 26–28; 100 CONG. REC. 2196–97, 2205 (1954) (remarks of Sen. George); *id.* at 2195, 2199, 2203 (remarks of Sen. Bricker); *id.* at 2202–03 (remarks of Sen. Ferguson); *id.* at 2195–97, 2200 (remarks of Sen. Knowland). Despite these rhetorical flourishes, these Senators were fully aware of the implications of Bricker's proposal. Senator Knowland, the Republican majority leader, opposed Bricker's version precisely because it would afford the President alternative routes for all agreements, thereby further consolidating interchangeability. *See id.* at 2195–97, 2199–2200 (remarks of Sen. Knowland). Several Senators based their opposition on this ground. *See, e.g., id.* at 2201–04 (remarks of Sen. Ferguson); *id.* at 2202, 2261 (remarks of Sen. Hennings); *id.* at 2259–60 (remarks of Sen. Case); *id.* at 2260 (remarks of Sen. Fulbright). In response, Senator George, author of a similar proposal, explained that it was too late to worry about the participation of the House; the problem of the day was to gain control over the executive's increasing tendency to act unilaterally. *See id.* at 2196, 2261. Others seemed to agree. *See, e.g., id.* at 2202 (remarks of Sen. Butler); *id.* at 2203 (remarks of Sen. Bricker); *see also* S. REP. NO. 412, *supra* note 449, at 29 (explaining that the Judiciary Committee's proposed amendment would permit the Congress to decide which agreements should be approved as treaties, which as congressional-executive agreements, and which as unilateral executive agreements).

[451] *See* TANANBAUM, *supra* note 445, at 175–90 (describing Sen. George's substitute proposal).

[452] To the minimal extent that courts became involved, they also confirmed the new constitutional consensus. During the 1930s and 1940s, they deflected challenges to the 1934 Trade Act that might have clarified some of the constitutional issues. *See, e.g.,* Ernest E. Marks Co. v. United States, 117 F.2d 542, 546 (C.C.P.A. 1941); Wislar v. United States, 97 F.2d 152, 154–57 (C.C.P.A. 1938). *But cf.* Louis Wolf & Co. v. United States, 107 F.2d 819, 826–27 (C.C.P.A. 1939)

patterns emerged as both the Senate and the Congress took advantage of a weakened executive. On the one hand, a few Senators launched a campaign to reclaim the old constitutional monopoly. On the other, members of both Houses reshaped the post-war precedents to make the congressional-executive agreement into a sophisticated instrument for the conduct of diplomacy.

The fate of these two initiatives tells a lot about the living Constitution. The Senate's unilateral effort to recapture its lost glory was a failure.[453] Its collaboration with the House, however, generated a breakthrough of great constitutional significance. In the Trade Act of 1974,[454] Congress and the President created a structure for trade negotiations that is far superior to the one envisioned by the Framers of the Constitution of 1787. This collaborative construction of a framework statute, as we will call it, will help us unlock the riddle with which this essay began: why didn't all those well-paid lobbyists and lawyers challenge the constitutionality of NAFTA?

B. Reclaiming the Past?

But let us begin on a different note, with the Senate's failure to recapture its constitutional monopoly. In 1961, the Senate had gone along with the enactment of the Arms Control and Disarmament Act, which explicitly authorized the President to present his agreements for ratification under a two-House procedure. Almost immediately, the Senate began to regret this concession. In 1963, it sought repeal of this provision but failed to persuade the House.[455]

(construing language in a treaty that referred to any "Commercial Convention" as including agreements under the 1934 Act and strongly suggesting their validity). In the 1950s, however, the Court of Customs and Patent Appeals expressly upheld the constitutionality of the 1934 Act against both delegation and Treaty Clause challenges. *See* Star-Kist Foods, Inc. v. United States, 275 F.2d 472, 482–84 (C.C.P.A. 1959), *aff'g* 169 F. Supp. 268, 277–80 (Cust. Ct. 1958).

[453] The Senate's efforts did, however, serve to undermine most congressional attempts to control executive unilateralism. The House took offense at senatorial efforts to exclude it from the approval of international agreements, refusing to support legislation that would require senatorial, rather than congressional, approval of the President's agreements. *See* FRANCK & WEISBAND, *supra* note 12, at 149–51; LOCH K. JOHNSON, THE MAKING OF INTERNATIONAL AGREEMENTS 147–50 (1984). The only legislative victory came in 1972 with the Case Act, which requires the President to provide Congress with executive agreements within 60 days of their conclusion. *See* Act of Aug. 22, 1972, Pub. L. No. 92-403, 86 Stat. 619. Past senatorial efforts to impose a similar notification requirement would have required the President to inform only the Senate, *see* S. 603, 85th Cong., 1st Sess. (1957); S. 147, 84th Cong., 1st Sess. (1955); S. 3067, 83d Cong., 2d Sess. (1954), and so foundered in the House. *See, e.g.*, S. REP. NO. 521, 85th Cong., 1st Sess. 2 (1957); CONGRESSIONAL RESEARCH SERV., LIBRARY OF CONGRESS, *supra* note 12, at 176–77 n.21. Learning from these mistakes, Senator Case required presidential transmittal to both Houses. *See id.* at 176–77.

[454] Pub. L. No. 93-618, 88 Stat. 1978 (1975) (codified as amended at 19 U.S.C. § 2101 (1988)).

[455] The Senate proposed amending the provision to eliminate the statutory reference to approval by act of Congress and replace it with a requirement of approval in accordance with constitutional processes. *See* 109 CONG. REC. 10,958–59 (1963). The ambiguity of this language provoked some debate before it was adopted in the Senate. *See, e.g., id.* at 10,963 (remarks of

With the two-House procedure remaining on the books, President Nixon made the most of it. In 1972, he submitted the SALT I arms limitations agreement with the Soviets as a congressional-executive agreement. The Senate went along, joining the House in creating another major precedent for interchangeability.[456]

But then came Watergate and the Senate's efforts between 1976 and 1978 to roll back the post-war precedents by enacting a Treaty Powers Resolution.[457] The Resolution would have allowed a simple majority of the Senate to declare that a particular international agreement should be processed as a treaty. Thereafter the Senate would have been barred from considering any appropriations bill relevant to the agreement if a single Senator raised a point of order. The result would have forced the President to use the Treaty Clause if he wished to implement his agreement.[458]

President Ford reacted vigorously. His Legal Adviser rejected this attempt to reclaim the Senate's lost prerogative,[459] but not on behalf of the President alone. He also invoked the rights of the House — citing the framework statutes that, with senatorial consent, had expressly invited the House into the tent.[460] In the following years, the State Department's counteroffensive was joined by Clement Zablocki, chairman of the House Committee on International Relations.[461] As Senator Pell explained, the Resolution was "an open invitation to the House of Representatives to retaliate with a resolution of its own to raise a point of order regarding funding the implementation of any

---

Sen. Long); *id.* at 10,959 (remarks of Sen. Fulbright); *see also To Amend the Arms Control and Disarmament Act: Hearings on H.R. 3299, H.R. 6982, H.R. 6294, H.R. 7430, H.R. 7531, and S. 777 Before the House Comm. on Foreign Affairs,* 88th Cong., 1st Sess. 185–87 (1963) (providing the Administration's interpretation). But the House refused to go along. *See* H.R. REP. NO. 863, 88th Cong., 1st Sess. 6 (1963); 109 CONG. REC. 22,508 (1963) (remarks of Rep. Morgan).

[456] *See* Joint Resolution of Sept. 30, 1972, Pub. L. No. 79-448, 86 Stat. 746. The Administration was somewhat inconsistent in explaining its reasons for choosing the two-House procedure. *See Agreement on Limitation of Strategic Offensive Weapons: Hearings before the House Comm. on Foreign Affairs,* 92d Cong., 2d Sess. 17-18 (1972) (testimony of William P. Rogers); Trimble & Weiss, *supra* note 12, at 658–60; Vartian, *supra* note 15, at 442–46.

[457] The various versions of the Resolution are described in ELEANOR C. MCDOWELL, U.S. DEP'T OF STATE, DIGEST OF UNITED STATES PRACTICE IN INTERNATIONAL LAW 256–63 (1976) [hereinafter 1976 DIGEST]; JOHN A. BOYD, U.S. DEP'T. OF STATE, DIGEST OF UNITED STATES PRACTICE IN INTERNATIONAL LAW 413–18 (1977) [hereinafter 1977 DIGEST]; and MARIAN L. NASH, U.S. DEP'T OF STATE, DIGEST OF UNITED STATES PRACTICE IN INTERNATIONAL LAW 787–99 (1978) [hereinafter 1978 DIGEST].

[458] *See* 1976 DIGEST, *supra* note 457, at 256–57, 263; 1977 DIGEST, *supra* note 457, at 413–14; 1978 DIGEST, *supra* note 457, at 788–89, 794, 797–99.

[459] *See Treaty Powers Resolution: Hearings Before the Senate Comm. on Foreign Relations on S. Res. 486,* 94th Cong., 2d Sess. 72 (1976) [hereinafter *Treaty Powers Resolution Hearings*] (statement of Monroe Leigh); 1976 DIGEST, *supra* note 457, at 257–62.

[460] *See Treaty Powers Resolution Hearings, supra* note 459, at 72–77, 79–80.

[461] *See* Letter from Rep. Clement Zablocki to Cyrus R. Vance, Secretary of State of the United States (June 27, 1977), *reprinted in* 1977 DIGEST, *supra* note 457, at 415.

international agreement which the House finds should be approved by both Houses of Congress."[462]

When faced with unyielding opposition from the executive and the prospect of internecine warfare with the House, the Senate blinked. After more than two years, it enacted a Treaty Powers Resolution that was a shadow of its former self: "in determining whether a particular international agreement should be submitted as a treaty, the President should have the timely advice of the Committee on Foreign Relations."[463] Nothing remained of the previous effort to allow a single Senator's objection to thwart the implementation of any effort to short-circuit the Treaty Clause.[464]

---

[462] 124 CONG. REC. 19,229 (1978). Pell told the Senate that Chairman Zablocki had already warned the Foreign Relations Committee that "he could 'easily imagine a similar House Resolution.'" *Id.*

[463] The Senate passed Resolution 536 by voice vote on September 8, 1978. *See* 124 CONG. REC. 28,545 (1978). Even before passage of the resolution, the State Department had agreed to a procedure for consultation as to "the form of significant United States international agreements." S. REP. NO. 1171, 95th Cong., 2d Sess. 3 (1978) (quoting Letter from Douglas Bennet, Assistant Secretary for Congressional Relations, to Sen. Sparkman, Chairman of the Senate Foreign Relations Committee). But it insisted that it would consult with both the Senate Foreign Relations Committee and the House Committee on International Relations. *See* 1978 DIGEST, *supra* note 457, at 795–96.

[464] The Senate has made other bids to regain its exclusive prerogative. But these efforts, more often than not, have tended to consolidate, rather than undermine, the legitimacy of the congressional-executive agreement. The opening salvo in a decade of battle was Senator Fulbright's 1969 National Commitments Resolution, S. Res. 85, 91st Cong., 1st Sess. (1969), which the Senator described as an attempt "to reestablish the proper role of the Senate." 115 CONG. REC. 16,615 (1969); *see also* S. REP. NO. 129, 91st Cong., 1st Sess. 26–30 (1969) (affirming that the purpose of the resolution was to reclaim the Senate's prerogative). Nevertheless, Fulbright's non-binding resolution provided that national commitments could be undertaken by means of "a treaty, *statute, or concurrent resolution of both Houses of Congress.*" S. Res. 85, *supra*, at 1–2 (as considered and agreed to, June 25, 1969) (emphasis added). Challenged on this point, Fulbright stated: "What we are saying is that, for any arrangement to be regarded as a significant commitment, Congress, in some form or another, should participate." 115 CONG. REC. 16,768 (1969).

The issue reemerged in 1972 when the Foreign Relations Committee considered the *Vienna Convention on the Law of Treaties*, U.N. Doc. A/CONF.39/27 (1969). Article 46 of the Convention provides that a state cannot escape its obligations under a treaty (defined by the Convention as virtually any international agreement) by claiming that it was entered into in violation of a rule of domestic law, "unless that violation was manifest and concerned a rule of its internal law of fundamental importance." *Id.* art. 46, *reprinted in* ARTHUR W. ROVINE, U.S. DEP'T OF STATE, DIGEST OF UNITED STATES PRACTICE IN INTERNATIONAL LAW 197–98 (1974) [hereinafter 1974 DIGEST]. The Committee took submission of the treaty as an occasion to launch another offensive. Instead of cutting the House out of the loop, however, it proposed an "understanding and interpretation" that reconfirmed the post-World War II constitutional solution. 1974 DIGEST, *supra*, at 195. While it declared the Treaty Clause to be "a rule of internal law of the United States of fundamental importance," *id.*, it also declared that no treaty as defined by the Convention would be valid "unless the Senate of the United States has given its advice and consent to such treaty, *or the terms of such treaty have been approved by law, as the case may be.*" *Id.* (emphasis added); *see also* CONGRESSIONAL RESEARCH SERV., LIBRARY OF CONGRESS *supra* note 12, at 21–25 (recounting the history of Senate action on the Convention). As a result of the Senate's insistence on this understanding, Presidents have thus far refused to ratify the Convention in an effort to defend their unilateral executive agreement-making powers. *See id.* at 22–25.

Nonetheless, the Senate has been willing to engage in guerilla warfare in less provocative contexts — especially when aided by presidential incompetence. Consider the fate of SALT II, negotiated by President Carter. When faced with growing senatorial opposition, Carter publicly considered submitting SALT II as a congressional-executive agreement. But when some Senators loudly protested, he submitted SALT II as a treaty — only to withdraw the entire matter after the Soviets invaded Afghanistan.[465]

The Senate continued to press its claims into the 1980s, when arms control returned to the agenda. It did so, however, in a procedural context that could not provoke serious presidential or House reaction. Because Presidents Reagan and Bush were confident of senatorial support, they chose to submit their arms control agreements with the Soviets as treaties. While the Senate went along with the Administrations' initiatives, it began to append an odd "declaration" to its assent. Beginning with the Intermediate-Range Nuclear Forces (INF) Treaty, the Senate declared that future arms control agreements must be processed as treaties![466]

The Soviet Foreign Ministry must have been puzzled by these senatorial pronouncements, which had to do with interbranch, not international, diplomacy. But the Presidents were happy with the ratification of their treaties, and therefore ignored senatorial "declarations" that had no international implications. So far as the House was concerned, the Senate's odd "declarations" could not serve to repeal the express terms of the Arms Control Act of 1961, which authorized the President to invoke the two-House procedure.

Putting empty senatorial pronunciamentos to one side, the law in this area remains where it was left by President Truman and the Eightieth Congress: if the President persuades a majority in both Houses to ratify an executive agreement, it gains unquestioned accept-

---

[465] The history is recounted in Trimble & Weiss, cited above in note 12, at 661–62. For a similar story regarding Carter's Panama Canal accord, see JOHNSON, cited above in note 453, at 140–41.

[466] *See, e.g.,* CONGRESSIONAL RESEARCH SERV., LIBRARY OF CONGRESS, *supra* note 12, at 211; Trimble & Weiss, *supra* note 12, at 685–87. The declaration attached to the INF Treaty still arguably suggested senatorial acceptance of the President's two-House option under the Arms Control Act, at least in certain circumstances. *See id.* at 686–87. The Senate eliminated any play in the language of the Conventional Forces in Europe Treaty. *See* S. EXEC. REP. NO. 22, 102d Cong., 1st Sess. 70–71 (1991); 137 CONG. REC. S17,846 (daily ed. Nov. 23, 1991) (remarks of Sen. Helms). Not surprisingly, both the House and the executive continued to believe that the two-House option was alive and well. *See, e.g.,* 134 CONG. REC. 7322–25 (1988) (remarks of Reps. Fascell and Berman) (referring to and reprinting a memorandum from Michael J. Matheson, State Department Deputy Legal Adviser, to Ambassador Kampelman (Apr. 14, 1988), asserting that neither § 33 of the Arms Control Act nor the Constitution compels the use of treaties rather than congressional-executive agreements).

ance as a binding international obligation that is the "supreme law of the land."[467]

This does not mean, of course, that individual Senators cannot launch constitutional crusades against particular agreements. To beat back a presidential initiative, however, it will not be enough to persuade "one third plus one" of their colleagues that the President has evaded the Treaty Clause. It will take a majority to reject the agreement under the new rules of the game fashioned in the aftermath of the Second World War.

C. The Trade Act of 1974

A second Watergate-era story contrasts strongly with the Senate's vain effort to roll back the precedents of the Roosevelt years. The subject here was international trade, not international security. Rather than fighting a losing war with the House, the Senate helped create a new and powerful mode of congressional supervision of the executive branch.

The Trade Act of 1974[468] reshaped existing practice in fundamental ways. Until 1974, the only important difference between the one-House and two-House alternatives had been the size of the majority required for approval of the agreement — two-thirds of the Senate or a simple majority of both Houses. The Trade Act moved beyond this single point and transformed the congressional-executive agreement into a highly sophisticated tool for modern diplomacy.

Consider the way the Act and its successors[469] organize the process through which legislators advise the President during the negotiation period. Although the Constitution requires senators to give their "advice" as well as their "consent" to treaties, this text lapsed into desuetude over the centuries.[470] Today's Senate often confronts completed agreements that it can reject or revise only on pain of international

---

[467] For the most elaborate recent State Department restatement of the interchangeability doctrine, see Department of State Assistant Legal Adviser's Reply to Second Memorandum of Senate Office of Legal Counsel Concerning Certain Middle [East] Agreements (Feb. 5, 1976), *reprinted in* 122 CONG. REC. 3374–79 (1976) and Department of State Legal Adviser's Reply to Senate Office of Legislative Counsel Memorandum on Certain Middle East Agreements (Oct. 8, 1975), *reprinted in* 121 CONG. REC. 36,718–21 (1975). The State Department's Circular 175 Procedures state flatly that the President may conclude international agreements "on the basis of existing legislation or subject to legislation to be enacted by the Congress." 11 U.S. DEPARTMENT OF STATE, FOREIGN AFFAIRS MANUAL § 721.2(b)(2) (revised ed. Feb. 25, 1985). The Circular 175 Procedures also set out a list of factors guiding executive discretion in the choice of methods. *See id.* § 721.3.

[468] Pub. L. No. 93-618, 88 Stat. 1978 (1975) (codified as amended at 19 U.S.C. § 2101 (1988)).

[469] *See, e.g.,* Omnibus Trade and Competitiveness Act of 1988, Pub. L. No. 100-418, 102 Stat. 1107, 1127 (codified as amended at 19 U.S.C. § 2901 (1988)). We refer to the Trade Act of 1974 and its successors collectively as the "Trade Act."

[470] *See supra* pp. 869–70.

embarrassment.[471] In contrast, the Trade Act provides a dynamic framework through which Congress can give effective advice before the President signs on the dotted line. In authorizing wide-ranging negotiations of the NAFTA type,[472] the Trade Act insists that the President consult with all relevant congressional committees,[473] include members of Congress in American negotiating delegations,[474] and provide ninety-day notice of an intention to sign any agreement.[475] In discharging these functions, the executive must generate reams of paper explaining how its evolving proposals satisfy the Act's detailed statement of objectives.[476] More important than the paper trail is the genuine discussion and serious horse-trading that goes on during the advisory period. Thus, this modern statute has redeemed the promise of *"advice* and consent" in a way that eluded the constitution-writers of 1787.[477]

By increasing Congress's advisory role in formulating international agreements, the Trade Act also helps curb a second failure of the traditional treaty system. As the Senate lost its effective capacity to give advice, it began to reassert its power in dysfunctional ways, renegotiating agreements after they were tendered by the President. This takes the form of adding "reservations" that change the deal foreign countries thought they had made with the President. If foreign nations do not accept the Senate's unilateral conditions, the agreement never becomes effective.

Adding reservations is not only counterproductive; it also encourages political irresponsibility. Senators need not take a highly visible stand against a treaty they dislike. They can camouflage their opposition by coupling an affirmative vote with crippling reservations that are unacceptable to treaty partners. Worse yet, these unsatisfactory outcomes are often shaped by strategic delays in committee and on the Senate floor. In short, the classic constitutional procedure not only generates unnecessary disaffection abroad but encourages political obfuscation at home.

The Trade Act strikes at these practices, but succeeds only because it encourages interbranch consultation at the policy formulation stage. The crucial device is its famous "fast-track" procedure. So long as the executive plays by the rules at the earlier stages, it can guarantee an

---

[471] To the Senate's chagrin, the President has begun to negotiate multilateral conventions that prohibit states from adding any reservations. *See* CONGRESSIONAL RESEARCH SERV., LIBRARY OF CONGRESS, *supra* note 12, at 224–26.

[472] *See* 19 U.S.C. § 2902(b)–(c) (1988).

[473] *See id.* § 2902(c)–(d).

[474] *See id.* § 2211(a)(1).

[475] *See id.* § 2903(a)(1)(A). Congress extended this period to 120 days for the Uruguay Round negotiations. *See id.* § 2902(e)(3)(A) (Supp. V 1993).

[476] *See id.* § 2903(a) (1988).

[477] *See* Koh, *supra* note 208, at 1200–08.

up-or-down vote, without amendments, after a relatively brief period for congressional hearings and floor debate.[478] No longer can legislators escape their moment of truth, yet both Senators and Representatives are given many opportunities to voice their concerns and threaten the executive with the prospect of ultimate defeat should their advice be ignored.

But the Trade Act is more than a theoretical breakthrough. It actually works. Its first test was the Tokyo Round of GATT, an ambitious effort to move beyond traditional tariff reductions and to focus on non-tariff trade barriers.[479] Rather than bogging down in a mass of strategic delays and special reservations, the Tokyo Round glided along the fast track in thirty-four legislative days.[480] This initial success motivated further use of the framework, with some modifications, in the path-breaking free trade agreements with Israel and Canada.[481]

All this stands behind NAFTA, the most recent of the successes on the fast track. Little wonder, then, that anti-NAFTA forces did not wish to discredit themselves by invoking the Constitution-with-a-capital-C. It was one thing to explain why NAFTA was a bad agreement, quite another to destroy one of the great successes of modern American government. Not only was the new framework transparently superior to the classical system of "no advice, but consent with reservations." The Senate had itself recognized this fact by voluntarily participating in the design of the new framework. As for the House, it

---

[478] *See* 19 U.S.C. §§ 2191, 2903(b)–(c) (1988).

[479] *See* Koh, *supra* note 208, at 1201–03. Even before the 1974 Act, Congress had approved a trade pact with Canada as a congressional-executive agreement. *See* Automotive Products Trade Act of 1965, Pub. L. No. 89-283, 79 Stat. 1016. The State Department's Legal Adviser again prepared a memorandum asserting the interchangeability doctrine. *See* Letter from Leonard C. Meeker, Acting State Department Legal Adviser, to Senator Fulbright (Feb. 24, 1965), *reprinted in* 111 CONG. REC. 9064–65 (1965). In response, the Senate Foreign Relations Committee Chairman sought an appraisal of the Legal Adviser's opinion. *See id.* at 9062 (remarks of Sen. Fulbright). Reflecting the solidity of the post-war consensus, the Legislative Attorney fully affirmed the Legal Adviser's views on interchangeability. *See* A Critical Appraisal of the Legal Arguments Presented in an Opinion Submitted by the Acting Legal Adviser to the State Department, Prepared by Norman J. Small, Legislative Attorney, American Law Division of the Library of Congress (Mar. 29, 1965), *reprinted in* 111 CONG. REC. 9065 (1965). He differed only in asserting that the President did not have the last word: "the President may be said to enjoy a choice of means only insofar as the Congress is disposed to sustain him in his election." *Id.* Thus, in the Legislative Attorney's view, a *majority* of the Senate always has the power to insist on the treaty form by refusing to approve a congressional-executive agreement. This is in accord with the prevailing view. *See* RESTATEMENT, *supra* note 5, § 303 cmt. e.

[480] *See* Koh, *supra* note 208, at 1203.

[481] *See* United States-Canada Free-Trade Agreement Implementation Act of 1988, Pub. L. No. 100-449, 102 Stat. 1851; United States-Israel Free Trade Area Implementation Act of 1985, Pub. L. No. 99-47, 99 Stat. 82. In recent years, Congress has also approved a number of other important trade agreements. *See, e.g.,* Omnibus Trade and Competitiveness Act of 1988, Pub. L. No. 100-418, § 1122, 102 Stat. 1107, 1143–44 (implementing the United States-European Community Agreement on Citrus and Pasta); *id.* § 1203, 102 Stat. at 1148 (approving the Convention on the Harmonized Commodity Description and Coding System).

would have been quixotic for opponents of NAFTA to suppose that Representatives would respond enthusiastically to a constitutional plea for a return to the good old days of senatorial monopoly.

VI. The Bigger Picture

We have been treating the congressional-executive agreement as a constitutional problem in its own right. But our story has larger implications, inviting us to rethink conventional accounts of American constitutional change and reexamine why the Constitution deserves our respect in the first place.

Traditional accounts of change fall into two broad categories. The first is formalist: the only legitimate path to revision is the one marked out by the Founders in Article V. The second is based on common law models of development. On this view, the broad themes established by the constitutional text take on meaning only as they are applied by seasoned statesmen and judges confronting particular cases. As time moves on, concrete decisions build on one another, generating doctrinal patterns that become more important than the abstract formulae originally pronounced by the Founders.

This gradual transformation of abstract text into concrete doctrine is a cause for celebration, not mourning. If Americans had followed the formalists' advice, and restricted themselves to the rules of Article V, they would have broken the Founding mold long ago, and followed the French example of enacting one Constitution after another to express changing social needs and political ideals. The only reason Americans continue to live under the Constitution of 1787 is that legally trained elites have adapted its leading themes to the "felt necessities" of each age, constantly testing received doctrine against changing circumstance.

The story we have told suggests the importance of a third form of constitutional transformation. Like the common law mode, our account has emphasized the significance, and legitimacy, of changes that do not run along the formal tracks established at the Founding. But it differs from the common law pattern in three respects. The typical picture of common law development is elitist, gradualist, and antitheoretical. Acting slowly and cautiously, thoughtful judges and statesmen pile one precedent on top of another as they sense the need to adapt the constitutional order to a changing world. Over the course of a generation or two, these cautious changes can add up to a very large doctrinal transformation; but the process is so gradual that nobody, except perhaps for a few members of the elite, ever understands that there is more involved than one small step after another.

Our story is more populist, less incremental, and places a higher premium on constitutional self-consciousness. The Senate did not surrender its monopoly out of deference to thoughtful elite prodding. It yielded in the face of a formal constitutional amendment that expressed a radical change in prevailing public opinion. Nor did the Senate surrender gradually over the course of many decades. It happened in four years — from 1943, when the Administration and the Senate began to experiment with a constitutional novelty, to 1947, when the Senate responded to presidential assertions of interchangeability by cooperating in the approval of congressional-executive agreements without significant protest. Nor did the Senate surrender without noticing the high constitutional stakes. Its every move was accompanied by self-conscious debate — in which both reformers and conservatives repeatedly exposed the key issues on the pages of newspapers and legal journals, as well as on the floor of the Capitol and in the corridors of executive power.[482]

In these respects, the process was closer to ones that have accompanied change in the constitutional text. Both the Founding Federalists and the Reconstruction Republicans sought and won basic change in a short time — between 1786 and 1790 in the first case, between 1865 and 1869 in the second. They would never have triumphed if they had contented themselves with the cautious judgments of elite opinion. They won by going over the heads of established institutions and appealing to their fellow citizens for a principled overhaul of constitutional arrangements.[483] Indeed, in one important respect, the New Internationalists of the 1940s beat the Federalists and the Republicans at their own game. Both the Founders and Reconstructers won razor-thin majorities in support of their constitutional initiatives; in contrast, the New Internationalists pointed to public opinion polls showing the support of decisive majorities that their predecessors could only dream about.[484]

And yet there is an obvious difference: our story does not involve a formal change in the constitutional text. While such a step was in the works, it lost its practical point when the Senate gave up a bitter-end struggle, and made a "switch in time." Rather than codifying the new change in a classical amendment, the Senate cooperated in the creation of a series of precedents that stabilized a new interpretation of old texts. Henceforth, Congress's enumerated powers would be read generously, with the aid of the Necessary and Proper Clause, to include

---

[482] For further contrasts with the common law model, see ACKERMAN, cited above in note 8, at 17–24.

[483] *See* ACKERMAN, *supra* note 8, ch. 2; ACKERMAN, *supra* note 393, chs. 4, 7, 14; Bruce Ackerman, *Constitutional Politics/Constitutional Law*, 99 YALE L.J. 453, 486–515 (1989); Ackerman & Katyal, *supra* note 33 (manuscript at 3–4, 116–25).

[484] For the narrowness of the Federalists' victory, see Ackerman & Katyal, cited above in note 33 (manuscript at 122 n.250); for the narrowness of the Republican victory, see JAMES L. SUNDQUIST, DYNAMICS OF THE PARTY SYSTEM: ALIGNMENT AND REALIGNMENT OF POLITICAL PARTIES IN THE UNITED STATES 98–105 (rev. ed. 1983). Compare the public opinion data reported above at notes 283–86 and accompanying text.

the power to approve binding international obligations negotiated by the President.

A. *The New Deal and the New Internationalism*

In this, and many other respects, our story bears the most striking resemblance to the way the American people defined, debated and resolved the basic issues raised by the New Deal's response to the Great Depression. This is hardly surprising. While the issues were different, the players remained the same. Franklin Roosevelt and Congress had learned some important lessons from the constitutional crisis of the 1930s. So did ordinary Americans. Having successfully emerged from the Depression with its democracy intact, Americans relied on this experience as they confronted the task of building a new world order out of the war's devastation.

This constitutional linkage between the New Deal and the new American internationalism was well understood at the time. As early as 1944, Edward Corwin was analyzing the Senate's response to the problem of treaty-making from the perspective of 1937, and warning the Senate to learn the right constitutional lessons from the Supreme Court's switch.[485] The passage of a half-century permits us to elaborate these family resemblances more fully. In doing so, we will locate NAFTA's ultimate constitutional foundations. To put our conclusion in a nutshell: the processes that legitimated the congressional-executive agreement were merely variations on the institutional and doctrinal themes developed by the New Dealers in the preceding decade.

1. Institutional Dynamics. — In defining the commonalities in constitutional process during the 1930s and 1940s, begin with the path not taken. In both decades, Roosevelt refused to put his weight behind a formal amendment. The President made this decision for compelling reasons. The rules laid down by Article V were peculiarly dysfunctional given the constitutional messages that he sought to codify. The tension between formal medium and constitutional message is especially easy to see in the 1940s: while a strong and sustained majority of Americans opposed the Senate monopoly on treaty-making, Article V was blithely instructing them to seek the consent of two thirds of the Senate to its own disestablishment!

It is true, of course, that Article V is alive to the problem of institutional self-dealing, and defines an alternative that breaks the congressional monopoly on constitutional revision. Under this option, two thirds of the states can prevail upon Congress to call another Constitutional Convention. A Philadelphia-like convention could then consider the Senate's treaty monopoly without pronounced institutional bias.

---

[485] *See supra* p. 883.

But a second convention could have done a lot of other things as well. Whatever else may be said about this constitutional wild-card,[486] it is hard to fault Roosevelt for refusing to play such a high-risk game in the middle of the greatest war of the twentieth century. So far as we know, there was only one point at which Roosevelt considered calling a second convention — in November 1936, after the Democrats' landslide electoral victory.[487] At that moment of sweeping reexamination of fundamental premises, such a call might have been appropriate.

But this moment had passed by the 1940s. By this point, Americans were proud of the way their system had weathered the storms of the 1930s. Rather than giving the old constitutional regime a sweeping vote of no confidence, Americans were focusing upon a single Founding mistake. In this context, it would have been silly for the President to consider a convention. This meant that Roosevelt was up against an institutional problem that the Framers foresaw but had failed adequately to solve: Article V gave "one-third-plus-one" of the Senate the right to veto the popular demand that it strip itself of the treaty-making power accorded to "one-third-plus-one" of the Senate. It is only the hardest-line formalist who would not sympathize with the President's effort to find a way out of this double-bind by adapting the transformative techniques pioneered during the New Deal revolution.[488]

This is a moment, moreover, at which the pragmatic revolt against nineteenth-century formalisms had reached its triumphant climax.[489] John Dewey, not Herbert Spencer or William Sumner, was the country's leading philosopher. Americans were proud to think of themselves as a "can-do" people whose common sense would save the world from Nazism. Scholars like Corwin and McDougal were carrying this pragmatic impulse into constitutional law. Rather than urging Americans into a bitter uphill battle against the Senate on formalist terrain marked out by Article V, they sketched a more realistic alternative that would get the job done just as well.

In elaborating the case for the congressional-executive agreement, these scholars were recapitulating themes that had recently become es-

---

[486] *See* ACKERMAN, *supra* note 8, *passim*; Akhil Amar, *The Consent of the Governed: Constitutional Amendments Outside Article V*, 94 COLUM. L. REV. 457, 458–62 (1994).

[487] *See* BARRY D. KARL, EXECUTIVE REORGANIZATION AND REFORM IN THE NEW DEAL: THE GENESIS OF ADMINISTRATIVE MANAGEMENT, 1900–1939, at 27 (1963). Roosevelt's rejection of this possibility, and his embrace of court-packing as an alternative, is the subject of a chapter of a forthcoming book by Professor Ackerman. *See* ACKERMAN, *supra* note 393, ch. 14.

[488] Indeed, it is even questionable whether formalism at this level is philosophically defensible. *See* PETER SUBER, THE PARADOX OF SELF-AMENDMENT: A STUDY OF LOGIC, LAW, OMNIPOTENCE, AND CHANGE 25–38 (1990) (elaborating the "pardox of self-amendment").

[489] *See* MORTON WHITE, SOCIAL THOUGHT IN AMERICA: THE REVOLT AGAINST FORMALISM 3–10 (1949).

tablished elements of New Deal constitutionalism. Just as New Deal scholars attacked the antimajoritarian character of the Old Court, now the New Internationalists attacked the antidemocratic veto granted the malapportioned Senate. Just as New Deal scholars mined the history of the Marshall Court to create a pedigree for a newly expanded Commerce Clause, now the New Internationalists scavenged for precedents that helped expand the scope of Article I yet further to support congressional-executive agreements. The point of both exercises was the same: to convince legalists that the constitutional tradition applauded the collective effort to correct the anachronistic formalisms of the past when modern Americans were demanding fundamental change.

But in the final analysis, it was not up to the President, much less the legal scholars, to make this choice between pragmatism and formalism in constitutional law. The ultimate decision rested with the institutions that had the most to lose from the change: the Old Court in the 1930s, the Isolationist Senate in the 1940s. Both had the acknowledged power to carry on a bitter-end defense of their traditional vision of the Constitution. There was nothing inevitable about the Court's "switch in time" in the 1930s or the Senate's in the 1940s.

Of course, further resistance by these conservative branches would have forced the politically ascendant New Dealers/New Internationalists to consider their own options. Throughout the 1930s, the New Dealers were prepared to push through formal constitutional amendments if all else failed to impress the Court of the need for fundamental change.[490] Similarly, as the Senate was considering the presidential package composed of the United Nations Treaty and the Bretton Woods Agreements, the House's formal amendment still hung over its head.[491]

In both cases, the conservative institutions had a choice. The Court could have continued its defense of the traditional Constitution beyond 1937, daring the New Dealers to push on with court-packing or a campaign for formal amendments. Similarly, the Senate could have remained intransigent, and forced the struggle to the bitter end. Indeed, it was not even necessary for Senate traditionalists to block the United Nations Charter in order to assert that they had a veto on the shape of the new world order. Instead of reenacting the Versailles scenario, they could have approved the United Nations Treaty and made an offer to support the Bretton Woods Agreements so long as the President submitted it as a treaty.

In neither case, however, did the key conservative branch escalate its struggle with the reformist branches to the formalist limit. Each made a switch in time, accepting a new vision of activist government at home and abroad — but only after the reformist branches had

---

490 *See* ACKERMAN, *supra* note 393, ch. 14.
491 *See supra* pp. 889–90.

demonstrated sustained support from public opinion by a series of electoral victories. There are important differences in the electoral patterns that are worth noting. Most importantly, while the New Deal agenda was inaugurated by the election of 1932, the election of 1940 did not perform a similar signalling function for the New Internationalists. It was Pearl Harbor, more than any endogenous act of political will, that began the popular process of constitutional reappraisal that was already proceeding in the minds of the political-legal elite. With the election of 1944, however, the New Internationalists could begin to claim the kind of deep and broad mandate from the American people that our constitutional tradition demands as a precondition for legitimate change.

At this point the Senate began an anxious reappraisal. Was it really willing to live with the constitutional compromise provisionally devised in the piecemeal efforts surrounding UNRRA, Panama, and the Connally Resolution of 1943? Or was it determined to make an all-out defense of its monopolistic reading of the Treaty Clause?

One thing was clear: Presidents Roosevelt and Truman were not about to let the Senate off the hook. With their popular mandate refreshed by an unprecedented fourth-term victory, they were going to repeat the scenario of 1937. Just as the Court faced its moment of constitutional truth in 1937, so too would the Senate confront some hard choices in 1945. Either it would accept a compromise that included the congressional-executive agreement or it would be obliged to fight for its traditional monopoly in a highly visible struggle before the American people.

In making its switch in time, the Senate followed the main line of American history. Indeed, there is only one case in which constitutional conservatives fought for their formal privileges to the bitter end. This occurred in the aftermath of the Civil War, and ended with the destruction of the southern state governments that sought to invoke their formal rights under Article V to veto the Fourteenth Amendment. But in the aftermath of the Second World War, there was no serious thought of such a bitter-end struggle. To the contrary, the political party that was most committed to traditional isolationism — the Republicans — had now embraced internationalism under the leadership of Senator Vandenberg.

This meant that the Senate's acceptance of Bretton Woods was not going to be a temporary swerve any more than was the Court's acceptance of the National Labor Relations Act a decade earlier. Just as the Court's five-to-four decisions in the spring of 1937 culminated in nine-to-zero affirmations of New Deal constitutionalism by 1941, so too the Senate's approval of Bretton Woods was confirmed by its subsequent behavior. Indeed, the new constitutional solution was consolidated even more quickly as the Republicans won control of the Senate in 1947. Rather than using this victory as the basis for a constitutional counteroffensive against Harry Truman, the Senate continued to cooperate with the House as the President codified the transformation. Just as all the relevant branches were treating New Deal constitutionalism as an established fact by 1941, so too all relevant branches were treating New Internationalist constitutionalism as an established fact by 1947.

To summarize the common constitutional dynamics of these two different movements during the Roosevelt Era: (1) The election of 1932 signalled the rise to public prominence of the New Deal agenda while Pearl Harbor signalled the rise of the New Internationalist agenda; this was then followed (2) by the President leading Congress to explore alternatives to the constitutional status quo; then (3) by a triggering election, which the victorious party used as a mandate for presidential proposals that pushed the leading conservative branch to a moment of constitutional truth; which was (4) resolved by a switch in time; that was then (5) confirmed as an enduring constitutional solution by the previously conservative branch after another election.

In taking these steps, the Senate and the Supreme Court acted in the best tradition of American constitutional law. Rather than fighting for a constitutional vision that had lost its grip upon the hearts and minds of the American people, the conservative branches faced the hard facts at their moments of truth, and then set out to reestablish the People's faith in their reliability as good-faith participants in a revised constitutional order.

2. Rereading the Text. — The similarities between the New Deal and the New Internationalism arise with equally compelling force on the level of constitutional doctrine. The domestic New Deal did not give rise to formal constitutional amendments, but expressed itself in the decisive triumph of a distinctive school of textual interpretation. Before 1933, Article I of the Constitution was read to grant the federal government strictly limited powers of intervention in domestic affairs, preserving to the states vast areas of exclusive legislative jurisdiction. By Roosevelt's third term, a reconstituted Supreme Court had unanimously rejected this traditional reading. After cases like *Wickard* and *Darby*,[492] mainstream constitutionalists have learned to read each of Article I's great grants of congressional power expansively, and then to expand them further by ringing reaffirmations of Marshall's understanding of the Necessary and Proper Clause: "Let the end be legitimate . . . and all means which are appropriate . . . which are not prohibited . . . are constitutional."[493]

---

[492] *Wickard v. Filburn*, 317 U.S. 111 (1942); *United States v. Darby*, 312 U.S. 100 (1941).

[493] *McCulloch v. Maryland*, 17 U.S. (4 Wheat.) 316, 421 (1819).

This same Marshallian reading of Article I provides the textual basis for the congressional-executive agreement. In the case of NAFTA, for example, Article I expressly establishes Congress's power over "Commerce with foreign Nations" and thereby satisfies Marshall's demand that NAFTA's "end be legitimate." Similarly, Congress could reasonably determine that it was "appropriate" to enter into binding international obligations with Canada and Mexico as a means of furthering its legitimate constitutional ends. Finally, congressional action satisfies Marshall's caution that it be "not prohibited." While Article II of the Constitution vests treaty-making power in the Senate, it does not by any means prohibit the Senate from joining with the House to exercise Congress's full powers under Article I.[494]

Within the terms of our narrative, the Marshallian reading of the text provided the Senate of the 1940s with ample constitutional grounds for concluding that a formal amendment was unnecessary before it could cooperate with the House and the President under Article I in support of congressional-executive agreements. Given the Supreme Court's decisive interpretive switch in *Darby* and *Wickard*, there was no longer any compelling need to insist on a formal change in the text. It was now enough to recall Marshall's great admonition in *McCulloch* that the Necessary and Proper Clause had been designed for "a constitution intended to endure for ages to come, and, consequently, to be adapted to the various crises of human affairs."[495] In acting upon a Marshallian interpretation of Article I, the Senate was operating under the very same interpretive principles that had allowed the New Deal Court to constitutionalize the domestic policies of the activist state without the need for formal constitutional amendments.

3. *NAFTA and the EPA.* — These common institutional and doctrinal themes lead us to conclude that the constitutional foundations of NAFTA are no better, but no worse, than those underlying domestic agencies of activist government. Even Chief Justice Marshall might be a bit surprised to learn that a toilet flushed into an intrastate lake may now be subjected to pervasive regulation by the EPA. But after the Court's decision in *Wickard v. Filburn*, modern constitutionalists take the legitimacy of such action for granted. So too with NAFTA. After the Senate's considered and repeated endorsement of interchangeability in the 1940s, the Marshallian reading of the Foreign Commerce Clause provides a fully adequate basis for congressional action.

---

[494] *See supra* Part I.B; *infra* pp. 919–21, 923.

[495] *McCulloch*, 17 U.S. (4 Wheat.) at 415–16.

B. Framework Statutes[496]

But there are important differences as well as similarities between the New Deal and the New Internationalism. One concerns the identity of the institutional players: while the Supreme Court played a central role in consolidating New Deal constitutionalism at home, it has been a remarkably silent partner in the constitutional development of the foreign affairs power. Although there are some supportive suggestions,[497] the Supreme Court has never squarely confronted the status of the congressional-executive agreement.

The Court's absence has left other institutions with the task of stabilizing constitutional norms. The result, in the trade area at least, has been strikingly successful. While most statutes content themselves with establishing new substantive law, the Trade Act of 1974 discharged a constitutional function, creating new rules for the law-making system itself. Such framework statutes, as we will call them, are at the jurisprudential core of the legal system — providing citizens with "rules of recognition" for determining the nature of their legal rights and duties.[498]

Within the area of international trade, the modern framework statute has been far more successful in discharging this constitutional function than the Constitution-with-a-capital-C — at least when judged by three fundamental criteria. The first is efficacy: if you really want to know how to pass an internationally binding trade agreement with Mexico and Canada, you would be silly to ignore the framework provisions of the Trade Act, but it would be counterproductive to stare too hard at the Treaty Clause. It is the modern, not the classic, framework that actually guides the conduct of legislators and citizens in the real world.

A second criterion is normative. It inquires into the intrinsic merits of the rules established by the modern and classic frameworks. Here too the Trade Act comes out way ahead. The two-House procedure it creates has not only made it more difficult for narrow regional interests to veto legislation that has gained the approval of a national majority of America's citizens. It has also provided a structure for organizing congressional advice and consent that is vastly superior to the treaty process as it has evolved over the last two centuries. In short, the modern practice is more democratic and more deliberative than the one it supersedes. Rather than mourning the slow decline of the classic rules into desuetude, we should take satisfaction in the

---

[496] For a preliminary effort to locate modern framework statutes within the contours of more general constitutional theory, see ACKERMAN, cited above in note 8, at 107. For a thoughtful discussion of their use in other areas of foreign policy, see Koh, cited above in note 208, at 1208–25.

[497] *See infra* pp. 927–28.

[498] H.L.A. HART, THE CONCEPT OF LAW 92–93 (1961).

thought that modern Americans have not lost the art of constitutional statecraft.

Third, the new rules were generated in a legitimate way. Although they do not have their source in a formal amendment, they build upon precedents from the Roosevelt era that express America's overriding constitutional commitment to popular sovereignty. In fashioning the congressional-executive agreement, political leaders in the White House and on Capitol Hill were responding to a profound shift in public opinion brought about by the transforming experience of total war. After four years of collective sacrifice, the majority of Americans had become thoroughly convinced of the need to break from the isolationist tradition set by Washington's Farewell Address and symbolized by the Senate's rejection of the League of Nations.

The rules for constitutional amendment, however, provided inept mechanisms for implementing this profound popular judgment. Given the acute dysfunctionality of Article V, the President was on sound constitutional ground in refusing the House's invitation to fight a bitter battle in the Senate for a formal amendment. At the very best, he would have won the formal battle at the cost of destroying the bipartisan coalition he and Vandenberg had built to support an internationalist foreign policy.

Rather than sacrifice the substance of foreign policy for a formal victory, the President and Congress modernized the treaty-making system by adapting the techniques they had used to transform domestic constitutional law in the 1930s. After all, it was these New Deal techniques that allowed the country to weather the economic storms that had destroyed democracy in Europe. It was therefore entirely appropriate to rely on them once again to express the will of the people rather than place undue pressure upon the peculiarly dysfunctional formalisms of Article V.

Efficacy, democracy, legitimacy: who can ask for anything more?

VII. THE FUTURE DEBATE

While we applaud the modern system of agreement-making, we have tried to distinguish our own views from the larger questions of constitutional process at the center of this essay. Just as highly intelligent men like Edwin Borchard vigorously protested against the introduction of the modern system, we expect that others of our generation will argue strenuously either for a reversion to the classical system or for another process altogether. In this respect, the silence surrounding the passage of NAFTA is misleading. As the practical significance of the modern procedure is increasingly appreciated, more and more Americans will explore its foundations and its alternatives.[499]

A. The World Trade Organization

Indeed, the conversation has already begun in connection with the Uruguay Round of GATT, which proposed a powerful World Trade Organization (WTO) to displace governing arrangements made in the 1940s. As in the case of NAFTA, much of the debate took the modern constitutional consensus for granted. But this time an odd coalition led by traditional protectionists like Jesse Helms and consumer advocates like Ralph Nader made a last-minute challenge to the Senate's decision to consider the WTO under the two-House procedure of the Trade Act. And they enlisted a group of distinguished constitutionalists, led by Professor Laurence Tribe, to join the effort to reassert the senatorial monopoly over "advice and consent." This campaign prompted a vigorous response from the Administration in defense of the congressional-executive agreement,[500] kicking off a spirited debate.[501] In the months before the Senate voted for the WTO in late November 1994, Professor Tribe launched an accelerating barrage of letters and memoranda on behalf of his new cause.[502] Unfortunately,

---

[499] The Trade Act has already spawned suggestions for extending fast-track procedures into other substantive areas. *See, e.g.*, Ronald A. Lehmann, Note, *Reinterpreting Advice and Consent: A Congressional Fast Track for Arms Control Treaties*, 98 YALE L.J. 885, 896–97 (1989); Vanessa P. Sciarra, Note, *Congress and Arms Sales: Tapping the Potential of the Fast-Track Guarantee Procedure*, 97 YALE L.J. 1439, 1453 (1988).

[500] *See* Memorandum from Walter Dellinger, Assistant Attorney General, Office of Legal Counsel, to Ambassador Michael Kantor, United States Trade Representative (Nov. 22, 1994) (on file at the Harvard Law School Library) [hereinafter Dellinger Memorandum of Nov. 22, 1994]; Memorandum from Walter Dellinger, Assistant Attorney General, Office of Legal Counsel, to Ambassador Michael Kantor, United States Trade Representative (July 29, 1994) (on file at the Harvard Law School Library) [hereinafter Dellinger Memorandum of July 29, 1994].

[501] Professor Tribe and the present writers have been ongoing participants. *See* Bruce Ackerman & David Golove, Joint Statement to the Senate Committee on Commerce, Science, and Transportation (Oct. 18, 1994) (on file at the Harvard Law School Library); Letter from Bruce Ackerman, Professor, Yale Law School, and David Golove, Professor, University of Arizona College of Law, to President William J. Clinton (Sept. 21, 1994) (on file at the Harvard Law School Library); Memorandum of Law of John H. Jackson, Professor of Law, University of Michigan Law School et al. (Nov. 11, 1994). Professors Ackerman and Tribe debated their views before the Senate Commerce Committee on October 18, 1994. Professor Tribe's written contributions are cited in note 502 below.

[502] *See GATT Implementing Legislation: Hearings Before the Senate Comm. on Commerce, Science, and Transportation*, 103d Cong., 2d Sess. 285 (1994) [hereinafter *GATT Hearings*] (prepared statement of Laurence Tribe, Professor, Harvard Law School); Memorandum from Laurence Tribe, Professor, Harvard Law School, to Walter Dellinger, Assistant Attorney General, Office of Legal Counsel, et al. (Oct. 5, 1994) (on file at the Harvard Law School Library) [hereinafter Tribe Memorandum of Oct. 5, 1994]; Letter from Laurence Tribe, Professor, Harvard Law School, to President William J. Clinton (Sept. 12, 1994) (on file at the Harvard Law School Library) [hereinafter Tribe Letter of Sept. 12, 1994]; Letter from Laurence Tribe, Professor, Harvard Law School, to Sen. Robert Byrd (July 19, 1994) (on file at the Harvard Law School Library) [hereinafter Tribe Letter of July 19, 1994]. Two of Professor Tribe's Harvard colleagues have joined the campaign.

Professor Tribe did not enter the debate with a fully informed opinion. Not only was his new position at odds with the most recent edition of his treatise,[503] but his legal views shifted from month to month as he learned more about the history and complexity of the issues.[504] As the Senate vote neared, Professor Tribe's emphatic certainties had dissolved into doubts:

> In short the issue is a close one. Although I continue to believe that the constitutional concerns that I have previously raised are deeply important, I cannot say with certainty that my prior conclusions should necessarily be adopted by others or are the ones to which I will adhere in the end after giving the matter the further thought that it deserves.[505]

Despite this retreat into uncertainty, Professor Tribe's aggressive intervention had served the public interest. The WTO is the most important step taken to construct a new world order in the aftermath of the Cold War. Even if the President's decision to submit it to both Houses had gone unchallenged, its approval as a congressional-executive agreement would have served as a major precedent in the diplomatic era that lies ahead. It was far better, then, that the Senate's vote of seventy-six to twenty-four[506] supporting the WTO came only after both sides of the constitutional argument had been vigorously

---

See Letter from Richard Parker, Professor, Harvard Law School, to Sen. Robert Byrd (Aug. 9, 1994) (on file at the Harvard Law School Library); Letter from Anne-Marie Slaughter, Professor, Harvard Law School, to Sen. Ernest F. Hollings (Oct. 18, 1994) [hereinafter Letter from Anne-Marie Slaughter], *reprinted in GATT Hearings, supra,* at 286.

503 *See* LAURENCE H. TRIBE, AMERICAN CONSTITUTIONAL LAW, § 4-5, at 228 n.18 (2d ed. 1988) (arguing that congressional-executive agreements are "coextensive with the treaty power. Such congressional-executive agreements are the law of the land, superseding inconsistent state or federal laws.").

504 For example, his earliest letter did not explicitly mention Article I as a basis for congressional action, and spoke as if the country had "fallen into an almost habitual pattern of regarding trade agreements as proper subjects for enactment through the concurrence of the President and a majority of both Houses of Congress," without any recognition of the transformative debates and decisions of the 1940s and the repeated failures of the Senate since then to reclaim its prerogatives. Tribe Letter of July 19, 1994, *supra* note 502, at 2. While his second intervention began to take notice of the Commerce Clause, *see* Tribe Letter of Sept. 12, 1994, *supra* note 502, at 3, it was only his third effort, the Memorandum of Oct. 5, 1994, that glimpsed the problem's true complexity. Even then, however, Professor Tribe dismissed as "a strategic move" the Senate's decisions in the 1940s to cooperate with President Roosevelt and the House to develop the powers vested in Congress by Article I, Tribe Memorandum of Oct. 5, 1994, *supra* note 502, at 7, and he has never seriously reconsidered this position. In framing its final response to Professor Tribe's critique, the Office of Legal Counsel was on firm ground in pointing out this weakness:

> Professor Tribe himself acknowledges that '[t]he issue whether major international agreements should be submitted for majority approval by Congress or for supermajority approval by the Senate was the topic of fierce debate in the halls of Congress, the popular press, and the pages of law reviews during the 1940s.' In light of that vigorous and protracted debate, it is strange that Professor Tribe should dismiss the political branches' practice as a mere matter of 'political convenience.'

Dellinger Memorandum of Nov. 22, 1994, *supra* note 500, at 5 n.16 (citations omitted).

505 Memorandum from Laurence Tribe, Professor, Harvard Law School, to Sen. George J. Mitchell et al. 1 (Nov. 28, 1994) (on file at the Harvard Law School Library).

506 *See* 140 CONG. REC. S15,379 (daily ed. Dec. 1, 1994).

developed and seriously considered on Capitol Hill and within the executive branch.

Even the Senate's overwhelming vote, however, will not be enough to silence the questions raised in the latest round of constitutional debate. As they retreat into the academy, the critics will undoubtedly generate a new wave of debate in the law reviews. For the present, we restrict ourselves to a few basic problems revealed by the brief but intense round of WTO polemics.

First and foremost, critics must do a better job confronting the Marshallian reading of the Necessary and Proper Clause that serves as the constitutional foundation of the congressional-executive agreement. Resolute sophistication is required because, as we have seen,[507] these same Marshallian principles support the key domestic innovations of the twentieth century — ranging from the Federal Reserve to the EPA. As a consequence, the critics must explain why their assault on the New Internationalism does not also undermine the basic premises of New Deal constitutionalism that justify modern American government at home as well as abroad.

Recognizing this challenge, Professor Tribe has noted that "the Necessary and Proper Clause authorizes Congress '[t]o make all *Laws*' necessary to execute its powers, but does not mention treaties."[508] Presumably the italics are supposed to explain why a Marshallian reading of Article I allows Congress to authorize the EPA but not the WTO. Even at the level of verbal manipulation, such a distinction is unconvincing. In approving the WTO, Congress is enacting a "law" that is formally identical to all others passed under Article I. If the act of legislation is unconstitutional, it must be for one of two other reasons: first, that Congress cannot properly find the WTO a "necessary and proper" way of pursuing its constitutional mandate to regulate foreign commerce; or second, that its action under Article I is prohibited by some other part of the Constitution.

As to the first point, the objection seems downright frivolous. If Congress cannot find that the WTO is a "necessary and proper" way of "regulat[ing] Commerce with foreign Nations," we will have to rethink all of the leading cases under the Commerce Clause from *McCulloch* to *Wickard*.

The second point, then, is crucial. Even the critics recognize that the Treaty Clause does not explicitly prohibit the exercise of congressional power under Article I. They seem to argue, however, that the

---

[507] *See supra* pp. 913–14.

[508] Tribe Memorandum of Oct. 5, 1994, *supra* note 502, at 5 (quoting U.S. CONST. art. I, § 8, cl. 18). He also seeks to use the Supreme Court's decision in INS v. Chadha, 462 U.S. 919 (1983), to restrict the range of the Marshallian interpretation to avoid its application to the present problem. *See* Tribe Memorandum of Oct. 5, 1994, *supra* note 502, at 8. We discuss the implications of *Chadha* below at pp. 926–28.

Treaty Clause functionally precludes an expansive reading of Article I. On their view, the Marshallian reading of Article I "render[s] the Treaty Clause meaningless."[509] If this were true, even the most devoted Marshallian would pause before adopting a reading that implies "that the Treaty Clause has essentially been amended out of the Constitution."[510]

But these extreme claims are simply false. Marshallianism does not render the Treaty Clause a dead letter. It simply insists that constitutionalists recognize both Article I and Article II for what they are: great and independent grants of power, each of which suffices to justify the creation of international obligations.

This is by no means the only case in which the text creates multiple legislative procedures for accomplishing the same end. The text provides no fewer than four ways of passing a constitutional amendment. And there are, of course, two ways of passing a statute — one with, and one without, the cooperation of the President.

Similarly, Articles I and II set up alternative systems through which the nation can commit itself internationally — one with, and one without, the cooperation of the House. Note, moreover, that the text prescribes the same super-majoritarian remedy whenever one of the normal law-making institutions is excluded from the process. In creating statutory law, a two thirds vote of both Houses of Congress is required to override the presidential veto. In creating international obligations under the Treaty Clause, two thirds of the Senate is required to offset the absence of the House.

Rather than demeaning the Senate, this Marshallian reading of Article I puts the Senators at the very heart of the entire process of international negotiation. If a majority of the Senate believes that Article II describes the most appropriate course, no progress can be made along the track described by Article I.[511] A congressional-executive agreement will emerge only if the Senate believes that constitutional values will best be served by cooperating with the House and President under Article I, rather than cutting the House out of the process under Article II.

In emphasizing the coherence of the modern reading of the constitutional text, we hardly wish to deny that another reading is possible. To the contrary, we have labored long and hard to reestablish the historical reality of an earlier constitutional world in which Americans overwhelmingly read Article II as precluding the exercise of power under Article I. But it mistakes our entire project to suggest that the traditional reading is the only plausible reading. Here, as elsewhere,

---

[509] Letter from Anne-Marie Slaughter, *supra* note 502, at 2, *reprinted in GATT Hearings*, *supra* note 502, at 286.

[510] *GATT Hearings*, *supra* note 502, at 310.

[511] *See supra* note 479.

the constitutional problem is more complex: because the text is open to competing interpretations, how to select the most reasonable one?

It is at this point that the emerging critique becomes paradoxical. Although the critics present themselves as resolute defenders of the Senate, they are in fact assaulting one of the Senate's most precious prerogatives — the right to engage in constitutional interpretation. As we have seen, Senators of the 1940s did not revise their traditional interpretation of Article I for frivolous or passing reasons. They adopted the Marshallian view only after a sustained and self-conscious political process had convinced them that the American people no longer supported the traditional reading. Moreover, the Senate's half-century of practice under Article I cannot be condemned as idiosyncratic or arbitrary. Instead, it elaborates Marshallian themes that lie at the center of modern constitutional development. Given these facts, the critics seem naively self-confident in supposing that the words of the Constitution have the single meaning that they have chosen to impose upon the text.

Especially when a closer inspection of their arguments reveals that the critics are much more Marshallian than one might suppose. Although they oppose a Marshallian reading of Article I in the case of the WTO, they do not yearn for a return to the good old days when Congress never sought to bind the nation internationally. Professor Tribe, for example, has emphasized that many of the congressional-executive agreements enacted over the last fifty years represent valid acts of authority.[512] But it is precisely this statesmanlike concession to reality that gets him into serious textual trouble.

To see our point, consider a congressional-executive agreement that has thus far managed to evade critical scrutiny: the United States-Israel Free Trade Agreement.[513] Assuming that this omission is not inadvertent, the critics presumably suppose that there is some text in the Constitution that authorizes the congressional action on behalf of Israel. But what text could this be, other than the provisions of Article I authorizing Congress to take "necessary and proper" actions in regulating foreign commerce?[514] To put it in Professor Tribe's terms:

---

[512] *See, e.g.,* Tribe Memorandum of Oct. 5, 1994, *supra* note 502, at 7; Tribe Letter of July 19, 1994, *supra* note 502, at 2.

[513] United States–Israel Free Trade Area Implementation Act of 1985, Pub. L. No. 99–47, 99 Stat. 82.

[514] The critics have occasionally pointed to the Compact Clause's distinction between "agreements" that the states may enter with Congress's consent and "treaties" that they can never conclude, *see* U.S. CONST. art. I, § 10, cl. 3, to support the proposition that there are some international deals that are "treaties" but not "agreements." *See, e.g.,* Tribe Memorandum of Oct. 5, 1994, *supra* note 502, at 6. The Compact Clause, however, does not give the federal government any authority to make agreements on its own behalf, but simply authorizes it to approve certain pacts made by the states. For the original understanding, see Abraham C. Weinfeld, *What Did the Framers of the Federal Constitution Mean by "Agreements or Compacts"?*, 3 U. CHI. L. REV. 453 *passim* (1936). If Congress has any power to make internationally binding commitments

if the Israeli Agreement constitutes a valid "law" under Article I, why doesn't the WTO Charter?

In short, the critics seem to adopt the very same Marshallian treatment of Article I when it comes to Israel that they deny when it comes to the WTO. But the textual basis for the two agreements is indistinguishable. This simple point makes their reading of the Constitution far less plausible than *either* the Marshallian interpretation dominant since World War II *or* the traditional view held before Versailles. Both the modern and traditional readings have a clarity and elegance to them — either (as moderns think) Congress can create binding international obligations *whenever* it thinks it "necessary and proper" under Article I, or (as was generally believed before Versailles) Article I is *never* a source of this power and the Senate must *always* give its advice and consent. In picking and choosing amongst congressional-executive agreements, the new critics fall between two textual stools. They reject the modern reading, but do not have enough courage in their convictions to return to a traditional construction that would condemn not only the WTO but all congressional-executive agreements.[515]

The ad hoc character of the critics' exercise is heightened further when they confess, in the words of Professor Tribe, that "drawing a clear boundary around the treaty category is difficult."[516] But if this is

---

on behalf of the United States, the source of this authority must be Article I. Once this point is conceded, we do not see how the words of the Compact Clause — designed for a very different problem — are relevant in determining the scope of congressional power under Article I.

[515] One should recall that the traditional reading would not only render unconstitutional the modern practice of ex post congressional approval, as exemplified by the WTO and NAFTA, but would also undermine the even more common practice by which the President enters binding international obligations pursuant to statutory authorization. Questioning this procedure, introduced by the Trade Act of 1934, would cast doubt on the mechanisms through which the United States has assumed the vast majority of its international commitments during the modern period. *See* 14 MARJORIE M. WHITEMAN, U.S. DEP'T OF STATE, DIGEST OF INTERNATIONAL LAW 196, 210 (1970).

[516] Tribe Memorandum of Oct. 5, 1994, *supra* note 502, at 17. Indeed, Professor Tribe's efforts to engage in categorization emphasize the difficulty. While in July he was confidently treating NAFTA as if it were obviously constitutional, *see* Tribe Letter of July 19, 1994, *supra* note 502, at 2, by October he was questioning its legitimacy as well, claiming that no "agreement of comparable scope and import [to the WTO] — with the possible exceptions of our 1988 free-trade agreement with Canada (CFTA) and of the 1993 North American Free Trade Agreement (NAFTA) — has been entered into outside the Treaty Clause," Tribe Memorandum of Oct. 5, 1994, *supra* note 502, at 14. Professor Tribe has also suggested that the Bretton Woods Agreements were "arguably treaty-like," *see id.* at 13, thereby casting America's membership in the World Bank and International Monetary Fund under a constitutional cloud.

Aside from his extremely casual treatment of very serious agreements, Professor Tribe's characterization of the WTO as possessing singular importance ignores other precedents. In many respects, the congressional-executive agreement of the greatest "scope and import" was SALT I, *see supra* pp. 900–01, in which President Nixon and Congress gambled on strategic defense limitation, despite the possibility that cheating would permit the Soviets to obtain an overwhelming military advantage. While this gamble turned out to be worth taking, we think that the risks

so, surely we should leave it up to the Senate to consider, on the facts of each case, whether Article I or Article II provides the more appropriate procedure. Recall that it is always within the power of the Senate to insist upon the Treaty Clause whenever a majority believes that treatment under Article I is inappropriate. Given the admittedly contextualized character of the constitutional judgment, the critics seem quite brave when they insist on their right to denounce as unconstitutional the decision of a Senate majority's finding that the WTO is most appropriately considered under Article I.

Bravery verges on hubris in the face of an express constitutional provision that makes House participation especially appropriate in the context of the WTO (and NAFTA). Article I, section 7 of the Constitution requires that all revenue bills originate in the House. Given the impact of these agreements on tariffs (and therefore revenues), the Senate seems on particularly strong constitutional ground in involving the House. Even apart from this provision, there is much to be said for the Senate's choice of Article I for all pacts that require complex and controversial implementing legislation. If the Senate approves such agreements under the Treaty Clause, it may quickly find the House refusing to cooperate in approving the necessary statutory back-up. The resulting conflict between Senate and House may force the nation to breach treaty obligations the Senate and President had only recently affirmed as binding. In seeking the early participation of the House, the Senate guarantees that the nation's promises will not immediately prove hollow.[517]

---

involved were of a scope and import more than comparable to the commercial risks presented by the WTO.

[517] Professor Tribe also attempts, unpersuasively, to support his reading by reference to the Appointments Clause, U.S. CONST. art. II, § 2, cl. 2. This provision, found in the same section as the Treaty Clause, grants the Senate the power of "advice and consent" in the appointment of officers of the United States. But unlike the Treaty Clause, it explicitly authorizes Congress to vest the appointment of inferior officers in the President, the courts, or the heads of departments. On Professor Tribe's view, the fact that the Treaty Clause contains no similar provision "provides at least a strong argument" for reading it to preclude any congressional role. Tribe Memorandum of Oct. 5, 1994, *supra* note 502, at 4–5.

But Professor Tribe reaches this conclusion only by assuming it from the beginning. To see this, indulge the opposite assumption and accept instead the argument that Article I contains an independent grant of power to make international agreements. The Appointments Clause then becomes evidence for the proposition that when the Constitution restricts Congress's powers under Article I — as it does in the case of appointments — it does so in unmistakable language. The fact that the Treaty Clause contains no similar language can now be taken to imply that Congress's Article I powers remain intact.

Even were Professor Tribe's extrapolation from the Appointments Clause persuasive, it still would not support his broader conclusions. Here, again, he seems to lack the courage of his convictions. Indeed, if the Appointments Clause teaches any pertinent lesson, it is that Professor Tribe is on the wrong track in distinguishing two different classes of agreements for Treaty Clause purposes — major ones (like the WTO), which require senatorial approval and lesser ones (like the trade deal with Israel), which can be dealt with by Congress. This distinction is the precise analogue to the one made by the Appointments Clause when it distinguishes between principal

Moving beyond textual dynamics, there are the many competing arguments of constitutional principle that most Americans last squarely confronted in the 1940s. On this level, we do not suppose that there will ever be a conclusive resolution of the debate. There will always be scholars like Corwin and McDougal and ourselves who will defend the primacy of the deep constitutional values expressed by the Marshallian reading of Article I. And there will always be scholars like Professors Borchard and Tribe who will respond by invoking the values of federalism and diplomatic caution expressed by the Treaty Clause. Over the generations, the balance of argument may slowly shift from one side to the other. During one era, the Corwins and McDougals may have a field day; during the next, the Ackermans and Goloves may — or may not — prove successful in making their case. As the agon continues, it will influence elite opinion more generally and may ultimately affect the way the Senate goes about deciding concrete cases.

But it is essential to distinguish between these long and slow shifts in elite opinion and those rare moments in American history when the mass of Americans get into the act. Precisely because the ultimate constitutional values are inevitably controversial, the legal elite should never forget the moments when debate about the Treaty Clause leapt beyond the law reviews and the Senate committee rooms and occupied the center of the public stage. We have no authority to displace the judgments made by the American people with our own legal conceits.

Friends of the Treaty Clause are free, of course, to mount a massive campaign on behalf of the Senate's abandoned monopoly. Just as an earlier generation successfully transformed Versailles into a compelling symbol of the need for constitutional change, critics of the status quo may convince Americans of the twenty-first century that Congress has abused its modern role in agreement-making and that the time has come to return to an older, and now abandoned, vision of the Treaty Clause. But the proponents of a senatorial monopoly should not expect to win their struggle without riding a wave of popular opinion equal in force, but opposite in direction, to that which prevailed in the aftermath of the Second World War. Until that time comes, the Presi-

---

and inferior officers. *If* the Treaty Clause's silence connotes disapproval of the Appointment Clause's solution, as Tribe suggests, then his distinction between major and minor agreements has no place in our constitutional jurisprudence. The Senate must give its advice and consent in all cases.

But it is more important to reject Professor Tribe's effort to create a tight relationship between two clauses designed to serve radically different functions. Whatever their relationship in the text, the Appointments Clause is far closer to the Impeachment Clause than it is to the Treaty Clause. Given the obvious practical and theoretical differences between approving appointments and approving treaties, it seems wiser to refuse Professor Tribe's offer of instruction in advanced tea-leaf reading and squarely confront the fact that the textual relationship between Article I and Article II is indeterminate.

dent is fully within his constitutional authority to submit the WTO to both Houses for their approval, and opponents will be obliged to convince fifty-one, not thirty-four, percent of the Senate to vote against the proposal.

B. *The Promise of Judicial Review*

There is only one force that could quickly reshape the existing terms of constitutional law: the United States Supreme Court. Over the past half-century, however, the Court has been extremely deferential on foreign affairs, allowing Congress and the President to fight out their constitutional battles on their own terms. Its deference, verging on abdication, has been much criticized by leading scholars for reasons we generally find persuasive.[518] Nonetheless, it is always possible to do worse than nothing. Here is a nightmare scenario. The Court awakens from its dogmatic slumbers only to focus single-mindedly on the intentions of the Framers. Elaborating upon the original understanding, the Justices find NAFTA unconstitutional and restore the Senate to a monopoly it has long since abandoned in the court of public opinion. Of course, once the Court overturns the constitutional status quo, the Senate will begin to act like other monopolists — clinging to its new-found power unless it is once again dislodged by an outraged public. Unless and until this happened, a misguided judicial decision would not only give isolationists a veto they did not deserve, but it would tear at the existing fabric of American international obligations. From Bretton Woods to the WTO, many of America's key commitments have taken the form of congressional-executive agreements. A Court decision striking them down would gravely destabilize the nation's international standing.[519]

Nor would it be easy for the Senate to reenact existing agreements under a two thirds rule that gave a host of regional interests new veto powers. Instead, the nation would be treated to a familiar constitutional dance in which Senators couple their consent to treaties with crippling reservations unacceptable to our allies.

---

[518] *See, e.g.*, THOMAS M. FRANCK, POLITICAL QUESTIONS/JUDICIAL ANSWERS: DOES THE RULE OF LAW APPLY TO FOREIGN AFFAIRS *passim* (1992); KOH, *supra* note 264, at 134–49.

[519] If the Court were to strike down the modern constitutional practice, what would be the status of all the unconstitutional agreements that have been negotiated over the last half-century? According to article 46 of the Vienna Convention of the Law of Treaties, conclusion of an agreement in violation of domestic law is not a basis for invalidating the agreement internationally, unless the domestic law violated is of "fundamental importance" and the violation was "manifest." As we have seen, *see supra* note 464, the Senate and the President continue to be at loggerheads over the meaning of this provision, and the United States has refused to ratify the Convention. *See* CONGRESSIONAL RESEARCH SERV., LIBRARY OF CONGRESS, *supra* note 12, at 32–34. This impasse, and many other matters, would be opened up by an ill-considered act of judicial intervention.

However much we would like to discount such a scenario, we cannot say that it is impossible. If the Court were so minded, it could reach this result through a wooden reading of its decision in *INS v. Chadha.*[520] The case involved another twentieth-century innovation: the "legislative veto." Congress had sought to respond to twentieth-century realities by designing new mechanisms of legislative control over administrative rulemaking. A series of framework statutes authorized a single House, or specialized congressional committees, to veto rules enacted by administrative agencies. Although the Founding Federalists did not imagine that they were establishing a constitution for a massive bureaucracy, the Court took their words as barring Congress and the President from dealing with pressing problems of democratic accountability in the modern activist state. In a narrow originalist opinion, the Court swept aside a host of statutory frameworks under which one or another House of Congress could effectively control administrative law-making activities.

Some of these frameworks did offend basic constitutional principles. But the Court did not seek to separate the wheat from the chaff. Instead of inviting Congress and the President to enact better framework statutes, the Court supposed that the intentions of the omniscient Founders of 1787 should serve as the omega, as well as the alpha, of constitutional interpretation.

If this can happen once, it can happen again — but this time, with more serious consequences. Congress has found many ways around *Chadha* and continues to exercise effective control over agency lawmaking on an ongoing basis.[521] In contrast, a *Chadha*-like fixation on 1787 in the case of congressional-executive agreements would not merely change the instrumentalities of congressional control but would change the balance of decision-making power itself — to the advantage of states with low populations and parochial interests that set them apart from the rest of the country.

Fortunately, there is more to *Chadha* than an atavistic return to the intentions of 1787. The opinion contains many resources for more constructive use. First and foremost is its emphasis on the central importance of Article I in the overall constitutional scheme. Second is its insistence on respect for the integrity of the Article's written text. Third is its emphasis on the crucial value that deliberation by both Houses and the President plays in the enactment of binding law.

Because the congressional-executive agreement is buttressed by all three of these points, it is readily distinguishable from the "legislative veto" struck down in *Chadha*. In that case, Congress was seeking to use its powers under Article I to authorize action by a single House or

---

[520] 462 U.S. 919 (1983).

[521] *See, e.g.*, Stephen Breyer, *The Legislative Veto After* Chadha, 72 Geo. L.J. 785, 792–96 (1984).

committee. In the present case, it is using its powers to vindicate the values of joint deliberation by both Houses and the President. In *Chadha*, Congress was seeking to change the law without complying with the textual requirements of Article I. In the present case, Congress and the President are complying with all textual requirements. In *Chadha*, Congress was diminishing the role of Article I in the future life of the nation. In the present case, Congress is vindicating the continued vitality of Article I in our constitutional arrangements.

But there is more than the principles of *Chadha* at stake. In supporting the congressional-executive agreement, the Court would be supporting the Senate under conditions that make its constitutional judgment especially worthy of respect. Of all the branches, the Senate had the most at stake in determining the relative importance of Articles I and II in the constitutional scheme. Of all the branches, it was the one that would be expected to place the highest value on Article II. As a consequence, it reached its decision in favor of Article I only after an extended period of debate and deliberation. Surely this is a particularly uncongenial context for the Court to engage in second-guessing.

For these reasons, we believe that the *Chadha*-nightmare is unlikely to become a reality. The greater danger lies elsewhere: instead of striking down the congressional-executive agreement, the Court could uphold it on overly broad grounds. Rather than adopting a Marshallian reading of Article I, the Justices might follow Justice Sutherland's suggestion in *Curtiss-Wright* that the text does not bind American government when it acts within the "vast external realm" of foreign affairs.[522] On this approach, there would be no need to look at the text in order to know that "the President alone has the power to speak or listen as a representative of the nation."[523] Taken to its extreme, this view would suggest that the President was almost doing Congress a favor in asking it to approve his executive agreements — because he would, in any event, be authorized to commit the nation on a broad front.

While this approach would certainly lead to a sweeping judicial validation of congressional-executive agreements, we find it almost as nightmarish as the *Chadha* scenario. Along with many other scholars, we deny that the Constitution grants the executive sweeping unwritten powers in foreign affairs. However, it is entirely unnecessary for the Court to confront this vexed question in order to resolve the present controversy. Rather than embark upon the uncharted seas glimpsed by Justice Sutherland, the Court can dispose of this case by a Mar-

---

[522] United States v. Curtiss-Wright Export Corp., 299 U.S. 304, 319 (1936); *see also supra* pp. 857–59.

[523] *Id.* at 319. For criticism of Sutherland's history and his presidentialist bias, see the sources collected above in note 264.

shallian reading of the text and leave the status of *Curtiss-Wright* for another day.

This is precisely the approach suggested by the modern case closest to our problem. *Dames & Moore v. Regan*[524] involved President Carter's deal with the Iranian government securing the release of Americans held hostage in Teheran. As part of his executive agreement, the President reached a settlement that deprived creditors of their claims in American courts, transferring them to an international tribunal in The Hague. When they sued, the Court supported the President, but in an opinion marked by great caution. Rather than speaking expansively about *Curtiss-Wright*, then-Justice Rehnquist relied heavily on Justice Jackson's famous concurring opinion in the *Steel Seizure Case*.[525] Speaking for the Court, Justice Rehnquist agreed with Jackson that the key variable in assessing the constitutionality of presidential action is the character of congressional support. Thus, even though Presidents had traditionally been conceded broad powers in settling international claims without any congressional or senatorial participation, Justice Rehnquist did not approve Carter's executive agreement on that ground alone. Instead, he carefully examined the quality of congressional support for the President's actions and conditioned the Court's approval on his positive assessment. While the Court could not find express statutory authorization for all aspects of the President's decision, it upheld his agreement only after concluding that Congress had "acquiesced in the President's action."[526] Given the tenor of its opinion, the Court would have been delighted to find that both Houses of Congress had supported the President's decision with the majorities provided in the cases of NAFTA and the WTO.[527]

Given its hesitations about *Curtiss-Wright*, the Court's embrace of a Marshallian reading of Article I should be seen as part of the solution, rather than part of the problem. By establishing a framework for foreign policy-making, statutes like the Trade Act of 1974 help avoid situations in which the President may otherwise be tempted to abuse his (uncertain) unilateral authority in foreign affairs. Rather than calling congressional power into question, a constructive Court opinion

---

[524] 453 U.S. 654 (1981).

[525] 343 U.S. 579 (1952). Indeed, the Court identified it, and not *Curtiss-Wright*, as the case "which . . . brings together as much combination of analysis and common sense as there is in this area." *Dames & Moore*, 453 U.S. at 661.

[526] *Dames & Moore*, 453 U.S. at 688.

[527] Another straw in the wind is Weinberger v. Rossi, 456 U.S. 25 (1982), in which a unanimous Court held that an executive agreement authorized by Congress constituted a "treaty" as a matter of statutory construction. While the Court did not explicitly consider the constitutional question, it showed great equanimity in finding that an executive agreement authorized by Congress bound the nation under international law. At the very least, the Court's treatment suggests no great anxiety about the underlying constitutional issue.

should encourage Congress and the President to build on the successes of NAFTA and the WTO and to construct new framework statutes in other fields of foreign policy. Only effective frameworks will discourage Presidents, and their underlings, from supposing that the Constitution grants the executive branch a vast prerogative for unilateral foreign adventurism.

But in the final analysis, there is more at stake than the avoidance of difficult constitutional questions. By affirming the Marshallian view of Article I, the Court would be endorsing the considered judgment of the generation that fought the Second World War. These men and women supposed that they had decisively resolved the question of constitutional interpretation that the critics of the WTO seek to revive. Though the Americans who fought the war and won the peace are now rapidly leaving the political stage, there is no reason to forget their enduring contribution to our constitutional tradition.